K2483812000

CW00865907

The Future of
WHITEHALL

OONAGH MCDONALD

The Future of
WHITEHALL

Weidenfeld & Nicolson Ltd
LONDON

First published in 1992 by
George Weidenfeld & Nicolson Ltd
91 Clapham High Street
London SW4 7TA

ISBN 0 297 81240 8

Typeset in Great Britain by Selwood Systems,
Midsomer Norton
Printed and bound by Butler & Tanner Ltd,
Frome and London

Contents

Introduction

Government is a contrivance of human wisdom to provide for human wants. Men [and women] have a right that these wants should be provided for by this wisdom. (Edmund Burke, *Reflections on the French Revolution*)

No government can long be secure without a formidable opposition. (Benjamin Disraeli, *Conningsby*, Book 2, Chapter 1)

Mrs Thatcher sought to revolutionize the way in which the highly centralized, but heterogeneous government machine, the civil service, works. This book seeks to evaluate the effectiveness of this enterprise, but it does more than that. The assumptions underlying the Thatcher reform programme are called into question as well.

'Management by objectives' and 'value for money' dominated the Thatcher reforms. Important though these nostrums are, they are both inappropriate and incomplete when applied to the civil service. Good government is much more than the efficient delivery of services, though that is an essential element in the process. Public services have to be delivered effectively and fairly as well. Questions of equity, justice and effectiveness arise in the provision of public services in a way in which they do not in the delivery of commercial services. The public has a right to the former, but cannot demand that the private sector provides unprofitable goods and services.

Services can only be delivered effectively if they fulfil the aims and objectives of government policy and, at the same time, meet the needs of the public. A service can be delivered efficiently but may not be effective, although the converse does not apply. Effective public services require efficient delivery. Determining whether or not public services are effective requires full public accountability in terms of public access to information, and an open review of the public service in question.

Good government must take the considerations of efficiency, effectiveness and equity into account. These aims can only be achieved if both the civil service and government are open to scrutiny. Government itself is much more than the provision of public services on which the Thatcher reforms focused throughout the 1980s. It is concerned with the management of the nation's economy, its relations with other nations and the determination of domestic policies. The civil service is designed to provide ministers with the necessary advice and information on which ministerial decisions rest. The Thatcher reforms neglected these functions of the civil service; indeed its efforts to provide advice and support were often treated with contempt as the Prime Minister imported her own advisers. Yet the whole approach and system of policy-making in this country urgently requires fundamental reform, which has implications for the conduct of parliamentary business as well.

Public access to information is fundamental to the reform of the civil service in this country. The culture of secrecy which imbues the behaviour of civil servants and ministers alike has to be destroyed. Neither Parliament itself nor Her Majesty's Loyal Opposition can function effectively without open government. The scope of this book is wider than the future of the civil service, however essential an element that may be in good government. It argues that the government machine can no longer cope with the demands of the late twentieth century, still less the twenty-first. It has to be completely overhauled, a task neglected in the 1980s. The reforms proposed in this book may seem obvious enough, but taken together they will help to provide a 'true contrivance of human wisdom to provide for human wants'.

Acknowledgements

I started working on this book as the Gwilym Gibbon Research Fellow at Nuffield College, Oxford. I would like to take this opportunity of thanking the College for a most enjoyable year and for enabling me to visit Sweden as part of my research.

ONE

Making an Efficient Civil Service

Raynerism and the Financial Management Initiative

'Whenever the Prime Minister sees a British institution, she wants to hit it with her handbag' – a colourful, if sexist description of Mrs Thatcher's attitudes to the Establishment. It arises from a combination of radicalism and prejudice. The civil service was just one of the institutions of which she was 'profoundly suspicious'. Patrick Cosgrave records that a friend asked her if she hated all institutions. Mrs Thatcher frowned and replied that she had a 'great respect for the monarchy and Parliament'. But 'for the City, the trade unions, the civil service and the Church of England she has a dislike that some would call hatred and certainly veers over into contempt'. Her attitude towards the civil service was 'ferocious'. Mrs Thatcher 'rarely bothered to justify [it] in terms of greater efficiency or savings'[1] – in private, one should add, since her public pronouncements argued just that.

These prejudices lay behind the then Prime Minister's determination to wean the civil service away from what she regarded as its pretensions to policy-making and to hone it down to a smooth, efficient machine for delivering and administrating such public services as should remain in the public sector. Apart from prejudices which apparently had much to do with the experiences of being patronized by senior civil servants, which Mrs Thatcher faced in the Ministry for Pensions and the Department of Education and Science, her attitude towards the civil service was all of a piece with her approach to managing the economy. The public sector was a burden on the economy as a whole, which should be ruthlessly pruned to allow for the full and free development of the private sector, 'to restore incentives, encourage efficiency and create a climate in which commerce and industry can flourish', to use the words of the Thatcher Government's

I

first Queen's Speech. The monetarist weaponry was used on the economy as a whole, at least in the early 1980s.

A year later, the implications of this economic strategy were spelt out in the Prime Minister's announcement about the future of the civil service to the House of Commons:

> In the past governments have progressively increased the number of tasks that the civil service is asked to do without paying sufficient attention to the need for more economy and efficiency. Consequently, staff numbers have grown over the years. The present Government are committed to a reduction in tasks and to better management. We believe that we should now concentrate on simplifying the work and doing it more efficiently. The studies that departments have already carried out, including those in conjunction with Sir Derek Rayner, have demonstrated clearly the scope for all this. All ministers in charge of departments will now work out detailed plans for concentrating on essential functions and making operations simpler and more efficient in their departments. When this Government took office the size of the civil service was 732,000. As a result of the steps that we have already taken it is now 705,000. We intend to bring the number down to about 630,000 over the next four years.[2]

The Prime Minister had promised to cut overall civil service numbers and to 'de-privilege' the service during the election campaign. The size of the non-industrial civil service was cut from 565,815 in April 1979 to 527,970 by April 1982, a 6.7 per cent reduction. The administration had increased considerably during the 1970s, up from 493,000 at April 1970, with much of the growth in the administrative grades below assistant secretary level. Such an increase indicates 'grade drift' due to the income policies of successive governments in the 1970s and a possible lack of grip on staff development, together with a belief in the need for government to undertake a wide range of functions – in public ownership, partnership with industry and so on. But the incoming Conservative Government was determined to 'roll back the frontiers of the state', promising in the Conservative manifesto in 1979 a 'reduction of waste, bureaucracy and over-government' as well.

The civil service was an obvious target, and since a strongly unionized civil service might resist the Government's determination to reduce the burden of the public sector on the taxpayer, it acted swiftly to reduce the power of the trade unions. The Priestley pay system was unilaterally abolished by the Government in 1981, despite trade union protests and a long drawn-out strike. The latter provided the Government with the justification for banning membership of independent trade unions at GCHQ. The defeat of the trade unions was consolidated by the Government's decision to disband the Civil Service Department and to transfer the responsibility for pay and conditions to the Treasury. But these were only part of the moves towards a smaller, more 'efficient' civil service. The Wardale Inquiry (1981) into staffing at the 'open structure', that is the 60 per cent of civil servants with an administrative background, and the Rayner scrutinies, were part of the Government's approach to reforming the civil service. The purpose of the Wardale Inquiry was apparently to establish whether or not the under secretary grade was really necessary. The report concluded that the under secretary role was a 'vital one in many areas', but that 'a number of Open Structure posts can be removed and should be'. The number of such posts did in fact fall from 823 to 743 between 1979 and 1982. From such beginnings, the Government's strategy for reform only slowly evolved from what was initially probably little more than a cost-cutting, number-crunching exercise. The Rayner scrutinies played a part in the development of that strategy.

During the 1979 election campaign, Mrs Thatcher was advised on civil service efficiency by the author of *Your Disobedient Servant*, Leslie Chapman. But, when it came to appointing an adviser, she chose Sir Derek Rayner, now Lord Rayner, a board member and now Chairman of Marks and Spencer, a company the Prime Minister uses and admires. Such admiration lay behind the appointment, according to Clive Priestley, himself the Whitehall Chief of Staff to Derek Rayner.[3]

The Rayner Scrutinies

Derek Rayner moved into No. 70 Whitehall on 8 May 1979, the day after Mrs Thatcher won the election with a majority of forty-three, together with a 'small but high quality' team of seven people, including support staff, to advise the Government on eliminating waste and reducing bureaucracy in the civil service. His task was a 'continuing critical examination of activities, functions and policies with particular regard to cost and need'. His sense of mission arose from his experience of working on defence procurement in the Heath Government, days which he recalled in *All the Prime Minister's Men* in 1986:

When I first arrived in the Ministry in 1970, I was amazed that in the Defence Department with enormous expenditure there were no kinds of financial management that I knew in business and that the head of finance was certainly not an accountant by training or experience ... and yet were dealing with 10-year forecasts involving billions of pounds ... [When I asked] about new projects, I was assured there was space for them in the long-term costings. My natural request was to see these long-term costings ... In due course, a large, wheeled skip arrived containing these very documents. Needless to say, in that form they were not much good for senior management to make any judgements at all as to whether there was no room for expenditure or not.

Lord Rayner had already revealed that 'no one at the time of my arrival knew how much it cost to run a government'.[4] He blamed 'ministers, politicians and officials for this, mesmerized by the glamour of "policy" and [for regarding] the costs of administering the policies, [as] simply the "candle-ends of public expenditure"'. Rayner did at least enable the Government to publish and identify the gross costs of running the administration. These amounted to £16.5 billion in 1983–84 and the gross running costs were expected to be £17.5 billion in 1990–1 according to the 1991 White Paper, now called Public Expenditure Analyses. The Public Expenditure Analyses 1991 also pointed out that the numbers of civil servants fell by 168,000, a reduction of 23 per cent between 1978–9 and 1989–90, but anticipated an increase in civil service staff from 565,000 in 1990–1 to 569,900 in 1992–3. The last figure is a calculation based on all the separate departmental reports. It is interesting to note that it is now much more difficult to estimate the total running costs for this reason. Indeed, the Government responded to a recent written parliamentary question, which asked the Chancellor of the Exchequer what proportion of total Government spending went on the administration of the civil service in each year from 1979–80 to 1989–90, and what proportion was spent on the wages and salaries of civil servants, by saying that the precise information was not readily available and that consistent data for all the years in question could be provided only at 'disproportionate cost'.[5] The reply is an interesting one since to set out the data on a consistent basis would show that, despite all the attempts to cut costs throughout the 1980s, the bill for administration has hardly changed at all as a proportion of total Government spending. We shall, however, consider what form those efforts took. Apart from pay, the costs of running departments in 1979–80 invited savings as well. Rayner concentrated his attention on cutting the administrative costs.

Shortly after Rayner was installed in Whitehall, a Note of Guidance was issued, which typified his 'no-nonsense approach': 'The purpose of the scrutinies is action, not study. It is therefore (a) to examine a specific policy, activity or function with a view to savings or increased effectiveness and to questioning all aspects of the work normally taken for granted; (b) to propose solutions to any problems identified; and (c) to implement agreed solutions, or begin their implementation, within twelve months from the start of the scrutiny.'[6]

Rayner added at the end of the Note, 'The reasoning behind the scrutiny programme is that ministers and their officials are better equipped than anyone else to examine the use of resources for which they are responsible. The scrutineers therefore rely heavily on self-examination and on applying a fresh mind to the policy or activity under scrutiny, unfettered by committees or hierarchy; on learning from those who are expert in it; on supervision by the minister accountable for it; and on contributions from my office and me.'

The scrutiny programme got under way in November 1979. Ironically enough, it was introduced just as the Programme Analysis and Review (PAR), one of Rayner's own innovations during his time as an adviser to Prime Minister Heath, was abandoned. But, significantly, the scrutiny programme was not a direct replacement for the latter, whose focus had been on the effectiveness of Government programmes rather than their efficiency.

The initial scrutiny programme consisted of about thirty projects in over twenty departments, each investigation being taken by one or two officials from the relevant departments, including the arrangements for paying social security benefits, the administration of the teachers' pension scheme, food procurement for the armed forces and charging for courses at the Civil Service College. Savings of about £80 million were identified by the end of 1979 which was thought to be sufficient to justify the retention of Lord Rayner. By the end of 1979, over thirty projects in eighteen departments were in progress. These included the delivery of unemployment and supplementary benefit, the administration of student awards, the administration of the regional development scheme and the monitoring of central government expenditure. By July, 1981, the Government was able to claim that 'since June 1979 there have been 68 scrutinies of particular activities at a cost of about £1 million. This year there will be about 40 more. Savings possibilities of around £190 million a year (11,000 staff) have been identified so far. Ministers have already taken firm decisions to save some £90 million a year (involving by 1984 manpower savings of about 3,000) plus £28 million once and for all.'[7]

All of these scrutinies took place against the background of cuts in public expenditure. In June 1979, the newly appointed Chancellor, Sir Geoffrey Howe, reduced his predecessor's spending plans for 1979–80 by £2.5 billion and announced the sale of £1 billion of assets. Further cuts were announced in November 1979 in the Government's first White Paper on public spending, which only proferred plans for one year ahead instead of the usual three. The political background to the Rayner programme was the Conservative Government's belief that reining back public spending would put Britain on the road to economic prosperity. So right from the start, efficiency was linked to cash limits and reducing civil service manpower. That, in turn, implied central controls on money and people, which conflicted not only with Rayner's emphasis on each Government department looking at its own systems, but also with the later reforms. Indeed, the conflict between devolved authority and central controls on public spending has still not been resolved.

The way in which these two elements were involved in the scrutinies can be seen in the detailed descriptions of their activities given by two civil servants who actually took part in the scrutinies. They had to ask radical questions 'to the point of challenging the activity's very existence' as the Note put it. 'Why is this work being done at all? Why is it done as it is? How could it be done more efficiently or at less cost?' Questions of this kind could only be answered if the scrutineers actually observed the work being carried out. They did in fact visit government laboratories and canteens, customs posts, motorway construction sites, post offices, schools, hospitals, museums and prisons.

Of course, the topics chosen for scrutiny 'related to areas where the department thought expenditure could be reduced'. There was, indeed, considerable pressure on them to choose topics of this kind, especially in view of the fact that the Government had set new manpower targets alongside the system of cash limits they had inherited. 'These were to have a major effect in reducing civil service numbers, and in proposing topics for scrutinies the departments were frequently seeking ways of meeting these targets.'[8]

But departments also used the opportunity provided by the scrutinies to deal with long-standing problems, sometimes problems caused by changes in the economic and social environment in which the departments worked. Many of these problems ultimately required political decisions, but were not fundamental political issues. Because they would simply create, to no great purpose, political problems for the minister concerned, they were always postponed. The programme of scrutinies gave the departments an opportunity to air these issues. The scrutineers, usually bright young administrators (principal grade) in the department concerned, had to produce a written report within ninety days of the completion of the scrutiny. This was then presented to the minister, with copies to Lord Rayner and the permanent secretary to the department concerned. They also took the precaution, contrary to the instructions they had received from Lord Rayner, of circulating reports within the department for comment, before they were submitted to the minister and to Rayner's staff. That at least concentrated the minds of the senior civil servants in the department concerned.

That this was the accepted procedure is especially clear in the scrutiny described by Norman Warner.[9] As Assistant Secretary in the DHSS, he had actually carried out the scrutiny he describes. With the aid of two other officials from his department, he examined the system of payment of social security benefits of various kinds over the post office counter. When they carried out the review in 1979, social security administration cost £750 million a year, of which £250 million went to the Post Office, as against a total budget of £15 billion for social security benefits. All the main benefits could be collected weekly from the Post Office, in spite of the fact that many more people at work were being paid monthly salaries and that three million occupational pensioners received their pensions on a monthly basis, many having their money paid directly into a bank or building society account. It seemed obvious that significant savings could be made by abandoning weekly payments.

To this end the team of officials interviewed trade union representatives in both the department and the central and local DHSS offices, and representatives of consumers, banks, building societies, National Girobank and the Post Office. The team came up with a number of recommendations, including the monthly payment of benefit into a personal bank account; less frequent payments except for those who really needed weekly giro cheques, such as elderly pensioners and those in receipt of supplementary benefit or income support; and allowing the Post Office to take on new counter business to make up the shortfall in their income. They did, however, attach a 'health warning' to the report: it could create political difficulties for ministers.

A short presentation of the report was given to the Prime Minister and the Cabinet, before it was finalized in the department. It was then submitted to the Secretary of State for his decision, but while he was considering it, the report was leaked to the press. A campaign against the report was soon under way. The 'health warning' which the civil servants had delivered was indeed percipient. Protest letters began to pour in to MPs as well as to the department before the Secretary of State had a chance to come to a decision.

The report had, of course, made it clear that ministers would undoubtedly face political problems because of the impact of the proposals on the Post Office's counter business. Norman Warner points out that 'it was the politics of change that sunk the report's main proposal of paying benefits less frequently ... The experience of this scrutiny highlights the importance of early ministerial involvement in reviews of what might at first sight seem innocuous internal management issues; in fact these issues involve disruption for powerful vested interests.'[10] But, of course, once such considerations are introduced, it becomes much more difficult to streamline the organization in terms of an efficient cost-cutting method of delivery. It is not just a question of 'powerful vested interests', though these obviously play a part, but of the community needs. It may have been this episode, amongst others, which led Rayner to observe in later years that the 'Government has to provide services which no sane business would undertake'.[11]

Rayner's scrutinies were often designed to deal with internal organization of a department rather than with the nature and extent of the services provided. The favourite target for the Rayner scrutinies was communication: removing obsolete forms, rewording circulars for the public or other Governmental agencies, cutting back on the collection of Government statistics – a move which the Government is now beginning to regret – or reforming a department's internal communication system. Rayner's own horror story concerns a Ministry of Agriculture circular, issued on 18 December 1981, called 'Festive Fare for Busy Cooks', which suggested planning ahead for Christmas! He pointed out that 'over 2000 million Government forms and leaflets are used by the public each year. That is thirty-six for every man, woman and child in the country', and, although the cost to the taxpayer was unknown, he reckoned that at 10p a form, it would cost in the region of £200 million. It was one of his most successful campaigns. Five years later, Richard Luce, as Minister for the Civil Service, announced that 27,000 forms had been cut, and 41,000 had been redesigned at a saving of £14 million.

Rayner was, however, even more determined to deal with the complaints about the amount of paper, its complexity and its irrelevance. As a result, no fewer than nine departments carried out reviews of their internal communications between 1979 and 1984, ranging from the Inland Rev-

8

enue's instructions to local offices, to the Treasury's review of paper handling and the Registry system.

What exactly did Rayner achieve by all this? Departments did not always accept the radical recommendations of the scrutineers. Clive Ponting, to be tried in 1985 for breaking the Official Secrets Act, found when he examined the supply of food to the armed forces, 'glaring examples of waste and inefficiency everywhere – warehouses full of food that was stored for years; three separate distribution systems and no one in charge of the system'.[12] He suggested immediate savings of £12 million and annual savings of £4 million, but his plans were not adopted. He concluded that Whitehall had simply swallowed up Raynerism, just as it had all the other plans and programmes for efficiency and reform.

Meanwhile, what of the renowned savings? There was the famous, over-expensive rat, a symbol of Raynerism. (The Ministry of Agriculture's veterinary laboratory at Weybridge reared their own rats for research purposes at £30 a time, whereas a 'private enterprise' rat could be purchased commercially at £2 a time.) Other savings were identified. During 1980, the first full year of the Rayner programme, thirty-nine scrutinies identified potential savings totalling £128 million per annum and proposed a cut in staff of 9500 posts. By 1983, when Lord Rayner's appointment had come to an end, according to the National Audit Office, departments had carried out 5 programmes comprising a total of 155 scrutinies, which had identified possible savings of £421 million a year. In the event, not all of these savings materialized. By 1983, at the time of the National Audit Office's examination, about 40 per cent of the action documents resulting from the scrutinies had been implemented, so the total savings actually achieved by 1983–4 were valued at £51.3 million a year, representing over 50 per cent of the total savings expected when all accepted recommendations were fully implemented.[13] By 1990, Norman Lamont, then Chief Secretary to the Treasury, claimed savings of over £1 billion since 1979 through the various economy measures the Government had introduced in the intervening ten years or so, a claim which it is difficult to substantiate in view of the fact that the proportion of total public spending on administration has hardly changed throughout the period.

But perhaps Rayner all along was less concerned with saving money and cutting down on staff, and had another aim in mind altogether. He was, in fact, looking for 'lasting reforms' and regarded the scrutinies as only the first step, paving the way for more far-reaching reforms. Something of that emerged in an interview he gave to *The Times* on 25 August 1981. 'The greatest example of waste I have found in government is so much talent at the service of the nation that, for one reason or another, is not being harnessed. My principal role has been to create an atmosphere in which this talent has been freed from normal restraints.' He wanted to see reform from within; hence the stress on the scrutineer 'taking the department with him or her'.

Yet the approach implicit in the Rayner programme meant that its impact was inevitably limited. It did not tackle the fundamental problems revealed by the scrutinies. The difficulties of communication within a Government department and, to a lesser extent, with the public, cannot be overcome by simply rewriting this or that set of instructions. The scrutinies showed that there are serious structural problems within departments. Setting up proper channels of communication within departments should have been one of the problems which was tackled during Rayner's time, in the interests of efficiency.

Some of the scrutinies brought to light an endemic problem in the process of reform. The DHSS scrutiny of benefit payments is a particularly striking example. The problems of streamlining payments appeared to be an administrative problem, but was in fact a political one, since the interests and wellbeing of so many of those involved in delivering the benefits to the public would have been damaged by a more efficient method. If, therefore, a Government minister were to propose various ways of changing the method of payment, he or she would have to be prepared to face the flak, and would, understandably, avoid taking what would seem to be unnecessarily difficult political decisions. The department, on the other hand, could not decide to rationalize their procedures or services without ministerial approval.

But even in Rayner's own terms, the scrutinies did not meet what he saw as the fundamental problem facing Whitehall. He described this, as far back as 1977, drawing on his own experiences in the Heath Government. 'Within Whitehall lies the responsibility for the management of businesses of a scale and diversity which are comparable to the largest in the private sector ... but [the managers] fail to match the achievements of the private sector, not because they do not possess the management ability ... but principally because they do not have the scope to operate as they do in the best-run businesses.'[14] An efficiency drive, however useful that may have been, was not enough.

The National Audit Office's Report on the Rayner scrutiny programmes, published in 1986, summed up the limitations of the Rayner approach:

More generally the scrutinies concentrated on the efficiency of aspects of a department's operations; relatively few scrutinies extended to the effectiveness of the expenditure in achieving policy objectives, and to larger and more difficult topics requiring substantial effort, often on an interdisciplinary basis ... The Rayner technique is in this sense one among many and it has increasingly developed as a valuable tool for securing a rapid and positive response to problems' ... [though] the full potential for improvement and development through successful scrutiny of techniques can be realized only if there is commitment at the top of each department – specifically on the part of ministers and accounting officers – to bring this about.[15]

The Rayner scrutinies had their value as a 'high level management technique to improve value for money',[16] but they certainly did not lead to any structural reform. A more comprehensive strategy was needed, and that came about with the birth of the Financial Management Initiative in 1982. By then, Lord Rayner had departed from Whitehall.

The Financial Management Initiative

This drew on the results of the scrutinies and on MINIS, the management information system for ministers, Michael Heseltine's brainchild. When he took over the Department of the Environment as Secretary of State in 1979, Heseltine soon found that he was dealing with no less than forty-eight under secretaries, and that he 'could not untangle the chains of responsibility within the department. It was impossible to figure out who was doing what, or why, or whether it needed doing at all. There appeared to be duplication of effect and conflicting estimates of costing. It was very rare to be able to find one person easily identifiable as being responsible.'[17]

Soon after his arrival in the department, he initiated a study of the information requirements for ministers. It was set up as a Rayner exercise, since the same analytic methods could be used to work out the kinds of information ministers would need to manage the department effectively. The aim was to provide ministers with a comprehensive, detailed and systematic picture of the workings of the department. They would then be able to judge the effectiveness of the department's policies. It would also be a useful tool for looking at staffing needs, and at a time of public spending cuts, deciding where to cut staff and limit its range of activities.

It was a time-consuming process. Each MINIS round took six months, beginning with sending out forms for completion in October and ending with the completion of MINIS discussions in March. The MINIS documents provided the basis for discussions between the permanent secretary, senior officials in the directorate, and, if necessary, with the Secretary of State and any other relevant ministers. With this detailed information at their disposal, ministers and senior officials could plan the directorate's future programme of action and any staff changes.

The MINIS system was developed at a time when departmental information systems were almost non-existent. Indeed, the need for such a system arose out of a Rayner scrutiny on 'The Provision of Management Information to Ministers', which proposed procedures for assembling detailed basic information about existing departmental activities, objectives and patterns of responsibility, rather than being entirely Michael Heseltine's invention. But the system led departments along the road of producing too much paper and not enough information. A MINIS report on the Department of the Environment quickly turned into a twelve-volume affair. It is hard to imagine that many ministers would ever want to plough through so many volumes of a report. The fact is that, since Michael Heseltine's sojourn in the department, few have.

Not many other departments were willing to try the MINIS system, arguing that they had their own administrative systems and did not need to take the time-consuming MINIS system on board. Nor was there much chance that they would be pressed to adopt it by their ministers, since, as the former head of the civil service put it, 'There are not many Mr Heseltines around.' The MINIS system, Sir Ian Bancroft added, 'is specifically tailored to the wishes of a minister who takes a very keen interest and devotes a great deal of time to the management of his department. The system, as it is in the DoE, would only be applicable to a department who had a minister in charge of it with Mr Heseltine's particular aptitude and attitudes'.[18]

During his time in the Department of the Environment, Michael Heseltine argued that the MINIS system enabled him both to cut staff and increase the efficiency of the organization. The department certainly reduced its manpower as a result of several types of economies identified by MINIS, which involved tightening the manpower budget, cutting out unnecessary services and, of course, transferring work to the private sector. Some officials in the department viewed the development of new systems like MINIS, and the time and importance attached to them by some ministers and senior management, as being an 'incentive' to work. For them, the new methods increased job satisfaction and enabled civil servants to work in a more 'professional' way.

This view that the new methods led to increased efficiency was not always shared by users of the department. Tony Mogfor, the then independent Chairman of Buckinghamshire County Council's Policy and Resources Committee, told *Management Today* in February 1983 that the 'Department of the Environment is quite impossible to deal with. Since 1975, we've cut back more than governments have asked for despite an increasing population – the DoE are working on figures two years out of date and 50,000 down on actual numbers, while at the same time, due to the fall in the rate support grant, we've lost £19 million a year. In response to a request from Heseltine, I sent the figures in nearly two months ago, and I still haven't had a response.'[19] Was that just an isolated incident, or does it reflect the point that these methods were more concerned with 'inputs' than with 'outputs'?

Of course, it has to be remembered that the MINIS system only covered 2 per cent of the department's expenditure. In 1982 the administrative costs amounted to £157 million compared with an overall expenditure of some £12.4 billion. It was concerned with the efficiency of the staff and with savings on staff but not with the effectiveness of the programmes for which the department was responsible.

In spite of these limitations, the MINIS system was enthusiastically welcomed by the Treasury and Civil Service Committee, which concluded that MINIS was a 'most important development'[20] and recommended that 'it should be adopted in all departments and, as appropriate, in other public sector bodies'.[21]

However, Sir Robert Armstrong said, in evidence to the Select Committee, 'I do not think they should be able to impose systems. I think they should be able to stimulate departments to improve their management information systems but I do not think in the end something which is imposed on a department, which it itself does not voluntarily espouse, will work.'[22] The MINIS system was not accepted by other departments, some of whom did not regard it as cost-effective[23] and was itself integrated into a full management accounting system, known as the Joubert system.

One of the most important aims of the MINIS was to provide ministers and senior management with detailed information about what was happening in their departments. It had other important effects as well. Sue Richards and Les Metcalfe, in *Improving Public Management*, argued that 'to the extent that MINIS procedures succeed in instituting due process in departmental decision-making, they represent a significant move towards establishing accountable management. They pave the way for clear delegation of authority and responsibility and provide a mechanism for differentiating systematically between levels of policy decision within departments ... Another unintended consequence of MINIS is to reinforce tendencies towards greater openness in Government. To the extent that Government departments assemble information on a systematic basis for their own purposes, the argument that open government is too costly loses a lot of force.'[24] These possibilities may well have been opened up by the introduction of MINIS and its adaptation through FMI to other departments. The Department of the Environment still publishes the MINIS reports annually, and therefore continues to provide a precedent for open government. But by 1988, the 'Next Steps' programme was introduced to pursue the objectives of devolving responsibility. In other words, the reforms begun in the early 1980s still have to reach fruition.

Once, however, departments had begun to develop modern, computerized, financial management and information systems, the MINIS system was inappropriate. It was designed to provide ministers and permanent secretaries with far more detailed information than they could possibly use. This explains why the whole system was regarded with a decided coolness by those who were responsible for operating it. One assistant secretary in the Department of the Environment at the time commented: 'Heseltine probably read some of the reports, but that was not true of anyone else.' But even if they had, they would probably not have found the reports helpful because, 'the performance reviews contained in the MINIS reports were too indigestible, nor did they contain proper programmes of work for which a minister required a quarterly or monthly report on progress'. Indeed, such deficiencies seem to be symptomatic of the way in which the system operates, since the same assistant secretary complained that he had suffered from 'too many bosses who had sat on reports or on decisions for weeks or even months'. There are pressures of work, but these fall on civil servants working in policy areas, who are 'constantly buffeted by ministerial demands, political pressures, timetables for achieving objectives, which are not under the control of the civil service ... The legislative timetable determines events'. This means that there is 'no systematic planning or management system',[25] a significant comment in view of the array of management systems in the department.

This may explain why the MINIS system gradually moved towards a full management accounting system, called the Joubert system, showing non-staff costs in addition to all the details of staff costs previously recorded, thereby enabling directorates to have full details of their expenditure.

These systems were developed to support new management processes and methods. Their success relies on departments being able to identify the individual managerial responsibility for the delivery of services. In other words, the MINIS and Joubert systems were not ends in themselves, but they inevitably paved the way for the 'grand strategy' of achieving an efficient civil service. These innovations were the inspiration for the Financial Management Initiative, set out in the Government's response to the Third Report from the Treasury and Civil Service Select Committee.[26]

The Financial Management Initiative was, in fact, just the kind of centralized push towards setting up similar systems in Government departments which Sir Robert Armstrong said was undesirable. It did, however, arise out of the Treasury and Civil Service Select Committee's recommendation that MINIS, which they regarded as a 'most important development', 'should be adopted in all departments and, as appropriate, in other public sector bodies'.[27]

The Government responded to the Select Committee's report by accepting that and most of the other recommendations. It pointed out that the Treasury and the Management and Personnel Office (MPO) had set up a unit to 'ensure the systematic and comprehensive application of higher standards of financial management'.[28] The aim is to 'promote in each department an organization and system in which managers at all levels have:

a) a clear view of their objectives and means to assess and, wherever possible, measure outputs and performance in relation to those objectives;

b) well-defined responsibility for making the best use of their resources, including a critical scrutiny of output and value for money; and

c) the information (particularly about costs), the training and access to expert advice that they need to exercise their responsibilities effectively.'[29]

A working document set out more details and had already been sent to departments, which had to report back by July 1983.

The Financial Management Unit was set up by the Treasury and the Management and Personnel Office to assist departments in developing a strategy to improve efficiency. John Cassels took up the post of Permanent Secretary at the Management and Personnel Office. He had been the Director of the Manpower Services Commission and had expressed the view that financial management should be extended to cover a wide variety of non-financial objectives.

The Financial Management Initiative followed on from MINIS in that it was a top management system, which is supposed to provide information for strategic management. When Michael Heseltine moved to the Ministry of Defence from the Department of the Environment in 1983, he found he had acquired a much larger department with a complex structure. He persevered with his plans to set up a management information system and eventually succeeded, triumphantly displaying an organization chart of the Ministry of Defence on the wall in his office.

Michael Heseltine further regarded the FMI as an extension of the system he had introduced and a justification of his ideas. He commented in his book, *Where There's a Will*: 'By 1984 most departments had, at last, adopted management information systems with some or most of the features of MINIS, and were using them to improve financial control. To quieten any suggestion of vulgar imitation, and to maintain understandable *amour propre*, departments found different names and different acronyms: thus the Department of Trade and Industry introduced ARM (for activity and resource management); Agriculture sprouted both MINIM and the rustic sounding MAIS; in the Home Office there is APR, and in the Health Department DMA. By 1985, the Lord Chancellor's Department had devised something which sounds a little more lordly: it is called LOCIS, for the Lord Chancellor's information system.'[30]

Later the MINIS system was combined with a complementary management system, the Joubert system known as MAXIS. Civil servants working on the Rayner scrutiny of non-staff running costs in the DoE, which reported in 1981, studied the scope for developing an organization structure based on local cost centres, the heads of which would be responsible for controlling their expenditure. The system, which was then adopted as a result of the Rayner exercise, divided the department into 120 responsibility units or cost centres, each of which has an annual budget to cover running costs, including those for staff. A computerized management system tells managers at all levels how expenditure is going against the plan and a central budget unit oversees the system. This enabled the Department of the Environment, in which the system was first introduced, to establish budgets and cost centres at assistant secretary level and to give civil servants at that level the responsibility for managing the budget. It is called the Joubert system after Christopher Joubert, Assistant Secretary, Management and Personnel Office, who invented it. The Joubert system, known as MAXIS, complemented MINIS because the cost centres were based on functional units within the DoE, for example, dealing with housing subsidies or inner city grants all of which were identified in the MINIS system. 'MINIS,' as a former under secretary in the Department of Environment described, was 'concerned with the specific objectives we set ourselves to achieve within a limited time period, and the resources we use ... When it is operating successfully, as we hope it will be in the next year or so, we hope to be able to look back and ask managers: "You said you would do such and such in the last six or twelve month period. Now why haven't you done it?" '[31] The MINIS system was invaluable in Geoffrey Chipperfield's view because it produced a framework in which ministers and permanent secretaries in the department can consider the allocation of the department's resources.

In many ways, it is the Joubert system, as a development of MINIS, which should be seen as a precursor to the Financial Management Initiative. The latter is also a decentralized budgeting system, requiring information about the unit costs of specific activities. So sets of activities were grouped into appropriate units and cost centres. The aim was to make the managers who were responsible for the cost centres' operations more aware of the costs involved. Managers, therefore, had to have direct control over the activities which determined the costs. New budgetary, accounting and financial information systems had to be designed, tested, modified and then put into operation. Each department would have an organization and a system for delegating to senior line managers the responsibility for planning the use of resources within agreed limits. In addition, central departments – the Treasury and the Management and Personnel Office – would oversee the division of the cash, manpower and objectives into 'block budgets' which were directly linked to the annual cycle of procedures for planning and controlling public expenditure. That is the nub of the Financial Management Initiative, from which it can be seen that the Treasury remained in overall control, and that there were considerable difficulties in having responsibility both for a cost centre and for meeting the requirements of the public-spending cycle.

For a large, complex central government department, changing the management and accounting system is a real upheaval, so it is hard to judge when such change really has improved value for money. The National Audit Office in its report published in 1986, four years after the new system had been in operation, thought it was too early to judge. The Public Accounts Committee thought that a number of departments were not that enthusiastic about the Financial Management Initiative.

The Treasury, at least up until 1986, chose to ignore the FMI. Part of the reason for that was that it is an annual planning exercise, whereas PESC (the Public Expenditure Survey Committee) is a medium-term planning exercise, looking three to five years ahead. A conflict therefore arises between the resource planning and the medium-term planning controlled by the Treasury, which is concerned with overall resource allocation. The Treasury will not give up its power over the latter and this inevitably limits the flexibility of the top management divisions. The budgetary approach of the management (resource planning/ allocation/control/monitoring/performance review) contained in the FMI conflicts with the Treasury's public spending cycle, and with its determination to control spending, and in particular to see the FMI as another means of control.

Indeed, the first report from the Financial Management Unit in 1984 stated that 'more needs to be done to work out and implement clear links between top management systems, the established Public Expenditure Survey and Estimates process and the new systems of information and control to review and set management plans and budgets of those down the line'.[32]

The civil service unions, too, clearly recognized the limitations of the Financial Management Initiative:

... the spark of life missing from this forlorn creature is, of course, the allocation of real money to managers ... But giving them real money would, of course, mean giving them real power down the line – the last thing that the central departments, or, for that matter, department-level managements, would contemplate. So we are left with the usual half-baked civil service compromise. Civil service managers are to have all the rigours and disadvantages of devolved power, without being allowed to exercise that power.[33]

Recognizing that problem eventually led the Government to the introduction of the 'Next Steps' programme. They would then come to realize that the lessons of the past had not been learnt with the introduction of the Financial Management Initiative. The Civil Service Department, which Mrs Thatcher abolished in 1981, was set up to achieve the results that the Government now expected from the Financial Management Initiative. Richard Wilding, who had himself taken part in these changes, commented that:

While finance was the responsibility of the Treasury and management was the responsibility of the CSD, financial management was apt to fall down the crack between the two. The CSD did its best – and not without success – to promote management accounting and internal audit, but mainly in a consulting and advisory mode. It was not until the redistribution of functions in 1981 that the leading responsibility for financial management was clearly located in the Treasury and the machinery for a sustained central drive could begin to be properly developed.[34]

The main thrust of this initiative was to establish cost centres, but it should also have led to far greater powers, responsibilities and personal accountability for line managers and, presumably in line with that, a departure from stable pay structures with annual increments, which allows for mobility and career development throughout the whole service. However, there is little sign of any such intention in the Cassels Report or the report on Civil Service Management Development in the 1980s from the Management and Personnel Office, published in 1983, which noted that the civil service is a career service, whose staffing policy is primarily based on recruiting people as they leave the education system and retaining them in the service until they retire instead of hiring people on a short-term basis. The Cassels Report, for example, recommended that departments should have greater flexibility to operate local recruitment, and find cost-effective ways of involving their own local line managers, with the support and advice of personnel staff. But those recommendations applied only to junior levels of staff. Executive officers should still be recruited by the Civil Service Commission. The report notes that: 'Changing patterns of upbringing, education and recruitment are yielding staff more ready to express views, question authority, seek involvement in the work process and carry more responsibility. I firmly believe that their energies and abilities must be harnessed by a more open and participative style of management giving more opportunity for staff to exercise responsibility in shaping their jobs.'[35] Such recommendations, however, have yet to be fully implemented.

The Financial Management Unit was established to assist departments in establishing top management systems. Its first report was published in 1984. It commented that by 1983 most departments had only completed initial or experimental rounds of their new or strengthened top management systems.

The limited scope for manoeuvre, because of the Treasury's role, becomes clear in the report from the MPO. The departments the MPO reviewed pointed out that there is a 'general forward shift of emphasis in the annual resource planning and allocation cycle from the Estimates to the PES stages. This is reflected by increasingly thorough and comprehensive arrangements for a review of PES expenditure plans (and associated manpower) by senior management and ministers prior to submission of plans to the Treasury in June ... As a consequence, financial and man-power totals for the first and subsequent years of the PES period, together with underlying policy assumptions and objectives ... are increasingly determined through PES' (that is, centrally).[36]

Four years later, in 1986, the National Audit Office published its report on the departments' progress in developing their management systems in response to FMI. The departments were making real progress with that task, but the National Audit Office did not examine how far they had succeeded in achieving value for money, the overriding aim of FMI. 'The arrangements to support this improved management, even those whose development was substantially complete, had not been in place long enough for their full effect, in terms of improved value for money, to become apparent.'[37]

Not only was progress slow towards the Government's main objective in introducing the Financial Management Initiative, but the pitfalls were still there. The control which managers could have over elements of their budgets varied considerably between departments, with some having little opportunity to transfer money from one budget to another. The report adds that 'some managers felt their control over staff costs was less effec-tive because of the continuation of central controls over pay, grading and manpower ceilings, and that they had little scope for controlling accommodation costs, particularly in the shorter term'.[38] The National Audit Office saw 'encouraging progress' on the part of departments in gaining an 'effective control' over administrative costs, but 'more still needed to be done to achieve the full potential benefits particularly as regards developing strong links between the input costs and the value of outputs'.[39]

The Financial Management Initiative had two failings, one of which con-cerned the Government. The lack of control experienced by managers over all matters affecting their ability to manage their budgets was one of the factors which led to the introduction of the 'Next Steps' programme. The second failing is the lack of concern with the effectiveness of programmes. Departments did endeavour to assess the effectiveness of programmes designed to fulfil the Government's policy objectives, but 'value for money', not the effectiveness of policies, was the overriding consideration.

The implicit assumption behind FMI is that if you get the budgetary process right, you get good management – it is simply a question of control, and control comes through budgets which make line management responsible and accountable for achieving budgetary targets. Of course, line managers may have to play some part in formulating their objectives, because practical knowledge has to be built into the budgetary process. However, consultation with the line managers is only part of the story. Top management actually works out the objectives, and then allocates these to middle managers for operational purposes.

In the past, the costs of running various units within the central departments were supervised by a few finance divisions, often linked with the system of accounting to Parliament (a nineteenth-century approach). It was difficult to assess these costs accurately, so they were estimated, with responsibility and accountability for such activities given to cost centre managers or budget holders. Having been given new responsibilities, these managers became aware of the link between the activities which they authorized and the costs of carrying them out. Principals and assistant secretaries received the requisite accountancy training, and familiarization training was given to a wide range of civil servants.

The Financial Management Initiative was designed to make senior civil servants concentrate on management, by requiring them to develop information systems, learn how to set objectives and allocate resources to achieve them, and carry out regular reviews of the extent to which objectives had been achieved. These are all time-consuming tasks, sufficiently absorbing to distract attention from the glamour of policy advice. Departments began to reorganize. They set up 'top management boards', with each board member having a responsibility for the line management of one particular area of activity. Each manager began to concentrate on his or her area of responsibility, leading to much greater compartmentalization within the department. This could well limit the exchange of ideas within the department, especially at principal and assistant secretary level. Top management alone were in a position to have an overview of the department's activities.

Attempts were made to ensure that line managers were really responsible for the services they provided. The Property Services Agency and the Civil Service College began to 'charge' for accommodation and training courses, although decisions about property were still taken by the Agency. Training courses, on the other hand, could be 'bought' by departments as they thought fit. There were further innovations following the Efficiency Unit's 1984 report on the consultancy, inspection and review services, which recommended that they should be limited to giving expert advice, rather than inspecting and controlling what civil servants were doing. The principal finance officers in departments were encouraged to 'challenge' other financial decision-makers and advise the top management board.

The National Audit Office's assessment of the Financial Management

Initiative, given by the head of the Government Accounting Service in 1986, has been, perhaps cynically, 'de-coded' as follows:

Wilson: Our findings suggest that the links between top management and budgetary systems are still developing, and for the most part, are not yet fully articulated.

Translation: Most top civil servants are not managing their departments.

Wilson: . . . while responsibility for decisions is progressively being transferred from central finance and establishment commands to the line management chain, the central divisions have still fully to come to terms with the requirements of their changing role.

Translation: Central divisions will not let go of their power.

Wilson: At the moment we see insufficient flavour of objective setting and performance review as the background to resource allocation.

Translation: The Treasury behaves as though the Financial Management Initiative does not exist.[40]

But is this cynical interpretation of the impact of the Financial Management Initiative justified? In particular, how significant was the unwillingness of the Treasury to devolve financial management to budget holders in the departments?

First of all, if nothing else, the Financial Management Initiative pushed departments firmly in the direction of setting up proper computerized accounting systems. Many central government departments had introduced such systems within four years of the commencement of FMI, turning their accounting systems into 'something substantially more than huge petty cash books'.[41] The size and significance of that task should not be underestimated.

'A large central government department advanced in the space of a year from a manual single entry accounting system, which comprised no more than about 400 accounts, to a computerized, financial and management accounting general ledger, processing three million transactions into 450,000 accounts.'[42] That gives some idea of the scale of the achievement. Such development put government accounting ahead of many private sector organizations at the time.

But of course these systems were designed to back up the new methods of decentralized management. And that is where the problem lay. Anne Mueller, then a Second Permanent Secretary in the Management and Personnel Office, conceded that:

There's still a long way to go in terms of giving greater freedom and discretion to individual departments and, within departments, to individual line managers. We are working on it. We're working quite hard on it. But it will take time just as it's taken time to set up the original systems for the Financial Management Initiative then the delegated budgets.

But at the end of the day, there is a limit. And it's a different sort of limit from the sort you'll find in the private sector, where you can simply rely on the profit measurement to determine what is and what is not acceptable for an organization as a whole.[43]

The Financial Management Initiative was intended to shift the Rayner emphasis from the costs of providing services to the development of indicators to evaluate the effectiveness of policies. The number of output and performance measures did increase with the introduction of FMI, up from 500 in 1985 to 1800 in 1987. But, on examination, many of these turn out to be manpower statistics, or the numbers of recipients of social security benefits, or hospital outpatients treated – information which has always been available in departments. These figures do not depend on a clear statement of the objectives of various policies and the appropriate measures of their effectiveness; they are simply activity indicators.

The inadequacy of these indicators was indeed recognized by the Treasury, but with the acknowledgement that 'information on final output measures over a large area is not actually going to be attainable ... we are bound to operate in large measure by intermediate measures'.[44] Admitting this to a Parliamentary Select Committee, however, did not prevent the Treasury and the National Audit Office from claiming real progress 'in identifying performance targets'.[45] In fact, the most progress has been made in measuring the administration of departmental work, especially in those departments handling specific services, such as Social Security's comparison of administrative costs to benefits paid to claimants, or the Department of Education and Science's estimates of unit costs per pupil.

But the 1986 National Audit Office report notes that administrative costs still amounted to 13 per cent of total Government spending, the same proportion as in 1980, the first year of the Rayner scrutinies. The report concluded that 'more still needed to be done to achieve the full potential benefits particularly as regards developing strong links between the input costs and the value of outputs.'[46] As Sir Peter Middleton admitted, 'Output measures are crucial to this, otherwise if you are applying too much judgement to the output side there is too much flab in the system to detect when management is good or bad.'[47]

Yet little further progress has been made since then in developing proper output measures, or indeed, adequate measures of the effectiveness of Government policies. Such measures do depend on the willingness of politicians to accept the need for clarity and precision in the statement of programme objectives in terms of 'what will be achieved, by when and at what cost'. Ministers willingly accepted these proposals in principle, but not in practice. In Government policies since 1982, there have been few signs of more clearly stated objectives fulfilling these criteria and, indeed, some policies have shown quite the reverse. The whole purpose of the policy has not been clearly set out, and the expected costs and achievements have apparently not been carefully assessed – the poll tax is a case in point. Sir Gordon Downey, then the Comptroller and Auditor General, while recognizing that tight controls may well limit a government's capacity to govern, pointed out: 'Nobody – particularly government – wants to volunteer the material by which they may be judged and found wanting. Nobody wants to set out clearly in advance what they mean to achieve, and then provide the information on results that show how far they may have fallen short. But the fact that evasion is natural does not mean that it is acceptable.'[48] But for this, the blame lies with politicians, not with the civil service.

The Financial Management Initiative could, however, make it more difficult to assess the effectiveness of programmes and policies, even if politicians stated aims and objectives more explicitly. The reasons for that have been usefully spelt out by Andrew Gray and William Jenkins. The Financial Management Initiative uses a 'code of accountable management', which 'emphasizes a responsibility ... for reducing inputs almost regardless of outputs, let alone policy effects ... Some of the applications of FMI appear to be mechanisms of financial restraint rather than elements in a programme of strategic management ... the thrust has been to create targets, to hold managers "accountable" and to define such targets almost exclusively in input terms ... The division of departments into "businesses" with "costs" that must be minimized and accounted for by "managers" reveals a particular view of the world that is input-dominated.'[49]

Management is regarded primarily as a means of control. But there is much more to management than control, although the Government did not see that. The problem is that the Government operated with too simple a view of private sector management, one which was inappropriate for management of public services in a political context. But there are much more suitable models of management that can be derived from the private sector, especially from financial services companies whose competitive edge rests on the quality of service they offer to their customers. Front-line staff are involved in key organization issues so that both quality and regulation are, to a large extent, self-imposed. These issues were entirely neglected by the Financial Management Initiative, despite the desire on the part of most civil servants to improve the quality of service they offered to the public.

Even the support civil servants gave to the Financial Management Initiative, especially middle managers for whom it represented freedom and opportunities for real management, was squandered by cuts in civil service numbers and the Government's continuing hostility to public services. It had been a step forward for these civil servants in particular – surprising though it may be. For the first time, they could see a connection between the work they authorized and its costs. A programme of familiarization training was established to make sure they understood the Initiative and would know what they were expected to do, if they became cost centre managers.

For civil servants themselves, the Financial Management Initiative presented other difficulties, a kind of threat to the traditional concept of a single career civil service, by separating the functions of management and policy advice, managers from senior advisers. Indeed, 'in some lights, the Initiative looks like a new set of roles which senior managers expect their subordinates to perform but over which they intend to remain in charge. In others, the Initiative looks like establishing a "career service" to manage the system of "cost centres", but from below and without any obvious ladders of promotion into the senior departmental posts above them.'[50] If those fears were present and in any way justifiable during the years of the Financial Management Initiative, they would be intensified with the introduction of executive agencies.

It had become clear, however, to many civil servants that solid managerial skills were not a route to the top. That was but one element in the widespread disquiet and low morale in the civil service as a whole. Civil servants leave the service at senior levels because they are not responsible for the results. A senior civil servant tends to advise rather than act and this can be very frustrating. Such frustrations lay behind the report on the progress of the Financial Management Initiative produced by the members of the Efficiency Unit.

This is the review in which Sir Robin Ibbs set Kate Jenkins and her team, Karen Caines and Andrew Jackson, loose on Whitehall. The process of gathering evidence on the achievements of the Rayner scrutinies and FMI 'showed clearly that there was something wrong with the organizational structure of Whitehall. Meetings with ministers and permanent secretaries in some departments led to both the minister and the permanent secretary pointing to each other and saying, "He's responsible for the management of the department." '[51]

Underlying the subsequent report, the 'Next Steps', is the conclusion that 'it is not possible for ministers to manage a department, even when they bring the requisite managerial skills to the task. It is too time-consuming for a minister to be involved in motivating and monitoring people's work, especially in a large department. That should be the role of the permanent official. The minister should be concerned with new policy directions and accountability to Parliament, bringing fresh criticisms of policy and strategic vision, leaving managing the department to the permanent secretary, whose role it should be.'[52]

Equally, permanent secretaries had to learn how to devolve power within departments, while the centre, the Treasury and the Cabinet Office continued to meddle in departmental affairs. Amidst such confusion, much more remained to be done if the managerial reforms instigated by Mrs Thatcher and Lord Rayner in 1979 were to be effective. It was no doubt these concerns which led to the development of the 'Next Steps' initiative.[53]

Notes

1 P. Cosgrave, *Thatcher: The First Term*, 1985, pp. 169–70.
2 HC Deb., 13 May 1980, Vol. 984, col. 1050.
3 A. Shenfield et al. (eds), *Managing the Bureaucracy*, Adam Smith Institute, 1986, p. 31.
4 D. Rayner, 'The Unfinished Agenda', Stamp Memorial Lecture, University of London, 6 November 1984.
5 HC Deb., 15 July 1991, col. 37W.
6 The Scrutiny Programme: A Note by Sir Derek Rayner, p. 2, 2 November 1979.
7 'Efficiency in the Civil Service', Cmnd 8293, p. 2.
8 A.M. Bray, 'The Clandestine Reformer: A Study of the Rayner Scrutinies', *Strathclyde Papers on Government and Politics*, 1987, No. 55, pp. 12–13.
9 N.Warner, 'Raynerism in Practice', *Public Administration*, Spring 1984, Vol. 62, pp. 7–22.
10 ibid. pp. 23–33.
11 D. Rayner, *The Administrator*, March 1983, pp. 3–6.
12 C. Ponting, *Whitehall: Tragedy and Farce*, 1986, pp. 215–16.
13 National Audit Office, Report by the Comptroller and Auditor General, 'The Rayner Scrutiny Programmes 1979–83', HC 322, 1986.

[14] D. Rayner, 'Making Room for Managers in Whitehall', *Management Services in Government*, 1973, Vol. 28, pp. 61–6.

[15] National Audit Office, op. cit. p. 6.

[16] ibid. p. 1.

[17] R. Pauley, 'Heseltine Uncovers a Few Home Truths', *Financial Times*, 18 November 1980.

[18] I. Bancroft, Q365, Treasury and Civil Service Select Committee, 'Efficiency and Effectiveness in the Civil Service', Session 1981–2, Third Report, HC236–II.

[19] Tony Mogfor, Whitehall's Mod Management, *Management Today*, February 1983, p. 72.

[20] p. xvi, Third Report from the Treasury and Civil Service Select Committee, 1981–2, HC236–I.

[21] ibid. p. xl.

[22] R. Armstrong, Treasury Committee, Q1220, ibid. vol. II.

[23] K. Barnes, Treasury Committee, Q897, ibid. vol. II.

[24] S. Metcalfe and L. Richards, *Improving Public Management*, 1987, p. 74.

[25] private source.

[26] Cmnd 8616, 'Efficiency and Effectiveness in the Civil Service', September 1982, pp. 5–6.

[27] p. xl.

[28] p. 5.

[29] ibid.

[30] M. Heseltine, *Where There's A Will*, Arrow Books, 1987, p. 23.

[31] G. Chipperfield, 'The MINIS and Joubert Programmes', in *Proceedings of a Seminar*, organized by RIPA and Peat Marwick Mitchell & Co., 1983, p. 22.

[32] 'Top Management Systems', Report by the Cabinet Office (MPO)/Treasury, Financial Management Unit, March 1984.

[33] The Bulletin of the Council of Civil Service Unions, February 1985, p. 17.

[34] R. Wilding, 'Management Information and Control: The Role of the Centre', in B. Hardcastle et al., *Management Information and Control*, 1983, p. 41.

[35] 'Review of Personnel Work in the Civil Service', Report to the Prime Minister, J.S. Cassels, 1983, p. 7.

[36] 'Top Management Systems', Report by the Cabinet Office (MPO)/Treasury Financial Management Unit, March 1984, pp. 20–21.

[37] National Audit Office, 'The Financial Management, Report by the Comptroller and Auditor General Initiative', 1986, p. 11.

[38] ibid. p. 5.

[39] ibid. p. 7.

[40] A. Harrison and J. Gretton (eds), *Reshaping Central Government*, 1987, p. 34.

[41] G. Oates, 'The FMI in Central Government', *Public Accountancy and Finance*, 20 June 1986, p. 17.

[42] ibid. p. 17.

[43] A. Mueller, 'Whitehall', LWT, Channel Four, 25 May and 1 June 1988.

[44] P. Middleton, Evidence to the Public Accounts Committee, 1986–87, p. 7, 13th Report, Financial Management Initiative, HC61.

[45] National Audit Office, 'The Financial Management Initiative', 1986, p. 5.
[46] ibid. p. 5.
[47] p. 8.
[48] G. Downey, 'Public Accountability: Fact or Myth?', *Public Money*, June 1986, Vol. 6, No. 1, June 1986, p. 37.
[49] A. Gray and W. Jenkins, 'Accountable Management in British Central Government', *Financial Accountability and Management*, Vol. 2, No. 3, Autumn 1986, pp. 182, 184–5.
[50] M.J. Lee, *Public Administration*, Winter 1984, Vol. 62, No. 1, 'Financial Management and Career Service', p. 6.
[51] Private information.
[52] Private information.
[53] 'Improving Management in Government: The Next Steps', Kate Jenkins, Karen Caines, Andrew Jackson, HMSO, 1988.

TWO

The 'Next Steps' Initiative

On 18 February 1988, the Prime Minister announced to the House of Commons that the Government had accepted four of the recommendations set out in the Efficiency Unit's report, *Improving Management in Government: The Next Steps*. The report was actually completed in May 1987, kept secret at the Prime Minister's insistence until after the June election, and finally released the following year after months of indecision and delay.

Four out of the five conclusions of the report are a damning indictment of the whole programme of 'management reform'. These are 'a lack of clear and accountable management responsibility ... the need for greater precision about the results expected of people and organizations ... the handicap of imposing a uniform system in an organization of the size and diversity of the civil service, and a ... need for a sustained pressure for improvement'.[1] What was clearly admitted in the report is what many had either known or suspected for some years: the Treasury had held on to its power. Delegation and decentralization of power meant little; '"management" had not yet caught on generally in the upper echelons of the civil service'.[2]

The Government finally agreed that, as far as possible, the executive functions of government should be carried out by designated units within departments – the executive agencies. They would 'carry out the executive functions of government within a policy and resources framework set by the department', the report said. This would see a real devolution of power to executive agencies concerning budgets, manpower, pay, hiring and firing. A chief executive would be responsible for the day-to-day operations of each agency, within a framework of policy objectives and resources set by the responsible minister in consultation with the Treasury.

The Prime Minister announced the appointment of a Project Manager, Peter Kemp (now Sir Peter Kemp), whose job it would be to ensure that the programme of change actually worked, and that staff were properly trained and prepared for the management of the delivery of services. The Prime Minister committed the Government to a 'progressive programme for attaining this objective'. By April 1991, 51 agencies had been established, involving 210,260 civil servants, with a further 24 under consideration. The Prime Minister promised Parliament that the agencies would be accountable to a minister, who would in turn be accountable to Parliament for the agency's performance. The agencies would generally be within the civil service and their staff would continue to be civil servants. In the brief statement Mrs Thatcher gave to the House, devolving administration to the agencies seemed entirely straightforward, without any complications for the traditional concept of a politically neutral career civil service or for parliamentary accountability. This apparent simplicity was indeed only apparent because these difficult issues were sidestepped by the Prime Minister.

At the time, though, setting up agencies seemed to be a logical step, following on from the devolved management implied in the Financial Management Initiative. Authority had been delegated to middle management. But it was clear that many managers still felt frustrated by 'unnecessary controls and by the intervention of ministers and senior officials in relatively minor issues'.[3] The answer seemed obvious – devolve the cost centres of the FMI still further and turn them into agencies, thereby giving managers real responsibility. Of course, that was not the only reason for this development, but it was plainly the most compelling one in the view of the Efficiency Unit.

'The process of gathering evidence [for the Next Steps] ... showed that there was something wrong with the organizational structure of Whitehall. It relied on what civil servants themselves thought about their work' – the frustration so many plainly experienced with the long chains of command and the consequent lack of real responsibility and decision-making. But its 'purpose was to change the way people behave ... It didn't depend on any other models, not even the "Swedish model". It relied on what civil servants themselves thought about their work. They would like to use their intelligence and judgement to bring to bear on policy, but instead they were surrounded by rules and regulations because their lines of management were insufficiently clear. The aim was to bring about a change in behaviour and perception, which would then have led to a change of structures.'[4] Commentators at the time certainly thought that the Government's plans to establish executive agencies had been influenced by the Swedish model of government. The *Financial Times* reported in November 1988 that Peter Kemp had paid a 'rapid visit to Sweden to see how its administration works' and quoted him as saying: 'We have to be careful about translating policies for one country into another', but Robert Taylor, the author of the piece, commented that Peter Kemp 'did not disguise his enthusiasm for the Swedish administrative system, which consists of small central government departments and a large number of semi-autonomous agencies responsible for carrying out their policy decisions'.[5] Subsequently, as we have seen, senior civil servants involved in the Next Steps programme denied any real Swedish influence. But, despite these denials, it is still worth examining the Swedish model and exploring comparisons between that model and the way in which the Next Steps initiative has developed since 1988. Some of these issues will be explored later in this chapter.

The 'Next Steps' document itself provided a range of justifications for introducing agencies, an idea which in the UK goes back at least to the Fulton Committee on the civil service which, in 1968, recommended accountable units of management. In its rationale for the introduction of agencies, the Efficiency Unit stressed the importance of service delivery. Attitudes and perceptions of the job must change, but this must be accompanied by organizational changes. The Efficiency Unit argued that the civil service was too large to be managed as a single organization; that ministerial overload prevented proper attention to management. The current reforms were being frustrated at middle management levels by unnecessary controls and intervention by top management. At senior levels a concern with policy work continued to dominate to an exclusion of interest in service delivery. All the pressures were mainly on expenditure and resource control rather than on the results being achieved.

The Efficiency Unit advocated radical changes in the way Government services were delivered in the major departments and at the centre of Government. Management could only be improved if:

the work of each department was focused on the job to be done

each department ensured its staff had the relevant experience and skills

there was a real and sustained pressure within each department for continuous improvement in value for money obtained in the delivery of policy and services.[6]

The original aims were clear enough. There would be a small, powerful core of the civil service, consisting of policy advisers in departments and the Treasury and Cabinet Office. They would operate with a limited set of rules, negotiate targets with the agencies responsible for delivering services, and simply monitor them to ensure compliance.

There would be a clear line of demarcation between policy and administration, in which the agencies would be designated to administer services. The agencies would be another significant step along the line of devolving responsibility and making it easier to emphasize the importance of results and check them.

The role of the departments in this framework has not been described in any detail by the Government, but it appears that they would set and monitor the framework, leaving managers to manage. The programme would have to be supported and driven by the centre of Government so that a planned programme of identifying and establishing appropriate agencies could be implemented, but no final decisions have been made on just how the departments would carry out that responsibility nor how they should characterize the nature of that relationship.

The 'Next Steps' initiative could bring about a change in the management style of the civil service. It means less emphasis on supervision and more on trusting line managers to 'get it right first time', by ensuring that they are aware of the implications of those requirements and are committed to their achievement. But that would require the line managers to understand the standards of service required and a commitment from the staff, which means clearly involving the staff in discussing how the standards are to be achieved and ensuring they have an input into that achievement. Quality cannot be imposed from above. Some, but not all, of the agencies are tackling the question of staff participation at all levels, but this is not a uniform development, and fewer still have seriously consulted their customers or clients.

The framework is supposed to leave 'ministers wholly responsible for policy' and 'officials are to show real qualities of leadership', but it is not clear 'who determines where the division comes between ministers who are responsible and the judgements and unpopular decisions which officials must be prepared to defend'.[7] Professor Chapman certainly put his finger on one of the fundamental problems of the programme of establishing the executive agencies, namely, that the original statement did not explain the policy/management relationship. Moreover, there has been no further explanation since then.

The Treasury's approach to the agencies is quite different from that of other Government departments. It inevitably has a central role in implementing the agency initiative, especially the negotiations for agency frameworks. The agencies naturally argue that they require more flexibility in recruitment, in personnel and pay policies and in budgeting, particularly the relaxation of annuality rules, and perhaps in some cases, more freedom for capital financing. The Treasury's main interest, however, seems to be in experiments with personnel policy, especially with pay, no doubt with the aim of reducing the costs of civil service pay.

The Government's interests are more difficult to determine, especially in view of the change of Prime Minister. Under the Thatcher administration, the underlying aim may well have been to restrict the role of the public sector still further and perhaps even to privatize certain functions. Under Prime Minister Major, the Government's intentions are still not clear – though leaks suggest the continuing possibility of privatization, with the same underlying hostility to the public sector. But no one has tackled the central question as to whether agencies are indeed the most appropriate way of achieving better management and service delivery. Nor has anyone examined the efficiency of existing agencies established in the early 1970s following the Fulton Report, or the extent to which any increases in efficiency arose from their agency status. Structural change pure and simple is assumed to bring the requisite improvements in its train.

Establishing so many executive agencies has raised much more fundamental questions about the structure of the civil service than were considered when the Government accepted the Efficiency Unit's report and embarked on the agency programme. Giving civil servants the power and the responsibility for making real decisions is plainly vital. The civil service, as Lord Rayner pointed out, still does not use its most valuable asset – its staff – to the full. A change in the attitude of the Government towards the civil service would be invaluable. To that has to be added reforms in management policies, especially those relating to personnel, whom the Government continued to denigrate throughout the whole of the 1980s, a process which was undoubtedly taken too far in the view of one senior civil servant[8].

Agencies could have other important advantages. Minister would be no longer expected to be responsible for managing their departments – an impossible task since there are only four or five ministers to a department, and those departments may range in size from the Treasury with its staff of about 3,400 to the Ministry of Defence with 165,000 (April 1987 figures). Ministerial workloads make such responsibility impossible, and it is, in addition, a distraction from the long-term strategic planning, which is almost always absent from the thinking of successive British governments to the detriment of the British economy. Britain's economic decline has more to do with the failures of politicians than with the deficiencies of the civil service. The structure of government simply does not allow for any long-term or strategic planning, nor is the Government provided with adequate information for this purpose. A fundamental change in the structure of government would enable ministers to engage in the requisite strategic thinking.

The authors of the 'Next Steps' report pointed out that 'there is nothing new in the suggestion that ministers should not be held answerable for many day-to-day decisions involving the public and public services'; and that, as far as accountability to Parliament is concerned, 'there is a good case for trying to reduce the degree of ministerial overload that can arise from questions about operations as opposed to questions about policy'.[9] The question of agency status and ministerial accountability was ducked in the Prime Minister's 1988 statement to the House of Commons, and has proved a source of continuing controversy since then. The Prime Minister's statement merely announced that the responsibility for day-to-day operations of the agency would be delegated to the chief executive and the minister would look after the framework of policy objectives and resources. The issue of ministerial responsibility cannot be so easily avoided.

The unanswered questions which lie at the heart of the Government's approach to the 'Next Steps' report showed up in the reply given by Richard Luce, then Minister for the Civil Service, to the Treasury Select Committee in 1988. He said that the aim was to 'take the delegation of authority a stage further', but that the 'basic principles of ministerial accountability to Parliament' still applied. The chief executive 'must take a large number of decisions ... but all of us as Members of Parliament have a right to challenge the minister who is ultimately accountable'. The Secretary of State, though, 'is entitled to override a decision of the chief executive if he thinks there is a wider Government and Parliamentary interest he has to take into account'.[10]

The Government sought to clarify the way in which the agencies would be accountable to Parliament on more than one occasion. For example, the issue came to the fore with the establishment of the Employment Service Agency in April 1990. Its Framework Agreement sets out the procedure in terms similar to those of other agencies: 'The Secretary of State will continue to answer questions from Members of Parliament on matters concerning the agency, but will encourage them to contact the chief executive or other appropriate agency managers direct on individual cases or operational issues'.[11] What this actually means was explained by the Minister of State in a reply to an adjournment debate in May 1990. The minister decides whether the question concerns a 'strategic, resource or operational matter'. If the question concerns the former, it will be answered by the minister. But if it concerns operational matters, the question will be sent to the chief executive, who will reply to the MP. At the MP's request, a copy of the chief executive's reply is placed in the Library of the House of Commons. The Minister claimed that this process is 'designed to ensure that Hon. Members deal direct with the person ... who is best placed to answer on the matter in hand'.[12]

The Select Committee expressed reservations about these arrangements. 'Replies from the chief executive, even if placed in the Library of the House, are not freely available to those outside the House, nor is it clear that they would attract parliamentary privilege in the same way as written answers published in the official report. Many answers on operational matters might have implications wider than the individual case concerned; changes in the opening hours of an unemployment benefit office, for example, might cause deep concern amongst members and their constituents.'[13]

The Select Committee on Procedure insisted that ministers must publish replies from the executive agencies to inquiries from MPs in Hansard as opposed to placing the reply in the House of Commons Library, for while members of the public may approach the Library or the public information office for an answer, they have to know that a particular question has been asked. That has meant, for example, that straightforward questions about the Royal Mint's budget, or the number of social security frauds, have been available only through the Library of the House of Commons. This adds to the limitations on the information which is available through written questions. The publication of answers to MPs' questions is a vital part of the process of wresting information from secretive governments, and the executive agency system cannot be used as an excuse for limiting information.[14]

The problem is that accountability is an essential part of public management, which makes it essentially different from private management. The failure to understand this has been one of the reasons for the failure of management reform in the past. Accountability makes devolved management difficult to introduce into the civil service. The 'Next Steps' report does imply less accountability to Parliament – at least at the level of detail. Accountability and well-managed public services can go together but it will require major adjustments to the way in which they are managed.

The role of the Treasury is vital for the successful development of the agencies. But Norman Lamont, then Chief Secretary to the Treasury, made it plain that such a role consists of examining the framework agreements and performance targets. The creation of agencies will not alter or lessen 'involvement and traditional roles in relation to public expenditure'.[15] The controls which the Treasury seeks to maintain over public spending extend beyond cash limits. Norman Lamont described them as 'strategic controls' in his speech to the Chartered Institute of Management Accountants on 9 May 1990, yet the framework agreements set out detailed arrangements for the management of agencies and their costs. Lamont, however, emphasized that the Treasury was 'moving towards a more hands-off approach, which allows for the maximum degree of delegation with essential central and departmental controls'.

Contact between the other central departments besides the Treasury and the agencies remains close. Twenty-two chief executives of the agencies that were up and running by April 1991 led the management consultants, Price Waterhouse, to conclude that, 'The volume of contacts between the agency and the "parent" department is ... very high. Virtually all those questioned reported weekly contacts with departmental officials, and two or three of them said there was daily contact. Twenty-five per cent had weekly contacts with ministers."[16] Much, of course, depends on the nature of the contact – whether the departments seek to manage the agencies from a distance or whether this is simply an exchange of information vital to the development of policy. In fact, what kind of contacts take place between chief executive of agencies and the ministers?

The new civil service will be 'unified, but not uniform'. The civil service will remain the same but will no longer have the uniformity of the past, whatever that may mean – but that is Sir Robin Butler's gift for ambiguity. The unified and uniform civil service is regarded as an essential part of the structure of government in Britain, but in fact it is a relatively recent phenomenon.

Indeed, the present Government appears to have no overall structure in mind for the civil service. The programme will lead, on the evidence of the list of the various agencies established so far, to a more fragmented system, with the risk that some agencies will acquire a greater degree of autonomy than the Government, and perhaps Whitehall itself, originally intended. This is because certain agencies will develop closer links with the private sector, and because they will be mainly staffed by certain professional or occupational groups. Just because the image of the grey-suited male bureaucrat working in Whitehall is so enduring, the public often does not realize that civil servants include meteorologists at the Met Office, to cartographers, mapping and charting officers at the Ordnance Survey Agencies, the Central Office, and scientists of all kinds at a wide range of establishments including the Hydrographic Office, the Chemical and Biological Defence Establishment and the Building Research Establishment. The degree of autonomy such agencies acquire will depend on the extent to which the central departments continue to be able to understand and scrutinize effectively what the agencies are doing. Furthermore, this very fragmentation will make it even more difficult than it already is to administer policies which require the coordination of a number of executive agencies. Such tendencies would certainly militate against any conformity to the Swedish model of the small, central policy-making ministries controlling a systematically developed range of executive agencies directly implementing policies.

The Swedish Model

Since the 'Next Steps' initiative will take a number of years to complete, it is worth considering in some detail whether or not it can be adapted to the Swedish model. That, too, is characterized by a sharp distinction between the policy-making function and the administration of these policies. The 14 central government departments form the policy-making core, employing about 2200 civil servants (excluding the Foreign Office and its diplomatic staff abroad) out of the 500,000 civil servants working in the general civil service. The second largest department after the Ministry of Foreign Affairs, the Ministry of Finance, has only about 250 employees; and the Ministry of Transport and Communications, with 75 employees, is responsible for state utilities such as the National Telecommunication Administration and the Post Office, employing a total of about 60,000. The Ministry of Foreign Affairs which, unlike other departments, also has executive duties, has about 875 employees. Virtually all state employees are included in the civil service salary scales, which reflect the hierarchical structure of the service – a pay structure which is being modified by the introduction of performance-related pay. That is so extensive that, according to one recently published study, 'the individual and performance-related system conflicts with the principles of the hierarchical system and thus with the legal protection of the legal rights of the individual'. The reason for its introduction was that 'during the 1980s the productivity goal has been growing in importance. This policy became possible with the introduction of the individual and performance-related system ... [which] will probably affect work forms in Government agencies and administration.' The implications of this are fundamental, according to this study, since previously the Swedish system conformed to the Weberian ideal type. The 'changeover to more individual and differentiated wages implies a break with this bureaucratic idea ... and [that it] will also alter the relationship between the administration and the world in which it operates'.[7] The author is Maivor Sjolund, currently a senior civil servant at the National Audit Bureau, and formerly at the Department of Government at Uppsala University, but this was, however, the only indication of concern about the implications of performance-related pay I encountered, for the concept of a unified career civil service has been taken for granted in Sweden, just as it has in the UK; others in the National Audit Bureau and the National Agency for Administrative Development regarded its introduction as an important, but not the only, contribution to increased efficiency. Non-financial rewards are built into the system, such as public recognition in the agency for good performance on the part of a local or regional office.

The central departments are concerned with policy development, preparing legislation and budget appropriations to be considered by Parliament. They lay down regulations and the general frameworks within which the executive agencies operate, once these have been approved by Parliament. They appoint officials to the executive agencies, but apart from that, they should have no further part to play in the day-to-day running of the agencies, which are responsible for administering policies, though 'demarcation disputes' are by no means unknown.

The most senior officials in the departments are the three under secretaries; the Under Secretary of State, the Permanent Under Secretary and the Under Secretary for Legal Affairs, the first being responsible for the overall planning and running of the work of the Ministry and coordinating the work of the various policy units. The Permanent Secretary ensures that the administrative decisions are both legal and consistent and is responsible for the final drafts of Government decisions which the executive agencies implement. Finally, the Under Secretary of State for Legal Affairs drafts the bills and regulations, for which the Ministry is responsible, for Parliamentary debate and decision. The three top advisers are all political appointments for a limited period only, usually terminated by agreement between the minister and the official concerned. They are assisted by three secretariats – for planning and budget affairs, for the legal formulation of ministerial policy and for the coordination of the department's international contacts.

The task of implementing Government policy is given to the executive agencies, totalling 170 in all, each with their own boards and director generals. Individual ministers have no formal rights to issue specific orders to the national boards, or to the agencies, but informally there may be extended contacts. After all, the ministries have the funds and the agencies know how to implement policy. The agency directors seek to find out as much as possible about the minister's plans and proposals. The ministers themselves are responsible to the Cabinet as a whole and the executive agencies take all the administrative decisions within the framework of laws laid down by Parliament.

The five largest and most important agencies are the National Social Insurance Board, the National Board of Education, the National Labour Market Board, the National Board of Occupational Safety and Health and the National Board for Universities and Colleges, comprising the most important part of the national welfare state organization.

The National Labour Market Board is at the heart of Sweden's economic policy, explicitly directed at full employment, and is therefore both politically powerful and well financed, though restraint on public spending is the order of the day in Sweden as elsewhere. The National Board of Education oversees comprehensive education for Sweden's pupils, over 99 per cent of whom attend state schools. There are no private universities or colleges, and Swedish universities lack the independence of British universities, so the National Board has a significant role in this area.

The National Board for Occupational Safety and Health operates under a 'framework' law, which simply lays down the procedures for dealing with questions of occupational safety. The Board itself issues all the detailed regulations governing health and safety at work. The National Social Insurance Board does not have the same freedom to issue detailed regulations, since benefits such has pensions and child allowances are covered in detail by parliamentary legislation. But a number of specific issues, such as questions about early retirement pensions or eligibility for disablement pensions, are decided by this board, which then sets out regulations for the regional and social agencies.

The boards of the executive agencies are generally composed of representatives from the political parties, civil servants, other than those employed in the agency in question, the trade unions (LO and TCO – the Swedish Confederation of Trade Unions and the equivalent organization for white collar unions) and the employers organization (SAF). In some special cases, however, such as the National Police Board and the National Central Bank, the boards are composed entirely of Members of Parliament.

Many of the national boards have special subcommittees, advisory councils as well as regional and local boards, all composed of 'laymen', the representatives described above.

Representatives of labour and management sit on these boards to investigate public policies and to make long-term administrative decisions in areas such as retraining, research and education, communications, energy, environmental protection and health services. The director-general is both chairman of the board and chief executive of the agency. The post is a political appointment for six years in the first instance, renewable for a further six years, but rarely beyond that. Moreover, the appointment can be terminated by the Government before the first six years is up. All board members are appointed by the Government to represent various interest groups in society, as are the senior officials of the agencies, although the latter are not political appointments.

Policy-making is not confined to the central core of civil servants, their ministers and their political advisers. It is a much more complex process than that, and one which is designed to reach a consensus before new policies are expressed in legislation which the Prime Minister and his Cabinet present to Parliament for debate and approval.

Once a new policy or reform, or even some administrative change, is under consideration, the Government sets up a 'commission of inquiry', composed of Members of Parliament both from the Government and Opposition parties; representatives from employers, the trade unions and other interested organizations; experts from the administrative bodies concerned and experts from outside the civil service, staffed by a secretariat from the ministry concerned. The commissions are guided by fairly detailed written terms of reference setting out the aims or the problems to be solved. The members of the commission, the time taken and the budget are decided by the Cabinet. The commission's proposals are distributed to various groups whom the Cabinet consider to have an interest in the proposed legislation and this range of views is taken into account both when the commission is set up and before the Cabinet reaches a decision. Even the commission's terms of reference as well as its very establishment are open to comments from executive agencies and outside organizations.

The commission thus established is usually quite small, five to ten members, with a majority of Government members. It has considerable freedom to carry out its inquiries through hearings, research and even travel. The commission works on the policy issue for a period of one to two years, sometimes longer, before publishing a written report. The proceedings of the commission are not open to the public, but the press takes a great interest in the progress of its work.

The results are published as a series of proposals for legislation, together with evidence and the supporting arguments. The commission's views are usually unanimous, but where they are not, dissenting members may publish their objections and alternative proposals in the report.

Once the report is completed, the ministry concerned deals directly with the executive agencies and non-governmental organizations to hear their official comments (the remiss). The right to comment, however, is not confined to those who have officially received the report: any organization may make its views known to the minister. All of these comments are published together with the commission's report when the ensuing bill is presented to Parliament. When the bill is debated, the minister has to take into account all the evidence and the views presented both in the report and in the 'remiss' in his presentation and defence of the bill.

This system of consultation involves a high degree of organization of the various social and economic interests to be taken into account in the policy-making process. Commissions are not a rare event in Sweden – in any one year, there may be over 300 at work. Reference has already been made to the presence of the employers' organization (SAF), the equivalent of the CBI, and LO or the TCO, the blue-collar and white-collar equivalents of the TUC, on the various commissions and the boards of executive agencies. Individual trade unions and employers' associations, whose members may be particularly affected by the proposed policy changes, will obviously comment, but so will a wide range of organizations representing social groupings of all kinds, from tenants to fishermen.

The process appears to be one of open consultation, as indeed it is, but the problem which lies below the surface is the extent to which the formal organizations truly represent public opinion or even the views of the members of the interest group in question. It is designed to avoid conflict and to reach consensus, and to achieve that end, time will certainly be taken to introduce reforms. The process of policy-making has sometimes been criticized for being 'susceptible to paralysis' and too 'poorly adapted to rapid change'[18] to allow for speedy policy changes. On the other hand, it is a remarkably stable system in which reforms, once introduced, survive because they command widespread, even though not universal, support.

The executive agencies, therefore, do play a part in policy formation, although they neither initiate changes, nor are they the prime movers.

The role they have is a limited one, but it is not insignificant. The five main executive agencies are expected to submit proposals to the Government about the policies the Government requires them to administer. Arising out of their practical experience of putting the Government's policies into effect, they may well propose specific amendments to the laws and regulations which Parliament has enacted. These recommendations are considered by the central policy-making core and are subject to examination and written report in the same way as the commission reports are treated.

The extent to which the executive agencies can and do comment on the Government policies they are expected to implement can be illustrated from the Report of the National Labour Market Board to the Government prior to the three-year budgeting period 1988/9 to 1990/91, an experimental scheme in which the Labour Market Board had been asked to participate by the Government. In setting out Labour Market Policy for the 1990s, the Board criticized a number of schemes to combat unemployment, to assist the long-term unemployed to return to employment, and the length of the waiting period for employment training. Youth team work for the young unemployed provided by municipal authorities was found to be inadequate and unrelated to future job prospects for the young. Better counselling resources and better economic incentives, it was suggested, would help to reduce the waiting period for training schemes from ninety days, the 1986 average. The report argued that putting more resources into services of this kind would save taxpayers' money.

The report also comments on the ineffectiveness of the temporary employment schemes, compared with training programmes. For a number of years, the Labour Market Board had observed that 65 per cent of those completing employment training programmes obtained permanent employment within six months, which contrasted favourably with the finding that 35 per cent of those employed on temporary employment schemes were registered as unemployed within three months of the termination of their projects.[19] The employment service, the report concludes, must systematically reduce waiting periods for training and new jobs, and improve the accuracy with which the Employment Service selects its programmes. Decisions of this kind are plainly within the scope of the executive agency, since the policy framework clearly permits the agency to have this degree of discretion.

The remit for the Labour Market Board is laid down by Government and by Parliament. Its principal task is, rapidly and efficiently, to help job seekers to find work and help employers to find the labour they need. Thus the employment offices of the Employment Service and the Employability Institutes are a service agency for job seekers and employers alike.

The Labour Market Board sees the service to employers as reinforcing the service it can offer to job seekers: 'If the Employment Service acts quickly and efficiently to help employers fill vacancies, this will enhance the employment prospects of disadvantaged groups. An employer receiving effective support from the Employment Service will be more interested in consulting the Service and relying on its opinions regarding the ability of different applicants to cope with a particular kind of work. The competence of the Employment Service in matters of counselling, job-modification and training/education is crucial here.'[20] The board then defines its specific objectives within the terms of its remit as laid down by Government and Parliament and with due regard for its recognition that an efficient service for employers can only benefit job seekers.

Several differences between the current British system, including the way in which the executive agencies operate, and the Swedish approach emerge at this point. The remit given to the Labour Market Board allows it considerable discretion in, for example, the kind of youth unemployment schemes and other measures designed to provide the unemployed with temporary work. Issues of this kind would be regarded as policy issues within the British system.

The agency, through its director general appointed by the Government, is answerable to the Government as a whole, not to the individual minister. The Government can only take its decisions collectively in Cabinet. Indeed, individual ministers cannot answer questions in Parliament about any aspect of the agency's operations, and MPs cannot table them. The formal relationship is one in which the administration of policy is devolved to the agencies. In practice, informal contacts between the ministries and agencies are frequent and necessary, since the available expertise on various issues is often found in the agencies.

The agencies are not directly accountable to the ministry or to the Secretary of State, but accountability is ensured in a variety of ways. First of all, the Government appoints its own official, the Chancellor of Justice, and the Parliament its Parliamentary Ombudsman, both of whom take up cases of maladministration at the individual's request or on their own initiative. Public accountability is further strengthened by Sweden's freedom of information provisions. These give any individual citizen the right of free access to public documents on demand, that is, all documents in public offices, of which the agencies are one example. This includes correspondence – even from Government ministers – sent to the agency.

All the operations of the agency are open to public view, thereby making it possible for the press to investigate maladministration of all kinds at every level in the agency. The agency's devolved responsibility for administration of Government policies is also one for which it is publicly accountable.

The agencies' work is scrutinized, too, by the National Audit Bureau, which reports to both Government and Parliament, and the results of whose work are published. The Swedish Agency for Administrative Development exists to support Government administration, which is directly concerned with increasing efficiency and effectiveness in the public services, and, in particular, with the development of administrative methods and data processing systems within the public sector.

A recent Act of Parliament (1987) sets out new guidelines for the relationship between the agencies and the Government. It requires Parliament and Government to set out more clearly what they expect the agencies to achieve, stressing that the politicians should concentrate on policy and not on internal administration, all of which suggests that even where devolving responsibility to the agencies has long been the practice, ministers and ministries have become involved in administration. Three-year budget schemes have been developed and the auditing procedures are being improved. Agency budgets were only being given a limited examination by the Government. Under the new scheme, the agencies would have to respond in detail to questions drawn up by the Government for each particular agency. On the basis of the replies, a three-year outline appropriation or budget proposals will be presented to Parliament for its approval. Control of the agencies will be radically changed by this method. With a rotating timetable, all agencies would be scrutinized within the three-year period, with the emphasis on policy considerations.

It is clear from the preceding outline that the division of responsibility between the executive agencies and the ministries in Sweden does occasionally become blurred. Recent legislation in the Swedish Parliament, however, is designed to clarify the direction of national administration and the Budget Bill of 1988 set out the Government's new guidelines for concerted changes in budget techniques.

Application of the Swedish Model in the UK

There are advantages to adopting this view of the work of the agencies in the UK. Devolved agencies would be responsible for administration, leaving ministers and the 'core' departments free to concentrate on policy.

Despite the views of some ministers, it is not possible to expect ministers to be managers of their departments, since they cannot be aware of all the administrative processes in their own departments. Relieving ministers of this responsibility is seen as a positive advantage by the Swedish. 'The great advantage of the Swedish system is that ministers and the Chancery are not burdened with a wealth of fairly uncontroversial executive decisions ... The system thus allows the ministries to remain fairly small units, mainly devoted to framing the future development of society, while the sense of responsibility engendered in the agencies also seems to make for greater efficiency.'[21]

This does raise problems, which have already been of concern to Parliament, about the accountability to Parliament of the work of the executive agencies. The Swedish solution is to provide the public with open access to all public documents, with a few exceptions. In addition, Swedish MPs are debarred from asking the minister to intervene in individual cases or, indeed, to raise any questions about the running of agencies. They do, however, adeptly find ways of debating the general issues concerning the operations of a particular agency.

A further problem is that the skills involved in policy advice are inevitably different from managerial and administrative skills. The 'quintessential skill of the senior civil servant involves being able to draft a letter or ministerial speech which means five different things to five different people', and with developing the 'arts of persuasion and negotiation, concepts loaded with ambiguity'.[22] Even if that is a somewhat cynical view, it seems preferable to abandon the pretension that analytic and presentational skills, the skills involved in protecting a minister's back and in preparing his or her views for defence or exposition in Parliament, traditionally required by senior civil servants in Whitehall, can be easily adapted to the managerial skills required to ensure that policies are effectively admin-istered. A proper career structure in administration would be an advantage in encouraging the achievement of the kind of goals which Sweden has set out in its 'renewal' programme for the public sector. The renewal programme, which will be described more fully later in this chapter, was undertaken by the Social Democrat Government in the mid-1980s. The programme was introduced in response to the public perception that the civil service had become increasingly remote and bureaucratic, and was designed to improve the quality of service to the public.

Executive agencies should be involved in policy decisions in an advisory role. The Swedish experience indicates that there is much informal contact between the ministries and the five main executive agencies, and, where relevant, between the ministries and the less central agencies. It would be more difficult to arrange such informal contact in the UK because of the greater number of staff involved both in the core departments and the large agencies which would come into being with the establishment of the Social Security Benefits Agency and other similar bodies. Formal procedures for consulting executive agencies on policy issues would be advisable. The practical experience of the agencies in administering policies is obviously a valuable resource for policy-makers. Consultation should take place at an early stage in the development of new policies, when a range of options are being considered under the normal conditions of confidentiality.

The five main Swedish executive agencies publish annual reports and budget submissions. Some of these reports give very positive accounts of the agency's work throughout the year, although even these may set out objectives which the agency plans to achieve; for example, the National Labour Market Board's Annual Report for 1989/90 refers to the Agency's aim of raising the cost-effectiveness of employment training by 10 per cent over the ensuing three years. Other published reports are more critical of the agency's ability to reach certain targets or suggest that some measures are more effective than others in achieving the policy objectives which the Government has set for the agency.

It should be possible to adapt some of these procedures to the process of policy-making in the UK. For many of the established agencies, this would not involve the agency in a policy debate over sensitive areas of Government policy. But with the establishment of agencies such as the Social Security Benefits Agency, however, such reports would impinge on sensitive areas. This can be illustrated from the controversy which broke out in the spring of 1991 over the role of the National Audit Office. Senior civil servants argued that its role should be limited to investigating the efficiency with which Whitehall and the agencies implemented Government policies. They accused both MPs on the select committees, including the Public Accounts Committee, which follows up the National Audit Office reports, of going beyond their remit to examine the effectiveness of government policy as well as the efficiency of its delivery. The MPs were unrepentant. Frank Field, chairman of the Social Security Select Committee, was quoted as saying: 'If you find, as the NAO did recently, that getting people to opt out of SERPS (the state earnings related pension scheme) has cost £6bn instead of a fraction of that, just establishing that fact is highly political. It is bound to raise policy questions. I suspect the problem is that the NAO is doing its proper job, looking at value for money in important policy areas, not just the use of paper clips'.[23] Agency reports of the kind proposed here could well give rise to a similar controversy but just as MPs insisted on the right of the NAO to raise questions about the effectiveness of policy, so too should the agencies be able to comment on the effectiveness of the policies they are required to implement. The value of so doing would justify the break with tradition.

Suitable ways of presenting such reports would depend in part on the way in which the Government set the framework for agencies of these kinds. If the agency was expected to consider and report on both the efficiency with which it delivered the various services or benefits laid down in legislation, and the effectiveness of its activities, then its reports would be a valuable contribution to policy-making. For example, the agency could carry out an efficiency audit on administrative costs involved in, say, a programme for the relief of family poverty and an effectiveness audit, showing how many, if any, families had their poverty reduced as a result of the programme. It would then not be necessary to breach the formal distinction between the central core of policy-making and the executive agencies responsible for administration.

Origins of the British Civil Service Structure

The development of a unified and centrally controlled civil service resulted from the famous Northcote-Trevelyan Report, which advocated the abolition of patronage and its replacement by a system of competitive examination as a means of recruitment to the civil service. This aspect of the Northcote-Trevelyan Report was not fully implemented until 1870. This Order in Council also gave the Treasury the power not only to control the finances of the other Government departments, but also to control the numbers and the types of people employed by those departments. These powers were strengthened when the MacDonnell Commission's recommendations were finally implemented in the years after the First World War, partly because of the impetus given to such developments by Sir Warren Fisher during his period at the Treasury between 1919 and 1939. A series of committees, including a Select Committee of the House of Commons, reporting in 1919, led to the Cabinet's adoption of a structure for the civil service in which the permanent secretary in each department was responsible for all the financial aspects of the department's work, and for 'economy in all establishment matters in his department'.

An establishments division was also set up within the Treasury in February 1919 to deal with the 'provision, payment and grading of officials throughout the public service'. Two further divisions, also headed by a controller with the status of a permanent secretary in a first-class department, were set up to deal with supply and finance. In addition, Sir Warren Fisher was appointed as a Permanent Secretary in overall charge of these three divisions to supervise, coordinate and direct all three divisions. He was also the Head of the Civil Service and advised the Prime Minister on all senior civil service appointments. By 1920, therefore, the Treasury, under Sir Warren Fisher's influence, had renewed its control over public spending and had achieved, with the cooperation of others in the civil service, a pivotal position in personnel management of the civil service. The broad structure of a unified, career service had been established.

The 'Next Steps' programme calls into question the concept of a career civil service, representing a shift in policy on the part of the third Thatcher Government. The point was made to the then Minister for the Civil Service, Richard Luce, by John Garrett MP during a meeting of the Treasury and Civil Service Select Committee on 10 July 1990: 'Mr Garrett: As chief executives of agencies achieve greater freedom, and as a departure from centrally laid-down rules becomes something to be applauded, will it be possible to maintain anything other than the superficial unity of the Civil Service? Is not this the beginning of the end of a national civil service? Mr Luce: I think that raises an important question. The term that has been used that it will be, and it is becoming, a unified not a uniform service'.[24] This does mark a shift in policy from the first two Thatcher Governments, which seemed to expect the career civil service to continue, but wanted a slimmed down, cheaper version of the service they inherited, and a restriction of its role in policy-making. It is this which the 'Next Steps' calls into question. They viewed the organizational structure of the civil service as that of a large company, with the permanent secretaries as 'top management', under and assistant secretaries together with principals as a 'middle tier' – responsible for policy implementation, as 'headquarters management' – and executive officers regarded as 'line managers'. All of this was designed to bring about greater managerial efficiency.[25]

But by the end of 1987, the Government came to see that making the civil service think in managerial terms and encouraging them to develop the principles of the Financial Management Initiative was incompatible with a unified career civil service. Attempts had been made at devolving management, at making line managers responsible for cost centres. As the Ibbs report noted:

There are controls not only on resources and objectives, as there should be in any effective system, but also in the way in which resources can be managed. Recruitment, dismissal, choice of staff, promotion, pay, hours of work, accommodation, grading, organization of work, use of IT equipment, are all outside the control of most civil service managers at any level. The main decisions on rules and regulations are taken by the centre of the civil service. This tends to mean that they are structured to fit everything in general and nothing in particular. The rules are seen primarily as a constraint rather than as a support; and in no sense as a pressure on managers to manage effectively. Moreover, the task of changing the rules is often seen as too great for one unit or one manager or indeed one department and is therefore assumed to be impossible.[26]

This led the Efficiency Unit to argue that the 'advantages which a unified civil service are intended to bring are seen as outweighed by the practical disadvantages, particularly beyond Whitehall itself. We were told that the advantages of an all-embracing pay structure are breaking down, that the uniformity of grading frequently inhibits effective management and that the concept of a career in a unified civil service has little relevance for most civil servants, whose horizons are bounded by their local office, or, at the most, by their department'.[27]

It is worth remembering at this point that the unified civil service with common standards of entry originated in the corruption of the mid-nineteenth century and was consolidated in 1920, when it consisted of less than 200,000 non-industrial civil servants. That was, of course, long before the founding of the welfare state, with its extensive administrative requirements, the demands of defence and greater governmental intervention in all aspects of economic life. It may well not be possible to sustain a unified civil service in the face of the development of the executive agencies. Sir Robin Butler described its continuance in ambiguous terms – 'unified but not uniform'. But not all have shown such discretion. When questioned by the Treasury and Civil Service Select Committee, Sir Angus Fraser, the Prime Minister's efficiency adviser, told the Committee that 'a unified civil service is not really compatible with the way we are going.'[28] Even in 1939, just before the outbreak of the Second World War, the main government departments had a mere eighty-six permanent, second or deputy secretaries between them. The Ministry of Pensions had one permanent secretary; the Ministry of Health had one permanent secretary and one deputy secretary compared with a staff of 86, 203 for the Department of Health and the Department of Social Security taken together in April 1990.[29] It is not, however, simply the development of the agency system which will bring about the destruction of the unified civil service, nor the limited experiments in performance-related pay and flexibility in pay between one agency and another. That would only happen if the Government pushed these developments further than it is prepared to do at present. These are the internal pressures. There are external pressures as well, such as the possible establishment of regional government, and the impact of developments in the European Community, from which the civil service is by no means immune, although that is not yet generally recognized.

The civil service of the 1920s faced none of these problems nor such potential for change. Managerial skills were not required in those early days. The tradition of valuing generalist skills, designed to assist with policy advice to ministers, began then and has dominated the attitudes of the service since. 'Senior management is dominated by people whose skills are policy formation and who have relatively little experience of managing or working where services are actually delivered.'[30] Policy advice, as one Grade 2 official told the Efficiency Unit, is 'the golden route to the top'.

'This kind of signal affects the unwritten priorities of a whole organization, whatever the formal policy may be,' the Efficiency Unit claimed. 'Managing large organizations involves skills which depend a great deal on experience; without experience senior managers lack confidence in their own ability to manage. Although, at most senior levels, civil servants are responsible for both policy and service delivery, they give greater priority to policy, not only because it demands immediate attention but because that is the area on which they are on familiar ground and where their skills lie, and where ministerial attention is focused. A proper balance between policy and delivery is hard to achieve within the present framework.'[31]

Obtaining the maximum efficiency in the delivery of services is the justification offered by the Efficiency Unit for the introduction of agencies, with the freedom to determine pay and conditions of employment to ensure that they can obtain the right staff. If the freedom is extended in the ways in which Dame Anne Mueller indicated in her report on 'Working Practices', then, indeed, there is a real threat of breaking up the single career service.

That freedom would only be available in the context of 'quite a different way of conducting the business of government' with the central core to which a 'range of agencies employing their own staff, who may or may not have the status of Crown servants, and concentrating on the delivery of their particular service' will respond. 'Both departments and their agencies should have a more open and simplified structure.'[32]

The responsibility for supplying the services to the department lay with the chief executive of the agency. To enable the chief executive to carry out that task in a cost effective way, Dame Anne Mueller stated that working practices should be changed to allow for recurring temporary contracts: nil hours contracts (that is, people being available for work but without any guarantees of work); annual hours contracts, involving rostering shift work a year in advance; part-time employment; part-time work for individual senior staff; fixed-term contracts; and provision for home-working.[33] The study argued that these changes in the patterns of employment would allow for better use of new technology, more flexibility in response to the workload, and an increased capacity to adapt to new demands in the labour market, especially by recruiting staff with scarce skills.[34] The report also claimed that 'some regulations, such as those covering shift disturbance, travel and subsistence, superannuation and maternity leave can constrain the efficient management of working time', and that 'the rules of annual leave, overtime and substitution may not always operate to ensure that the needs of work take precedence'.[35]

The study assumes that changing working practices in this way will in fact result in the increased efficiency which is rightly demanded. In fact, the study seems to assume that all private sector firms adopt employment conditions of this kind to improve efficiency, but some of the best private sector firms reject working practices of this kind because they look for a long-term commitment and loyalty, as well as efficient working from their employees. A more thorough examination of the way in which private sector firms actually achieve greater efficiency and look to developing the human resources already available to them shows that the emphasis is placed on training.

In fact, as yet, none of the executive agencies have moved that far in the direction of the working practices laid down in the Mueller report. The career civil service at present has as much standardization as it is possible to have with its inevitably complex structure. The study team realized that if they simply retained a core civil service, developing different working patterns in the agencies would 'create two classes of employee' – the 'haves' and the 'have nots'. In fact, if the recommendations of the 'Working Practices' study team were adopted, it would create two classes of civil servants, making it impossible to claim that there was a 'uniform' civil service and increasingly difficult to suggest that the civil service is unified.

The development of an agency system does not itself destroy the traditional concept of the career civil service. That will occur only if managerial initiative is directed towards altering employment conditions in the belief that that alone will bring about cost-effective services. Some flexibility in pay, conditions of work and entry to the service can be accommodated within the unified career service. The effectiveness and efficiency of service delivery depends far more on the attention the agencies pay to their customers and the nature and quality of service they require. So far the agencies have yet to ascertain who their customers are, let alone consult them about the nature of the service they require. Customers themselves may be too hesitant to make justifiable demands. For example, it took considerable pressure from certain quarters in the police force to obtain a twenty-four-hour, seven-days-a-week information service concerning vehicle ownership from the Vehicle Licensing Agency. The demands met with resistance from senior personnel at the Agency at first, but more junior staff were pleased to offer the kind of service they knew their customers wanted.

In general, the aims of an efficient and cost-effective service are more likely to be realized if senior staff at the agencies consult their customers and involve all the staff in planning and developing the agencies' work. But the civil service is still far too reluctant to look away from its own rules and procedures and turn its attention to the world outside, and in particular to its range of customers or to the wishes of the public, if it is the kind of service which deals mainly with ordinary members of the public.

The development of the agency programme runs the risk of fragmenting the service in such a way that a national civil service could be destroyed, its accompanying commitment to public service undermined and the possibility of coherent and coordinated policy development nullified. The envisaged conglomeration of agencies may well need to be restructured with a strong planning and strategic mechanism and a central department or the management of the civil service. As *The Times* editorial wrote when the 'Next Steps' initiative was announced, the 'virtues of loyalty and executive potency' of the civil service should not 'be lightly dismissed'.[36]

Review of the 'Next Steps' Initiative

In reviewing the development of the 'Next Steps' initiative so far, two problems arise; first, the meaning of 'agency' status seems to be quite unclear. As Professor Dunleavy pointed out: 'There is no common administrative logic that can possibly bind together into a usable category organizations as dissimilar as the 50-strong Fuel Suppliers Branch of DoE and the 72,000-strong Social Security Benefits apparatus.'[37]

Second, the development of the agencies is so patchy and uneven as to suggest that there is no clear pattern or purpose in mind – apart from the general aim of increasing efficiency in the delivery of services. Dunleavy himself compares the impact of the 'Next Steps' process with the pattern found in US Federal Government, where departments are 'basically congeries of bureaux and administrations loosely controlled by a central department administration',[38] though the developments in the UK are unlikely to follow that pattern in every detail. The administrative developments will lead to a fragmented organizational structure, far more so than at first thought.

The Swedish model was thought to lie behind the 'Next Steps' initiative, especially in view of Peter Kemp's discussions with senior civil servants and ministers in Stockholm shortly before the establishment of the first agencies in 1988. Press reports at the time referred to Peter Kemp's 'rapid visit to Sweden to see how its administration works',[39] with the *Guardian* carrying a description of the Swedish system under the headline: 'Socialist Sweden has the blueprint for Whitehall's dissolution',[40] a headline which would have alarmed No. 10.

Although the visits were made and an exchange of ideas took place, the evidence from Sweden suggests that the visit was too brief to allow for an in-depth study of the Swedish administrative system. Even at the time, Peter Kemp warned that, 'We have to be careful about translating policies from one system to another.'[41] If anything, his views on that point have hardened, and indeed, there seems to be little sign of following the Swedish approach to establishing the executive agencies.

The development of the agency programme in Britain leaves a number of fundamental questions unresolved. The 'Next Steps' report recommended that 'Agencies should be established to carry out the executive function of government within a policy and resources framework set by a department ... we use the term agency not in its technical sense, but to describe any executive unit that delivers a service for government'.[42] But which of the executive units within a department becomes an agency is a matter for negotiations, often delicate, between the department and the project manager of the 'Next Steps' programme. That in itself suggests that the criteria for an agency are not clear; there would only be scope for a disagreement about timing between a department and the project manager if they were clear.

Once established, however, executive agencies share certain characteristics. Each has an identifiable chief executive, who is also the accounting officer, and as such, directly accountable to Parliament for the work of the agency. In addition, the executive agency constitutes a discrete organization with a defined task set out in the 'Framework Document'. This is a formal agreement between the department and the agency, which sets out fine-sounding targets for achieving improved service provision, but does not explain how the targets are to be achieved. Furthermore, neither the details of the relationship between the sponsoring department nor the organizational design of the sponsoring department given its new roles and relationships have been clarified.

Framework documents are variable in quality and usefulness; John Mayne, who retired from the Department of Health and Social Security in July 1989, argued that the framework document should recognize that the chief executives in politically sensitive departments such as the Employment Services and the Social Security Benefit Agency will not be free agents when political troubles arise, but should include a 'proviso that such political clawback will be temporary and that as much as possible of the agencies' work will go on undisturbed, with maximum flexibility pushed and kept down the line'. He adds that the 'chief executives must have a say in policy and the policy-makers have got to understand operations. And each set can only do that if they have had direct experience on the other side of the line'.[43] Some framework documents do set out the chief executive's role in relation to policy. The Employment Service document gives the chief executive the right to make proposals to the Secretary of State for 'changes in the policies and programmes operated by the Agency' and adds that the 'chief executive is consulted before any policies affecting the agency are put to the Secretary of State', but the Social Security Benefits Agency, significantly enough, is given only a minimal role in policy-making. Such an agency could have a far more proactive and valuable role in policy-making. In addition, the framework documents could be a much more effective tool for defining the agency's tasks, discerning its achievements and making civil servants more responsible for policy implementation and the quality of service provided to the public, particularly, perhaps, if departmental select committees were allowed to consider draft framework agreements and if their views were taken into account before these plans were finally agreed. The framework documents should set out more sophisticated performance measurement techniques than are available at present. With a large number of case-load services among the new agencies it is likely that simple throughput will be the core effectiveness indicator in the 1990s. The Treasury and Civil Service Select Committee cites examples of these, such as Companies House's aim to reduce the time taken to process documents by 20 per cent. A careful study of other performance indicators, which measure quality and consumer satisfaction, is also required. The constraints on measuring consumer satisfaction may not only be technical, but may well arise from internal organizational politics or a lack of resources. On the information currently available on the operation of the agencies, it is impossible for Parliament to judge their true performance accurately.

By contrast with the notorious secretiveness of the British system of administration, the open and guaranteed access to information about the operations of the agencies in Sweden is an important element in ensuring the efficient and effective delivery of services. In addition, the overall structure of Swedish administration is more coherent, given that the five main agencies are responsible for the management of the welfare state, for which there has been continued and consistent public support, as well as a highly developed and flourishing private sector. Of the five main agencies the Labour Market Agency has a key role to play, since it is not only responsible for administering employment services and training, but plays a key role in Sweden's macroeconomic policies, which have held unemployment down to 2 per cent (1991) or generally below 2 per cent. Both the Labour Market Agency and the two agencies concerned with education play their part in ensuring a supply of highly educated and trained labour. The Next Steps programme should emulate the Swedish system with a clear identification of the key agencies for bringing employment and training together.

Sweden has not been complacent about its administrative system; indeed, the constraints imposed by limited financial resources during the 1980s did not allow that. Public expenditure is still being curbed and the public sector faces a 10 per cent cutback this year. Concern about the poor quality of service, the increasing complexity of organizations and the lack of responsiveness to public demand all led to the introduction of the Renewal Programme in 1985. The first phase focused on four objectives: increased freedom of choice; widened democracy; efficiency and quality; less bureaucracy and better service. The second stage, introduced in 1987, was concerned with the internal structure of the agencies. It delegated personnel and pay policies to the agencies and increased participation, 'flattening the pyramid' to allow individuals to participate more freely in them.

Evaluation of the Swedish public sector has been carried out by the 'Expert Group', which has been in existence since 1980 to advise the Ministry of Finance on developments in public sector productivity and on suitable measurements. In addition, the National Audit Bureau examines

55

the effectiveness of the work of the agencies by means of in-depth studies and the National Agency for Administrative Development promotes best practice in the agencies, a gap which the British civil service would do well to fill.

Overall, the Swedish approach has been to develop and apply a 'social responsibility' model of public management. 'It is different from the "market-led" private sector models in its concern for economic efficiency; for responsiveness to need as well as demand; for both outputs and outcomes; for humanistic values in organizations; and prefiguring an improved social reality in terms of how organizations manage these affairs.'[44] This, rather than the private sector model and market disciplines, should be adopted by the executive agencies here, but to do that effectively in this country would require a shift to public accountability and away from the myth of ministerial accountability.

The 'Next Steps' programme faces a number of problems apart from its inadequate concept of management. Despite all the efforts of the past three years, the latest report from the Efficiency Unit remarks that 'it was acknowledged that a great deal remains to be done to make staff more customer orientated'.[45] Nor was the level of service adequately measured: 'Few targets included adequate measures of service quality and others were too imprecise to provide a proper basis for monitoring performance.'[46] Yet the rhetoric surrounding their establishment was that the public would obtain better services and not just value for money.

The Project Manager, Sir Peter Kemp, has frequently stated that within ten years he hopes that at least three-quarters of the civil service will be working in the new agencies. To achieve that goal the Project Manager needs firm political support, which he may well have with a change of government, though that could lead just as easily to a different concept of the aims and goals of the agencies and their operation within the confines of full public accountability.

Whatever the developments, the 'Next Steps' programme will still have to contend with the Treasury, which has lost a battle but is determined to win the war by holding the purse strings of public expenditure as tightly as possible. It is to that issue we shall now turn.

Notes

[1] 'Improving Management in Government: The Next Steps', 1988, p. 7.
[2] C. Priestley, 'Government Management Must no Longer Be Left to Chance', *Independent*, 20 February 1988.

[3] op. cit., 'Improving Management in Government', p. 3.

[4] private source.

[5] *Financial Times*, 'Appeal of the Swedish bureaucrat', 23 November 1988.

[6] op. cit., 'Improving Management in Government', p. 1.

[7] R. Chapman, ' "The Next Steps": a review', *Public Policy and Administration*, Vol. 3, No. 3, Winter 1988, pp. 3–23, p. 27.

[8] private information.

[9] Annex A, paras 4, 10.

[10] Treasury and Civil Service Select Committee, Eighth Report, 'Civil Service Management Reform: The Next Steps', 1987–8, Vol. 2, p. 64.

[11] Employment Agency Framework Document, Employment Service Executive Agency: a framework document to the agency, para. 4.3, 1990.

[12] HLDC, 21 May 1990, cc. 150–51.

[13] Treasury and Civil Service Select Committee, Eighth Report, 'Progress in the Next Steps Initiative', 1989–90, Vol. 1., p. xix.

[14] Select Committee Procedure, Parliamentary Questions, July 1991, HC 178.

[15] p. 53.

[16] Price Waterhouse, 'Executive Agencies, Facts and Trends', Survey Report, 1991, p. 19.

[17] Statens Lone-Politik 1966–1988, Maivor Sjolund, Uppsala, 1989, p. 178, English summary.

[18] Brooking Institution, *The Swedish Economy*, B. T. Bosworth and A. M. Rivlin, Washington DC, 1987, p. 23.

[19] National Labour Market Board, 'Labour Market Policy for the 1990s – Aims and Aspirations', pp. 12–13.

[20] p. 4.

[21] P. Vinde and G. Petri, 'Swedish Institute, 1978, p. 17.

[22] S. Richards, 'The Financial Management Initiative', in A. Harrison and J. Gretton (eds), *Reshaping Central Government*, 1987, pp. 37–8.

[23] *Independent*, 4 February 1991.

[24] Treasury and Civil Service Committee, Eighth Report, 'Progress in the Next Steps Initiative', 1989–90, Q. 145, p. 46, HC 481.

[25] Efficiency Unit, 'Making Things Happen: A Report on the Implementation of Government Efficiency Scrutinies', 1985, p. 1.

[26] Efficiency Unit Report, 'Improving Management in Government', 1988, para. 11.

[27] para 12.

[28] Next Steps Initiative, Seventh Report from the Treasury and Civil Service Select Committee, HC 496, August 1991.

[29] Source for 1939 figures, Principal Officers in the Home Civil Service, 1939, H.E. Dale, *The Higher Civil Service*, Oxford, 1941, Appendices A and B.

[30] ibid. Next Steps Initiative.

[31] para. 5.

[32] para. 4.

[33] Working Patterns. A Study Document by the Cabinet Office (MPO) 1987, p. 10.

[34] ibid., paras 2.4, 3.14, 3.21.

[35] ibid., para. 4.9.
[36] *The Times*, 4 February 1988.
[37] Treasury and Civil Service Select Committee, Eighth Report, 'Progress in the Next Steps Initiative, 1989–90', p. 70.
[38] ibid.
[39] R. Taylor, 'Appeal of the Swedish Bureaucrat', *Financial Times*, 23 November 1988.
[40] *Guardian*, 29 November 1988.
[41] op. cit., *Financial Times*.
[42] Efficiency Unit Report, 'Improving Management in Government', 1988.
[43] J. Mayne, 'The Role of Managers and Management Audit', *Management in Government*, November 1983, Vol. 38, No. 4, p. 226. Summarized and quoted by Peter Hennessy in 'Managing when the going gets rough', *Independent*, 28 October 1990.
[44] C. Fudge and L. Gustafson, 'Administrative Reform and Public Management in Sweden and the United Kingdom', *Public Money and Management*, Summer 1989, Vol. 6, No. 2, p. 32.
[45] Report to the Prime Minister, 'Making the Most of the Next Steps: The Management of Ministers' Departments and their Executive Agencies', May 1991, p. 10.
[46] ibid., p. 12.

THREE

Public Spending

A Case Study

Public expenditure is plainly central to the activities of any government. A government must have at its disposal adequate means of planning and controlling public spending – and be responsive to public concern about the share of public expenditure in economic activity – its rate of growth and its composition. The media directs the public's attention to the impact of public spending on tax demands, and the markets closely watch the implications of a government's public spending plans for the amount it will expect to borrow. This chapter explores the way in which the British Government sets about determining how much it will spend in any one year, what its priorities shall be, and the kind of back-up it receives from the Treasury, on whose advice ministers inevitably depend, perhaps to the extent of allowing the Treasury to bring about 'the private government of public money' to use Heclo and Widalsky's famous phrase. Hugh Heclo and Aaron Widalsky are two American academics and authors of numerous studies of British, American and Swedish systems of government. Since their seminal work, of that title published in 1974, fundamental changes in the planning of public expenditure have taken place.

The 1980s was marked by a deliberate move on the part of the incoming Thatcher Government in 1979 to shift resources from the public to the private sector. The justification for this approach to public spending took a variety of forms throughout the decade, beginning with the claim that public sector borrowing crowded out the private sector. The Medium Term Financial Strategy was introduced at the time of the Budget in March 1980, but the underlying concepts had been brought into the Treasury by the new ministers and their special advisers. Keynesian demand management, using public spending as a 'pump primer', and a commitment to full employment, were abandoned overnight.

Unemployment rose sharply to peak at three million in 1983, and, over a decade later is expected to rise to well over two million by the end of 1991. The Medium Term Financial Strategy was effectively abandoned in 1986, but the attitude to public spending in the first Budget of the Major premiership was extremely cautious, an attitude which was cast aside in the Autumn Statement, 1991, with its commitment to increase public spending by £10.5bn (including privatization) in 1992/3 at the cost of a public sector borrowing requirement of approximately £20bn.

Public Spending in the 1970s

The Conservative Governments of the 1980s were not, in fact, the first to seek to control public spending. Changes to the Public Expenditure Survey had to be introduced in the mid-1970s owing to the continuing repercussions of the Barber boom of 1971 and the international oil crisis of 1973, in which the OPEC countries restricted their output to force up the price. In his autobiography, Denis Healey pointed out that in November 1975, Wynne Godley, who had himself served in the Treasury as an economist, showed that public spending in 1974/5 was 'some £5 billion higher in real terms than had been planned by Barber in 1971'. This was 'due to the Treasury's inability either to know exactly what was happening, or to control it'.[1] Healey continued: 'This was one of the reasons why I decided to fix cash limits on spending as well as pay, since departments tended to use inflation as a cover for increasing their spending in real terms. Cash limits worked all too well in holding spending down. Departments were so frightened of exceeding their limits that they tended to underspend, sometimes dramatically so. In 1976/7 public spending was £2.2 billion less than planned.'[2]

This did not end the demands for further cuts in public spending, owing to the heavy pressure on sterling in the markets in the spring of 1976, in response to the high forecast for the Public Sector Borrowing Requirement in 1977/8. Public spending as then defined was 'taking over 60 per cent of GDP' and the 'official Treasury forecast ... overestimated that year's PSBR by over £2 billion. In fact it later turned out that public spending actually fell by nearly 2 per cent in 1976/7 ... Such major errors in the official forecasts were to play a major role in the IMF crisis which followed.'[3]

The White Paper on Public Spending in February 1976 stated that 'the ratio of total public spending to GDP at factor cost has grown from 50 per cent in 1971/2 to about 60 per cent in 1975/6'. By defining public spending in the same way as many other countries did, 'our spending was reduced by some £7.7 billion at a stroke. And when we costed GDP, like public spending, at market prices, the ratio of public spending to GDP fell from 60 per cent to 46 per cent. By 1978/9 my successive cuts had brought it down to about 42 per cent – about the same as West Germany but far below Scandinavia and the Netherlands.'[4]

A definition of public spending and a switch from one way of estimating future public spending to another may seem an esoteric matter indeed. But to anyone who remembers the political agonies of a period in which public expenditure plans were cut in response to the falling pound, an economic crisis that seemed much more serious than it need have been, such issues are fundamental to deciding how much the country can afford to spend on the public sector and what its priorities should be. Even in 1976, both the current account deficit and inflation were falling. The balance of payments deficit was eliminated in 1977, and by 1978 the economy was growing by over 3 per cent a year. But in order for this to happen, proper controls over public expenditure had to come into operation and be seen to work.

The first step was the introduction of cash limits in 1976. To understand this first step it is necessary to understand the way in which public spending was determined prior to that date. Public expenditure was calculated in what was known as 'funny money', that is, planning took place in constant survey prices. (Public Expenditure White Papers were presented in constant prices. They set out the programmes in volume terms and priced these in constant prices; for example, the 1975 White Paper set out the Government's spending plans for the years 1974/5 to 1978/9 at the prices holding at the end of 1973. The 1976 White Paper set out the Government's plans for 1975/6 to 1979/80 but revalued all the programmes at the prices current in 1975.) Consequently no one really knew what any public expenditure programme cost. Allocations were first made in volumes and then subsequently translated into cash. It left ministers bemused, made planning difficult, and was not an effective means of controlling public spending, quite apart from the Treasury miscalculations which obviously made planning and economic management impossible. The cash limits system was grafted on to the system of volume planning which had come into existence following the Plowden report in the 1960s. Forty per cent of total public expenditure, divided into blocks, was cash limited in the first year of each new Public Expenditure Survey, with allocations for the following years still expressed in terms of 'funny money'. They were intended to be a weapon in Labour's attempts to cut public spending, perhaps as a 'back-door' method, although the implications of cash limits were quickly recognized. It was an effective method for all that, bringing about a shortfall of expenditure of, on average, 3–4 per cent in each of the three years 1976/77 to 1979/80.

The Treasury, however, was not satisfied with the degree of control cash-limited volume planning had given in the years between 1976 and 1980. Public spending fell sharply between 1976 and 1978, but it then began to rise sharply between 1978 and 1980, by 5.9 per cent in real terms in 1978–9 and by 3.3 per cent in the following year. The increases were largely due to public sector pay; first, the collapse of pay policy in 1979, then the impact of the Clegg Comparability Commission awards to civil servants, and also the fulfilment of the incoming Conservative Government's promises to give pay increases to the police, the armed forces and the fire brigades. The Conservative Government's determination to cut public spending and the Treasury's desire to obtain more effective control over public spending coincided. The Treasury had failed to deliver cuts of £2.5 billion, part of the Government's overall economic strategy, for the March 1981 Budget. It had proved impossible to control public spending since the mid-1970s through volume planning or even through volume planning plus cash limits.

The 1980s

The preparations for the March 1981 Budget provided an opportune moment to change the methods of planning public spending and to introduce cash planning. The decision, taken at the insistence of the Prime Minister, was duly announced in the March 1981 Budget, and was perhaps a more controversial decision within the Treasury than appeared to be the case at the time. However, the Treasury's decision to adopt cash planning fitted in well with the Government's Medium Term Financial Strategy. The justification for their decision was set out in the Monthly Progress Report in March 1981. The system would enable ministers to discuss the amount of money they would actually spend, which would also have to be covered by taxation and borrowing. 'Finance,' the Treasury declared, 'can [then] determine expenditure and not expenditure finance.'[5]

Volume planning worked the other way round and enabled spending departments to lead the Treasury by the nose. Even cash limits plus volume had not helped the Treasury to restrain spending plans as much as had originally been hoped. Its experience with cash-limited volume planning in constant survey prices was that it enabled departments to argue from the basis of entrenched entitlements. Once the Treasury and a department had agreed the volumes of goods and services that department was responsible for providing, the Treasury found it hard to resist the pressures from the departments to continue to provide the same volumes, but with the costs adjusted to take account of the changes in the movements in pay and prices which had taken place during the previous year. Public sector pay increases, in particular, created serious problems for the Treasury between 1979 and 1981. The pay increases meant that more money had to be raised through taxation and public sector borrowing to cover the increased costs of the same volume of goods and services. Cash planning included pay as well as other public sector costs. The new system meant that it was no longer necessary to revalue public spending programmes between one year's White Paper and the next. Once the decisions had been taken in the public expenditure survey about the overall planning totals for each of the three years ahead and the spending programmes for each government department, they could be translated into the total amounts of goods and services which could be bought with that sum of money – and into the Parliamentary Estimates for public expenditure which Parliament has to approve, before the Government can spend any of the taxpayers' money.

The new approach to planning public expenditure had one further advantage, which the Treasury mentioned almost as an afterthought. The new system, it was claimed, would encourage managers to look at the level of service which could be provided for a fixed sum. The same 'volume' of services would not continue to be provided no matter what the costs; managers would therefore face pressures to reduce costs and to look for ways of providing 'value for money'. They would have an incentive to examine their achievements and to look for useful indicators of output. The 'cash planning' approach and the Rayner scrutinies, already well under way, went hand-in-hand. In every way, from the global figures the Treasury considers during the public expenditure survey, to the detailed departmental expenditure plans and budgets, the pressure was on the civil service to cut costs.

Cash planning was linked to cost-cutting measures on the one hand and to monetarism on the other. It followed from, but does not logically depend on, the Medium Term Financial Strategy, which was promulgated at the time of the March 1980 Budget, with its commitment to a reduction in the growth of money supply as a means of reducing inflation. The latter was a repudiation of real resource planning. The aim of the Medium Term Financial Strategy was to decide on the total amount of public spending after the appropriate decisions had been made on the desirable targets for money supply, borrowing and taxation. It was hoped that the public spending could be squeezed to accommodate the Government's judgements about the desirable target figures for each of those variables. (In fact, the Government found that even these targets and the substitution of cash planning for volume planning did not enable them to squeeze public expenditure as much as they expected.) The important point is that thinking in cash terms developed from the belief that macroeconomic policy could not influence the stability of output and employment. Keynes had lost his impact. Policies derived from his work had lost their magic. Indeed, a properly working market mechanism would simply absorb any such attempt to manage demand so that it led to inflation instead of the anticipated output and employment changes. The Medium Term Financial Strategy was based on these beliefs.

The Treasury's choice of methods for planning and controlling public spending during the 1980s must therefore be seen as part of an ideological approach to public expenditure. It was plainly not a neutral selection of the most effective instruments of financial control and planning. That was certainly part of the initial reaction to their introduction. For example, David Heald, then lecturer in the Department of Management Studies at the University of Glasgow and a former specialist adviser to the Treasury and civil service select committee, took the view that cash planning would lead to cuts in volume. '[It] makes revaluation shortfalls cumulative in their impact. Revaluation only takes place at the predetermined cash limit factors. The method through which major volume cuts can be secured is quite clear: the revaluation factors set in the 1982 White Papers [Cmnd 8494] indicate that this is likely to happen unless they are, in the event, revised.'[6]

Other commentators were even more blunt, basing their remarks on the views expressed by departmental officials and ministers. 'It was to bring home to departments and unions that the trade-off between wages increases and jobs that the recession and a non-expansionist economic policy had forced upon the private sector.'[7]

For the Chancellor, though, the changes were all good news and part of the Government's plan for keeping a firm grip on public spending. Cash planning ' ... will change the framework of decisions, and is seen as a major contribution to improving financial management, supporting the other efforts being made to increase cost consciousness and accountability throughout the public sector'.[8]

The fact that cash planning was substituted for volume planning with cash limits does not by itself vitiate its use for planning public spending in a different ideological context, one which places a value on the public sector and public spending, because it sees the public and the private sectors as an integrated whole in which the efficiency of the private sector depends on the provision of efficient and effective public services which the market could not provide.

Cash planning does have certain disadvantages, as the Treasury and Civil Service Select Committee were quick to point out. The Committee argued that cash planning makes life even more difficult for programme managers since they would not know for certain what their cash allocation would be for the following year, nor what they would be able to purchase with it. Planning in cash terms involves forecasting the rate of inflation three years ahead. It is extremely unlikely that the Treasury would get that right since it has consistently failed to get the rate of inflation right for the current year in the Budget statement. Getting it right is crucial for the cash-planning system of public spending, since if inflation is over- or underestimated, there are consequent and unplanned decreases or increases in the volume of spending, unless departmental ministers can persuade the Treasury to make full adjustments for the actual rate of inflation.

The 'intention [with cash planning], as clearly documented in official statements and evidence to the Treasury and Civil Service Select Committee, is that decisions about future expenditure will be taken in cash terms without any detailed separation of price or cost changes on the one hand and volume changes on the other ... It is quite clear from this that cash planning merely represents the extension of cash limit principles to a medium-term horizon.'[9] It has serious consequences for infrastructure planning and is perhaps one of the reasons for its deterioration since 1979, since 'as far as the volume of purchases is concerned ... the effective planning horizon is only one year and it is very difficult to plan some programmes [particularly capital expenditure programmes] on the most efficient basis'.[10] But from the Treasury's point of view, 'The cash planning system represents a more stringent regime than might be suggested by the bare figures of overall increases in public spending ... by putting the onus on spending ministers to make out the case for extra money to finance higher costs.'[11]

The Select Committee argued in favour of planning in 'cost terms' since this allowed for the 'simplicity of cash planning linked to cash control, with the added realism of allowing for general inflation by reducing cash plans to constant prices by a single price index, the GDP deflator'.[12] In this system the actual amount of cash the departments received would depend on the general rate of inflation. Departments would not be compensated for increases in their costs beyond inflation.

The Treasury, however, was not interested in the respective merits of cash and cost planning. As Colin Thain and Maurice Wright point out in their thorough study of the introduction of cash planning, the Treasury, and indeed Treasury ministers, had other aims in mind. 'The Treasury's real [as opposed to ostensible] aim was to improve its control. It was quite prepared to trade greater uncertainty in planning for greater certainty in control. Planning in cash terms provided it with a blunter but more effective instrument for holding down the rising costs of public expenditure. This was to stand Plowden on its head. Where Plowden had insisted that control was inherent in the planning process and procedures, the Treasury's choice implied both the need and superiority of Gladstonian cash control.'[13] But the Treasury has consistently refused to listen to the pleas of the Treasury and Civil Service Select Committee for the inclusion of comprehensive cost term figures.

Further adjustments were made during the 1980s, designed to make it possible for departments to manage their expenditure in a more rational and effective manner. These included the end-year flexibility scheme, which was introduced in July 1983, enabling central government departments to carry forward a certain amount of underspending on capital programmes from one financial year to the next. More recently, special schemes have been introduced to overcome the problems faced by some departments, such as the Ministry of Defence procurement programme, and a limited version of the end-year flexibility scheme, enabling some departments to carry forward under-spending on running costs. Special arrangements were made for the Ministry of Defence as a result of Sir Frank Cooper's doughty and successful battles with the Treasury in which he argued that it was absurd to engage in defence procurement without 'a deposit account [and] overdraft facility', and with 'no means to carry anything from one year to another'.[14] This point is a significant one, with wider implications for the planning of public expenditure, as the Treasury partially recognized in further consideration of the need for flexibility in annual budgeting for public spending.

The Treasury responded with some concessions to the demands for flexibility. These were announced in the House of Commons by the Chancellor in July 1983. It allowed departments to carry over up to 5 per cent (or £2 million, whichever was the greater) of underspending on 'eligible' items. These are capital items such as 'new construction, land, buildings, and defence procurement', and, of course, departments have to meet a number of detailed requirements before any carry-over of underspending is allowed by the Treasury.

The scheme is limited in its scope, applying in 1988–9 to about 21 per cent of cash-limited votes (that is, £16.1 billion out of a total of £74.7 billion). A further special scheme for the Ministry of Defence was introduced in 1986, allowing the MoD to claim up to £400 million to carry forward for the following three years to assist the Ministry in managing the new procurement policy. Further schemes were introduced for the Department of Health for up to 0.5 per cent of its Vote in 1988, and a Running Costs scheme for all departments of up to 25 per cent covering such costs as contracts for computer installation and maintenance.

The Treasury has always impressed on departments the necessity of passing down to line managers the additional funds from the 'end-year' flexibility schemes, rather than retaining monies centrally, indicating that the Treasury does not carry out detailed scrutiny of departmental expenditure, but relies on its rules. The scheme, however, does imply an overall cost to the Treasury, since, as Colin Thain and Maurice Wright point out, 'the Treasury relies on a certain amount of "give" in the planning total in order to allow for some overspending elsewhere [from demand-led programmes, for example] . . . so that it can operate on a tightly budgeted reserve'.[15]

The problem is that such rationality in public spending may not survive. For as Thain and Wright point out, the Treasury may 'take back part or all of the flexibility granted as the public spending squeeze is reimposed under the pressure of high inflation and a shrinking PSBR'.[16] By 1991, however, the economic situation had changed, with other pressures arising from a deep recession and a return to a PSBR.

Further changes were made during the 1980s. In 1986, the Treasury altered the departmental bidding procedures by separating bids for baseline spending from those for additional spending. Baseline bids for the allocations for the first and second year are the same as those already published, together with any changes since publication and the beginning of the new survey. It is possible that these changes were made to enable the Treasury to reject criticisms that cash planning led to cuts in established as well as new spending. But because so little is known about the negotiations between the Treasury and departments before the imposition of cash limits for individual blocks of expenditure and the allocation of resources to non-cash limited programmes it is impossible to judge the truth or otherwise of the Treasury's claims.

Departments have to argue their case for both baseline expenditure and additional resources with detailed information about the quantity of goods and services provided for each unit of output, as well as some judgement about their quality and the effectiveness of those outputs to achieve the declared objectives. Principal finance officers and their line managers almost certainly have not abandoned volume measures since the introduction of cash planning, since what a cash allocation bought last year and what it is likely to buy next year are obviously practical considerations for efficient management and the development of programmes. Once allocations have been agreed between the Treasury and the departments, cash limits are assigned to blocks of spending for the coming financial year, as are cash allocations for the second and third years, based on the Treasury's estimates of, or targets for, inflation, which are supposed to be set in stone. But even the Treasury has to bow to reality, and these allocations are adjusted to take account of general pay and price factors, policy changes and changes for electoral reasons or as a response to political pressure. The Contingency Reserve has continued to grow to allow for such eventualities, but as Likierman points out, the generosity is only apparent, because 'a general allowance gives much greater control from the centre than the individual allocations if potential overspenders have to come and bid for resources against other overspending departments'.[17] It is because this kind of negotiation takes place that Pliatsky once remarked 'volume planning has only gone underground'.[18]

The Treasury has also used the developments in civil service management, from the Financial Management Initiative to the establishment of the executive agencies, as both a means of controlling departmental expenditure and devolving the responsibility to programme managers for operating their budgets. It is a new way of ensuring 'value for money' as far as the Treasury is concerned and one which has 'ramifications for the accountability of public agencies, for relationships between the Treasury and departments, and for relationships between the finance divisions of departments and agencies and their policy divisions, and for the politics of resource allocation'.[19] The Treasury is clear that the objective of this control is to exert downward pressure on administrative costs, while allowing departments greater freedom to allocate resources within their overall limits. It provides them with an 'envelope of cash', as one official put it, but that cash has to be used for wages and salaries and other administrative costs, not programme expenditure or capital items.

The Chief Secretary to the Treasury, John Major, announced in 1987 that departments could develop three-year deals with the Treasury covering running costs. 1986–87 was the first full year of operating running cost controls. Manpower targets were agreed by the Treasury with departments as well as the running cost limits in 1986–7 and 1987–8. The three-year deals announced by John Major in 1987 took effect in 1988–9 and covered both running costs and manpower targets as an integrated whole. To achieve the Treasury's agreement to a three-year deal, the department had to offer a suitable 'management plan', giving details of the way in which manpower was to be used to achieve the department's objectives, and the way in which efficiency gains were to be made in terms both of cost savings and output gains, although the savings on the manpower element was only introduced in 1988–9. The three-year deal also assumed that the department would produce year-on-year efficiency savings of 1.5 per cent of their running costs. Of course, the possibility of such deals has potentially far-reaching consequences for spending planning and control. So far little work has been carried out by the Select Committees to assess the value of these deals, or to consider their application to the executive agencies. The advantage of being able to plan running costs over a three-year period is that it enables sensible forward planning. It is interesting to note that three-year budgets have recently been introduced in Sweden and will be applied to budgeting for all the executive agencies in respect of their running costs, a term which can have a wider connotation when it applies to the activities of an executive agency.

Under the Swedish system, the budget for each agency is first discussed and agreed by its management board, composed of lay representatives from both sides of industry, following a presentation by the director general. The next step is for the executive agency to agree its budget with the sponsoring department, which must examine the agency on the results of its work. The sponsoring department enters into negotiations with the Ministry of Finance and the results become part of the Budget proposals. This basic system has been modified through a special government ordinance on budgetary reform, which took effect in July 1989 as a result of an experiment in 'three-year budget frames', for all administrative expenditure, which was initiated in 1985. The budget frame is expressed in real terms, not as a total amount of cash; for the first year in the period the frame will be equal to the appropriation, and the appropriation for years two and three will be adjusted according to inflation. The frame set by Parliament can only be changed to take account of pay agreements. This method allows the agency to use any savings it may make on administrative costs in the following year and credits up to a limit of 5 per cent between fiscal years without further action on the part of Parliament or Government. The purpose of this approach is to increase budget discipline and discretion for managers – familiar themes indeed.

These 'frames' are developed through joint consultation between ministry and agency executives, politicians and experts. Multi-annual resource levels are agreed on the basis of comprehensive reviews of all agency activities every three years. These reviews will concentrate on the results obtained and the ability of the agency to adjust to the new demands arising from the establishment of the multi-year 'appropriation frames'. The reviews, as with the documentation for all aspects of the work of the executive agencies, will be publicly available, enabling proper evaluations to be made of the agency's success.

The flexibility the British Treasury has allowed so far could well be extended along similar lines to the executive agencies, which would then develop their budgets together with the sponsoring department and take the responsibility for a three-year budget for administrative costs. The same openness about the agency's successes and failures would enable proper assessments to be made, and encourage efficiency in the agencies.

Cash planning and a limited flexibility over running costs are the tools the Treasury has developed as it has sought to increase control over public spending during the last twelve years. The use of these tools, however, is only part of the process of planning public spending, which takes place annually on a tight schedule. It is to that process we must now turn.

Planning Public Spending

The public expenditure survey, as the annual process of planning public expenditure is called, is supposed to follow a certain timetable during the year. The review by top management in each department begins in January. During this period, the department examines its aims and objectives, activities and resources, and as far as they are meaningfully available, output measures and performance indicators are compared with planned targets. The Treasury circulates the latest forecasts of prices, unemployment and interest rates and departments with demand-led spending plans, such as Social Security, are then expected to make realistic plans for future expenditure. Each department also has a baseline for its cash plans, derived from the previous Autumn Statement (the Public Expenditure White Paper is no longer published), adjusted for the Budget and any policy changes. In other words, the amount of public expenditure the country can afford depends on immediate past decisions, what was spent last year and what is currently being spent, as well as what was previously planned to be spent in the two years ahead. The actual movements of pay and prices in the previous year are not automatically reflected in the new planning totals. That gives the Treasury scope to reallocate resources between programmes, and perhaps allow for a larger increase than the rate of inflation for some programmes.

Nothing much is known about the way in which departments set about this review, nor are departments inclined to reveal their hand. But they probably only consider adjusting expenditure at the margins on the programmes for which they are responsible, despite the claims of a former Chief Secretary to the Treasury: 'Although the Government does not operate a formal zero-based budgeting system of the kind that has been tried abroad, we do ensure that a number of areas of policy are fundamentally reviewed each year. These reviews will ask: is this programme essential, does it have to be carried out in the public sector, have its objectives kept pace with changing circumstances and can these objectives be achieved more economically?'[20] Such questions may very well have been raised, but not, one suspects, as part of an internal departmental review of public expenditure, more as a distinctively political decision.

In February and March, departments begin to prepare their cash bids and the background papers supporting their claims for Years 1, 2 and 3. They begin to work out any additional bids they may have or even indicate reduced requirements. The Cabinet also considers public expenditure, and on that basis, the Treasury issues further guidelines to departments on the terms on which the public expenditure survey is to be conducted. The Budget, which usually takes place in March or April, will also feed in further information to the departments in the form of forecasts of prices, unemployment and interest rates. The departments finalize their baseline reports and submit these to the Treasury in April. Bids are never finally agreed at these meetings between officials; they are, instead, used to brief ministers and to prepare the ground for the ensuing battles. All that happens at this stage is that the bids are aggregated into the Survey baseline report by the Treasury to be presented to the Cabinet in June.

In July, the Cabinet discusses the report on the Public Expenditure Survey, which brings together the departmental spending plans and the Chancellor's report on prospects for the macroeconomy, indicating the expectations of economic growth, and therefore the resources available for private and public consumption and investment. The Chancellor will also relate the cash sums for each department to monetary developments over the medium term, and the additional bids for resources. The Cabinet decides on the overall spending limit, which is generally less than all the departmental bids.

At the end of July the Chief Secretary to the Treasury will write to the departments to point out the gap between the planning total limit of the Cabinet and the aggregate of departmental spending bids. Each department will be asked to cut back on their bids in certain ways, and the 'bilaterals' begin, in which departmental ministers and officials will discuss the proposed 'cuts' with the Treasury.

The whole process of bilateral discussions will go on throughout September and October until the November Cabinet meeting, usually the first or second Thursday in the month, when the final decision is taken. The Autumn Statement is made to Parliament in November. Details of departmental expenditure are published in separate booklets in the following March. The debate on the Autumn Statement is the main opportunity Parliament has to debate the whole picture of the Government's public expenditure plans, a debate which takes place quite independently of the Budget, which is, of course, designed to raise taxes to pay for the public spending plans. But as soon as the annual spending round is over, the departments begin the whole process all over again, planning their tactics for getting a larger share of resources next time. They will review the costs of existing programmes, examine whether or not they gave value for money, estimate their future needs and consider the costs of any new policy initiative departmental ministers may have up their sleeves.

So much for the bare bones of the process of planning public spending. Ministers obviously play a part in the whole process, although their scope for action is limited. About two-thirds of all public expenditure consists of programmes, such as social security benefits, which are demand-led or to which the recipients are entitled. Ministers may wish to adjust expenditure on these programmes, but can only do that through legislation to alter entitlements, such as breaking the link between the increases in the basic state pension and increases in average earnings; but these are long-term decisions. Other adjustments can be made, such as the decision to freeze child benefit, or to increase the amount for the first child but not for subsequent children. These, however, are rather different decisions from merely altering the total to be spent on programmes of this kind. Another 20 per cent of the total budget consists of long-term commitments, such as payments to the European Community, although it might be possible to achieve short-term adjustments in these amounts, if, as Mrs Thatcher did in 1984, one demands one's money back. The remaining 10 to 15 per cent can be altered speedily, and the arguments within departments, between the Treasury and departments, and between ministers, focus on this amount.

The ministerial role comes to the fore during the bilateral discussions, though there may well have been heated ministerial debates in Cabinet over the planning total. The extent to which that takes place depends on the economic circumstances of the time; if times are hard, then the meetings will be frequent, exhausting and tough. Barbara Castle describes 'another ... [of those] wretched PESC Cabinets. They are getting so drearily familiar! Denis reported he had reached agreement with ministers on some £870 million towards the saving of £1000 million he was demanding but the bilateral talks had still left him short of what he needed'.[21]

During the summer and autumn, the serious national newspapers are full of accounts of ministerial warfare, with ministers nobly defending precious areas of public spending, such as the National Health Service or Education, from the voracious appetites of the Treasury. It is always difficult to interpret the sounds of distant warfare, since ministers claim to fight battles which there is no necessity to fight, or claim victories when the threat was more imaginary than real.

Others see it less as a form of warfare, more as another part of the marketplace; hence Kenneth Clarke's description of bilaterals as 'haggling in a Turkish bazaar' in the autumn of 1990, when he was embarrassed by a leak of a draft letter setting out his negotiating tactics in the annual battle with the Treasury. That episode was one further example of the way in which ministers affect the public expenditure round, if only at the margins. Those with political clout, determination and the ability to manipulate the media or alarm colleagues with tales of Treasury machinations to cut spending on some politically sensitive programme or other, will emerge as 'winners'; those who seek to appease the Treasury with sacrifices will simply find a voracious god demanding more. The Treasury, on the other hand, will claim that each bid is considered on its merits, with a careful examination of the proposals to see if they will give value for money and if they will fit in with the pattern of the department's declared priorities.

If the Chief Secretary and the departmental ministers fail to agree during the bilateral negotiations, then the matter is referred to the 'Star Chamber', an *ad hoc* ministerial committee, known as Gen 48 or MISC 55, first established by Lord Whitelaw in 1981.

The Star Chamber

It is the 'nearest a government gets to a collective discussion or determination of priorities'.[22] The members of the committee are ministers who are not themselves involved in the dispute, and their secretary is a senior Cabinet official. They can overrule the Treasury and the spending ministers in settling these disputes, but they cannot set aside the planning total agreed by the Cabinet. Departmental bids are always greater than the total the Cabinet has endorsed. There may be a certain latitude, but the real problem is how to get the departmental demands to fit into the overall totals. The Chief Secretary deals with all the departmental ministers, and gets agreement with a great many of them, sometimes all of them. All of the ministers have something the Treasury can live with – perhaps there is an overriding claim which should be granted in that particular year, or perhaps the minister concerned is of sufficient standing in the Government. That comes into it as well. Yet despite all the Chief Secretary's efforts, a certain number of disputes may well be left outstanding. It was thought, therefore, that a senior minister should seek to adjudicate, mediate and generally find some sensible agreement between the warring elements in the Cabinet and the Treasury.

The Star Chamber was established because it was thought to be a more appropriate setting than the full Cabinet to deal with such disputes. The disadvantage of the full Cabinet is that there are too many members, so the meetings are too large, and all the Cabinet ministers have a vested interest in the outcome. They would not participate in any discussion on the issue in any meaningful way, because they are 'all terrified of saying anything which would upset their own position'.[23] Nevertheless, the right of a departmental minister to take his case to Cabinet must be retained, even if he or she is strongly advised that it would be unwise to do so.

The task of chairing the Star Chamber is obviously a difficult one, involving hours of discussions over a period of about three weeks. It is not a task which one minister can take on alone, since it could lead to isolation within the Cabinet – a split between the minister responsible for settling the disputes and the disgruntled spending ministers, who could 'gang up' against the minister concerned. The Star Chamber refers to a group of ministers, preferably with 'strong enough shoulders' to share the burden. Its membership always includes the Chief Secretary, who is automatically a member; the Leader of the House of Commons and the Leader of the House of Lords; the Lord Privy Seal, and possibly the Secretary of State for Scotland, who never faces the same pressures as other spending ministers since Scotland always has an allotted proportion of public expenditure. Sometimes spending ministers who have already settled their bids with the Chief Secretary are invited to attend.

The Star Chamber is often regarded as an important step forward in the process of planning public spending. Sir Leo Pliatsky, a former civil servant, gave a favourable assessment of the Star Chamber. 'The Star Chamber seems to me to have been an important and effective development in the final determination of priorities. The whole process through which priorities have become established from beginning to end, and the influences which play a part, are more complex than that . . . But something like a Star Chamber seems to me to be an instrument which future governments of whatever political complexion should have available.'[24]

This assessment contrasts sharply with a political assessment of its value. The Star Chamber had a certain task to perform, namely to bring down the overall total, and it is simply not in a position to judge effectively what the priorities between departments should be. The Star Chamber is concerned with cutting down on the demands made by one particular department, and the political and strategic judgements involved are very different from assessing priorities in public spending. It is, however, a useful reserve power, as it were, to encourage ministers to settle in bilateral negotiations, rather than facing the Star Chamber. It is a rough and ready way of getting something settled, which could not be done in Cabinet. The Star Chamber inevitably takes only political considerations into account, and 'cannot consider the actual effects of the cuts since the pressures of time are so tremendous'.[25]

The Star Chamber is essentially a means of facilitating agreement between spending ministers and the Treasury. It has not turned out to provide the kind of mechanism which a former Chief Secretary to the Treasury, Joel Barnett, described and which he considered to be a necessary addition to the public expenditure survey. 'My suggestion was to set up a small, but very senior committee of non-spending ministers, to sift through all major programmes, and then put proposals to Cabinet. They should examine programmes in depth, and seriously consider major changes so that Cabinet could take decisions that would not simply be on the margin.'[26] But senior, non-spending ministers would not have the time nor perhaps the expertise to 'sift through' the major programmes. Such a group of senior ministers could, however, consider the fundamental reviews conducted by another body, and make recommendations on the basis of the evidence before them to the Cabinet as a whole.

The whole process of setting the public expenditure totals for each department and ensuring that departments remain within the overall total which the Cabinet has set for the forthcoming financial year smacks of little more than horse-trading between ministers and the Treasury. The horse-trading itself is largely irrelevant to most departmental spending programmes, partly because almost all public expenditure is already determined by legislation or by the commitments arising from membership of the European Community. The former can only be changed if the Government makes major policy changes, not as an incidental part of the public expenditure survey. Changes to departmental expenditure are made only at the margins. The 'margins' – a new motorway, new hospitals or prisons – are important to many people, but they are not fundamental changes. The survey retains existing programmes of expenditure and priorities for public spending do not emerge as a result of this process. Indeed, the whole process is subject to what Sir Douglas Wass neatly summed up as 'two arbitrary principles. Number one: "as things are, so broadly they remain"; and number two: "he who has the muscle gets the money".'[27]

Thain and Wright describe the criticisms which are often made of this system, that it lacks 'rationality', that 'decisions made about the financing of public expenditure programmes should be taken in some more "objective" way, in which the merits of individual cases are assessed according to some agreed economic or financial or other criteria, compared and ranked.'[28] They reject such criticisms, claiming that there are 'no such acceptable criteria, and valid comparisons are problematic given the lack of comparative data on performance and output ... Often what those who argue for a "rational" system are trying to do is to remove politics from what is the most political of activities – fighting for resources. Ministers in bilaterals are negotiating, seeking to establish the terms of settlement, and perhaps strike a bargain.'[29] Thus what would have been astonishing about the revelation of Kenneth Clarke's negotiating tactics would have been for the leak to have revealed that he had none.

Of course, Thain and Wright are quite correct, given the way in which the public expenditure survey actually works in Britain. Setting up the process in that way inevitably means that haggling over the margins is the order of the day. There will certainly always be an element of the strongest minister with the best tactics being able to wrest the lion's share of the resources for his or her department, perhaps regardless of the way in which those resources will be spent. But, given that the resources available for public investment or for current public expenditure are likely to be limited, then it is vital to find more rational ways of deciding both how much to spend and where to concentrate resources. This is very much in line with the repeated recommendations of the Treasury and Civil Service Select Committee in the early 1980s. In 1984, they recommended that there should be 'a reappraisal of the machinery for determining public expenditure priorities, as reflected in the Autumn Statement, with particular reference to the need to improve the allocation across departments and a more open discussion of the best machinery for achieving this'.[30] They did not, however, provide a solution to a problem which has long been recognized. Barbara Castle, for instance, complained back in 1975 that, 'Ministers were never given the chance of discussing priorities or overall economic strategy. Instead we were faced with *ad hoc* demands from the Chancellor from time to time, pleading sudden crisis or necessity. In particular I pleaded that we should look ahead to 1979 and decide what objectives we would wish to have achieved by then and which ones we were prepared to sacrifice.'[31]

The problem seems to be twofold: finding a suitable body to conduct an overall review of public expenditure, and then finding the means of assessing the relative effectiveness of the various programmes. Such a review cannot be conducted by the Treasury, since it has traditionally been concerned with the aggregate of public expenditure, not its component parts. Having set the total for the years ahead, its task is to squeeze departmental bids into the total, taking a cut wherever it can, as Nicholas Monck, a Treasury official, put it in 'But Chancellor'.[32]

This is, however, just the sort of issue which ought to be considered by a central think-tank, despite the difficulties facing the last attempt to do so. That review was secret, but it was leaked, and the leaking aroused suspicions that this was the Government's 'hidden agenda'. It was hardly surprising that such fear was engendered by the leaks, given Mrs Thatcher's well-known hostility to almost any form of public provision.

There is no easy solution to the problems caused by the arousal of entrenched opposition to a review which calls major programmes into question. The only possible way of opening up any kind of rational debate is for the review to be conducted in public, with departments and other interested parties submitting evidence, and for such reviews to be a continual process. The work of the National Audit Office, the Public Accounts Committee and departmental committees would also be relevant to this process, although the emphasis and purpose of their work is to examine policy and not just the costs and priorities.

The more fundamental question concerns the method by which priorities could be decided, if indeed any such method is available. The

Treasury and Civil Service Commission put this question to Chancellor Lawson on one occasion, asking him, 'What the machinery first of all available to the Government is for comparing the relative priorities of expenditure under different departmental heads, and also tell us where those decisions are taken ... Who is providing the analysis so that ministers can make judgements about the relative priority of different heads of expenditure?' The Chancellor replied: 'I do not think that the procedure can be as scientific as you imply', and went on to decry the notion that there could be any 'mechanism' which would provide the answers to such questions about priorities.[33]

It is, of course, quite inappropriate to talk about a 'mechanism' for deciding on priorities in public expenditure; in the last resort, the decision of priorities will reflect differences in values between the political parties, but it does not follow from this that the judgements involved are non-rational, though they may be irrational and merely reflect the status of a particular minister. The present system of 'planning' public expenditure gives far too much scope for irrational decisions about public expenditure of this kind to be made. In other words, 'there is no alternative to a process of politico-economic judgement, but there are procedures for rendering the judgement well informed rather than ill informed, and for making the choices a little more rational rather than less.'[34]

Planning Public Expenditure – An Alternative System

Decisions concerning public expenditure could be informed by an attempt to assess the costs and benefits of a range of departmental programmes, using the familiar and well-established techniques of cost-benefit analysis. The significant elements in cost-benefit analysis of public expenditure policies – the systematic identification of alternative options, the quantification of physical impacts, the monetary evaluation of those impacts, the setting of monetary values in a consistent framework, and the assessment of major uncertainties – are all relevant elements in judging the value of one expenditure programme against another. These techniques are not only available but have long been used in government departments to aid choices between programmes designed to achieve certain limited objectives. Much of this material has never been published, yet its publication would enable other analysts to examine the assumptions underlying the analysis, the methodology and the conclusions, as well as informing public debate.

There is, however, a further hurdle to be overcome, and that is the lack of suitably qualified personnel in the Treasury itself. In 1988, *The Economist* pointed out that, although 'the staff turnover rate is still low ... among high-flying young graduates, it is rising. In both 1986 and 1987 it lost 16 of the 120 key officials in the assistant secretary, principal and economic adviser grades – more than double the yearly losses of the early 1980s.'[35] There is no reason to believe that the situation has eased since then. It leads to serious and fundamental problems; for example, a severe, one-third cut[36] in the man hours spent on interpreting the data provided by the Treasury model, which could partially explain the inaccuracies of Treasury forecasts.

Decisions about which programmes to continue to fund within a department on the basis of cost-benefit analysis are relatively simple compared with interdepartmental comparisons. The extent to which these techniques can be applied to such decisions is open to question, but the elements singled out above do seem to have some part to play in the decisions about which programmes should be given priority in public spending. The process is certainly not one of calculation alone, for 'valuing the different impacts [or outputs] of policy, was inescapably not value-free. That was particularly true when it came to adding up positive and negative outputs, and setting gainers off against losers. As a rule this stage of policy evaluation is carried out on the basis of political judgement.'[37] Political judgement could be improved if a better institutional framework was found. Graham Walshe, who argues strongly for the use of cost-benefit analysis in planning public expenditure, almost despairs at this point, for 'if ministers are risk-adverse by nature they will refuse to countenance such priority ordering systems. The way out of this impasse is not clear. If the role of the Treasury was more powerful, that is, if control over priorities was the subject of greater central direction, there might be improvement. But an expanded role for the Treasury need not provide a solution. Some more imaginative institutional initiative may require consideration.'[38]

Reference has already been made to the role of a central think-tank, advising the Cabinet. The Central Policy Review Staff did in fact prepare papers on public expenditure priorities in the 1970s, jointly with the Treasury during the Heath Government and independently during the period of the Labour Government between 1974 and 1979. The problem with presenting Cabinet with policy decisions of this kind has been well described by Lord Hunt, former Cabinet Secretary, who stressed the limitations of the Cabinet as a body which could make strategic decisions, such as are required in planning public spending. 'Unless the Cabinet can provide a clear strategic oversight over the policies of getting on for thirty departments of state – let alone all the other bodies for which the Government is directly or indirectly responsible – there is an inbuilt risk that decisions may be taken in an arbitrary, uncoordinated or even contradictory manner.'[39]

'Cabinets are not well placed to exercise this role of continuing strategic oversight alongside the taking of specific decisions. Cabinet ministers are heavily preoccupied with their departmental work and find it difficult to take time to think about the problems of other ministers when those do not concern them directly: and of course the more they get involved with their own work the harder it is for them to see the strategy wood from the departmental policy trees ... It was also argued that the Public Expenditure Survey did more to illustrate the inflexibility of public spending pro- grammes than to provide ministers with clear alternative choices: and furthermore that the subsequent public expenditure arguments in Cabinet were settled by muscle rather than relevance to the Government's strat- egy.'[40] Lord Hunt added, after a survey of the various efforts which had been made to deal with the problem during the 1970s, 'I have little doubt that there is a problem and we have not solved it yet.'[41]

Sir Douglas Wass, former Permanent Secretary at the Treasury , and obviously concerned with the public expenditure process, outlines the individualism of the Cabinet: 'The form and structure of a modern Cabinet and the diet it consumes almost oblige it to function like a group of individuals, and not as a unity. Indeed, for each minister, the test of his success in office lies in his ability to deliver his departmental goals ... No minister I know has won political distinction by his performance in Cabinet or by his contribution to collective decision-taking. To the country and the House of Commons he is simply the minister for such-and-such a department, and the only member of the Cabinet who is not seen in this way is the Prime Minister.'[42]

It is difficult to find a way through the institutional maze and discover suitable arrangements to facilitate the kind of thinking about public expen- diture that would ensure the country's resources are to be used effectively. The Cabinet will not only act as a 'group of individuals', but when it is more likely to act collectively, it will be in response to a crisis of some kind, in which all must sink or swim, or in the run-up to an election. A central think-tank, and a small group of senior, non-spending ministers considering the comparative reports produced by the think-tank, could help to produce a more rational ordering of priorities and the most effective concentration of resources. Inevitably, politicians will respond to public pressure, so the publication of as much information as possible during the public expenditure survey would enhance public debate.

The reports of the National Audit Office, the Public Accounts Committee and the departmental select committees are relevant as well, particularly the first, since the National Audit Office has attempted to deal with the effectiveness of public expenditure and not merely with efficiency. The Treasury and Civil Service Select Committee examines the Autumn Statement, the Budget and other macroeconomic decisions taken by the Government, such as the decision to join the Exchange Rate Mechanism. Its reports are published, although they do not always deal with public spending issues, preferring instead to concentrate on the Government's macroeconomic policy. None of these documents, however, are central to the public expenditure survey, and indeed it is doubtful that any of them make much difference to any Cabinet decision, though they may help to inform the public debate. The most effective contribution to a public debate would be the cost-benefit analyses which departments carry out or commission, and since the Public Expenditure Survey report to Cabinet in July each year is leaked, or at least the most interesting parts of it are leaked to the media, it might be worth taking the truly radical step of publishing it in full anyway, since leaks are always partial, politically motivated and therefore misleading.

Little reference has been made to Parliament in this discussion about planning public spending. This is because, despite the formal constitutional position, which is that Parliament grants the monies to the executive, Parliament in fact has formal control over part of public expenditure and none at all over the rest. The House takes note of the Autumn Statement, and formal authorization is given by the 'supply procedure'. Even then, Parliament cannot increase public expenditure, although it can reduce it, so obviously an unpopular move for almost all areas of public expenditure except defence spending that few politicians seriously consider a reduction as opposed to a reallocation. When, in July 1981, the Select Committee on Procedure proposed an overhaul of the 'antiquated and defective' financial procedures (which has since taken effect), they added, 'While we reject the concept of binding control by the House over the totality of public spending, we believe that there should be more scope for effective scrutiny.'[43] The problem is that, given the nature of the process of planning public spending, and the separation of the Budget from public expenditure decisions, 'effective scrutiny' by Parliament is as much a chimera as 'binding control'.

Planning Public Spending in Germany and France

The separation of public spending decisions and the budgetary process and the excessive secrecy which surrounds both processes of decision-making, is quite unlike the way in which such issues are tackled in other advanced democracies, such as Germany and France. In Germany, the Budget process begins about nine months before the beginning of the financial year with a group of independent economic and financial experts giving advice to the Ministry of Finance in the spring. It is an advisory report, covering, amongst other aspects, the question of the extent to which public sector borrowing should be increased. On the basis of this report, negotiations with the various spending ministries take place, but taxation decisions are considered in conjunction with the spending decisions. If important spending decisions are likely to raise the public expenditure borrowing requirement, then the taxation implications have to be faced. Linking taxation to public spending in this way establishes the purpose of taxation in the public mind as providing public services, unlike the British system of separating the Budget from any consideration of public services, so the focus of the Budget is always on the extent to which the Government may cut taxes, on the immediate financial benefit to some taxpayers.

The Budget, or *Finanz Bericht*, is presented to the Bundestag. This contains a summary of the Government's conclusions, a proposed budget based on these conclusions and outline proposals for budgets for the three subsequent years. The advisory group's report about the development of fiscal policy is published in advance of the Budget so that the Bundestag and the public can take part in an informed debate until the final vote in December, ready for the beginning of the financial year in January. The final decision does actually take into account parliamentary preferences, informed public opinion and independent forecasters, with monetary policy controlled by the Bundesbank. Parliamentarians have a real contribution to make to the whole process of 'getting and spending', unlike the British system in which all but Cabinet ministers are excluded from the process, and the Chancellor alone makes the final decisions (in consultation with the Prime Minister) about the shape of the Budget, which is then only revealed to the Cabinet on the morning of the Budget statement.

The Budget process in France is in many ways similar to that of Germany. The process begins in the spring with the *lettre de cadrage* from the Prime Minister to the various spending departments, setting out the nominal total by which all public spending should increase in the light of the economic forecasts, leading to the annual departmental bids for cash. Taxation decisions are taken at the same time. The Government presents its taxation and spending proposals in September and public debate and further negotiations take place in which the Government's proposals may be altered. The process of decision-making is less open than in Germany and the Bank of France is less independent of the Government than the Bundesbank, but the principle of an informed public debate in which the Government may set the public spending priorities, but in which the public have an effective part to play, is one which should be emulated here.

Such a process is at present impossible in this country, partly because of the separation of the Budget from public expenditure, which effectively makes a nonsense of planning. Take Terry Ward's comment in 1988 (specialist adviser to the Treasury and Civil Service Committee) on the Government's Expenditure Plans: 'Nor is it clear how far the competing merits of expanding public expenditure on the one hand and reducing taxes on the other were seriously evaluated, and if so on what basis. Separating the decision-making process on the two sides of the Budget as at present does not seem to be designed to encourage such an evaluation to be made.'[44]

This comment is in line with recommendations made by the Armstrong Report of 1980 for a 'unified budget' of which the three main requirements are:

(i) An economic framework in which to formulate and present tax plans alongside public expenditure for the medium term as well as the short term.

(ii) A change in timing so that taxation and expenditure plans are presented together.

(iii) The provision of a period after the Budget is first presented, to permit consideration, in Parliament and outside, of economic and fiscal policy.'[45]

Two documents would be provided – a December Budget statement would be the key document on economic and financial policy in the year, and would be followed by a second containing firm Budget proposals for the forthcoming financial year, taking account of the public debate. These proposals form the basis of a more rational approach to planning public spending.

Any possibility of Parliament's, or the public's, involvement in a proper debate about public spending is further vitiated by the lack of adequate information. The Government's overall plans are announced in the

Autumn Statement, which now forms the basis for the set-piece Parliamentary debate about public spending, and in 1991 the departments became responsible for publishing their own reports. The first set of such reports has proved to be deeply disappointing in terms of the kind of information they make available. Reforming the public spending and budgetary processes so that they become more open and more rational will require far higher standards of information provision than is available at present.

Notes

[1] D. Healey, *The Time of My Life*, 1989, p. 401.

[2] ibid., p. 401.

[3] ibid., p. 427.

[4] ibid., p. 401.

[5] Monthly Progress Report, March 1981.

[6] D. Heald, *Public Expenditure*, Martin Robertson, 1983, p. 196.

[7] S. Lewis and A. Harrison, 'How Real are Real Resources?', *Public Money*, September 1983, p. 54.

[8] Economic Progress Report, March 1981.

[9] Notes and Surveys, *Public Administration*, Spring 1983, Vol. 61, pp. 86–7.

[10] A. Likierman, 'Squaring the Circle', *Policy and Politics*, 1986, Vol. 14, No. 3, p. 286.

[11] L. Pliatsky, *The Treasury Under Mrs Thatcher*, 1989, p. 63.

[12] Treasury and Civil Service Select Committee Report, 1982, para. 3.14.

[13] C. Thain and M. Wright, 'The Advent of Cash Planning', *Financial Accountability and Management*, Autumn 1989, Vol. 5, No. 3, p. 160.

[14] F. Cooper, 'Matters Relating to the Ministry of Defence', Public Accounts Committee, Sixteenth Report, 1980, HC648, Q. 2291.

[15] C. Thain and M. Wright, 'Conceding Flexibility in Fiscal Management: The Case of Public Spending End-Flexibility', *Fiscal Studies*, November 1990, Vol. 2, No. 4, p. 77.

[16] ibid., p. 81.

[17] op. cit., A. Likierman, p. 295.

[18] L. Pliatzky, *The Treasury Under Mrs Thatcher*, p. 63.

[19] C. Thain and M. Wright, 'Running Costs Control', *Financial Accountability and Management*, Summer 1990, Vol. 6, No. 2, p. 116.

[20] HCDCL, 20 February 1986, col. 507.

[21] B. Castle, *The Castle Diaries 1974–76*, 10 April 1975, p. 360.

[22] private information.

[23] private information.

[24] L. Pliatsky, op. cit., p. 47.

[25] private source.

[26] J. Barnett, *Inside the Treasury*, Andre Deutsch, 1982, pp. 154–5.

[27] D. Wass, *Government and the Governed*, 1984, pp. 13–14.

[28] C. Thain and M. Wright, 'Haggling in Mr Clarke's Turkish Bazaar', *Public Money and Management*, Winter 1990, Vol. 6, No. 4, p. 54.

[29] ibid.

[30] Treasury and Civil Service Select Committee, First Report, 'The Government's Economic Policy', 1984–5, HC44, p. vii.

[31] B. Castle, op. cit., p. 522.

[32] Hugo Young and Anne Sloman, 'But Chancellor, An Inquiry into the Treasury', BBC, 1983, p. 56.

[33] Treasury and Civil Service Select Committee, First Report, 'The Government's Economic Policy', 1984–5, HC44, p. 45, para. 312.

[34] L. Pliatsky, 'Optimising the Role of the Public Sector: Constraints and Remedial Policies', *Public Policy and Administration*, Spring 1988, Vol. 3, No. 1, p. 38.

[35] *The Economist*, 18 June 1988, p. 32.

[36] private source.

[37] *Public Money*, June 1986, p. 59.

[38] G. Walshe, *Planning Public Spending in the UK*, 1987, p. 45.

[39] Lord Hunt of Tamworth, 'Cabinet Strategy and Management', CIPFA/RIPA conference, Eastbourne, 9 June 1983, p. 2.

[40] ibid.

[41] ibid.

[42] D. Wass, *Government and the Governed*, 1984, p. 21–40.

[43] Report by Select Committee on Procedure, July 1981.

[44] T. Ward, Treasury and Civil Service Select Committee, Appendix, 1988–89, p. 33.

[45] *Budgetary Reform in the UK*, 1980, p. 13.

FOUR

The Policy Advisers

Since 1988 the focus of attention has inevitably been on the 'Next Steps' initiative to the detriment of the role of the policy advisers, who will remain in the core departments when the devolution of Whitehall to the executive agencies is complete. The efficient delivery of effective services is, of course, vital, but the quality of advice ministers receive must not be neglected either. Policy advice may still be the 'golden route to the top' in the eyes of ambitious civil servants, but just how they arrive at the top is still a mystery.

The Way to the Top

In 1985 the Royal Institute of Public Administration set up a high-level working party to examine the whole issue of senior appointments and promotion. The traditional view is, of course, of the politically neutral career civil service offering objective advice to ministers, a view originally propounded by Sir Warren Fisher in his submission to the Tomlin Commission in 1930. It was echoed by Sir Douglas Wass, former Joint Head of the Civil Service, who stressed its value in his claim that the 'politically uncommitted civil service can evaluate ... factors with the objectivity which can sometimes escape the enthusiast'.[1] Similarly, the Management and Personnel Office, in the course of arguing for the continuance of the career civil service, claimed that 'a predominantly career civil service is ... more able to act impartially than one in which large numbers have divided loyalties between past, present and potential future employers'.[2]

But during the 1980s, particularly in the early to mid-years of the decade, many doubted that the civil service remained politically neutral. It was feared that the civil service had become politicized during the Thatcher regime in the sense that the administration of the day ensures that the senior civil servants are their political sympathizers. Some former civil servants claimed that there had been a growing interest in top-level appointments. Lord Callaghan, when Prime Minister, took a closer interest in these appointments than either Edward Heath or Harold Wilson, as his evidence to the Treasury and Civil Service Committee indicates:

> I took considerable interest in this, perhaps because I have known a lot of people in the civil service in my official capacity ... the degree of interest would depend on my knowledge of the persons involved. If I did not know them I would be willing to accept the advice of people who did know them ... If somebody was put up to me to become Under Secretary in the Ministry of Agriculture and I had no idea about the three people who had been put up I would choose the one recommended which had already gone through the permanent secretary in the department and a small group of permanent secretaries who knew these people together with the Civil Service Department ... I do not think I ever overruled them. If they were aware of my interest and knowledge I think they were a little reluctant to make a recommendation; they would put the facts in front of me and ask 'What do you think?' I cannot say I ever overruled them. I do not think that happened.[3]

Mrs Thatcher seemed even more involved, but certainly did not interview candidates or 'look for blues'. Indeed, one former senior civil servant pointed out that, on one occasion, when Mrs Thatcher needed another private secretary at No. 10 (which is staffed by civil servants from other departments, who spend a year or so there) she accepted a young man whose name was put forward by the department, although he is a well-known Labour supporter. She did, however, like to get to know candidates whom she had not already met. Arguments about candidates could become heated, but that was because she was apt to make 'ten-second judgements'. No one could think of a case in which a definite recommendation from senior civil servants had been overturned. Nor could anyone say that the people she appointed were not extremely capable.

Yet some senior politicians and their advisers expressed serious anxieties about the extent and degree of politicization. A memorandum written by William Wallace for the Liberal Party in 1985 and leaked to the press stated: 'We will want to replace a number of permanent secretaries on arrival in office as they are politically unacceptable; to do that we need ... to discover who our friends are and who are our most awkward political enemies.'[4] This obviously raised difficulties about the criteria for discovering 'political enemies' in the civil service, and the memorandum was quietly abandoned.

But a year earlier, Dr David Owen had also stated that he, too, would like to remove senior civil servants, but on quite different grounds. 'Key civil servants, the ones who make decisions and are paid reasonably high salaries, must be subject to early retirement, not on grounds of negligence or inefficiency, but for the more important and likely reason that their job could be better done by someone else.'[5]

The suspicions lingered on until the late 1980s on the part of some politicians, such as Dr Jack Cunningham, who declared that it would be impossible for him to work with Sir Terence Heiser at the Department of the Environment given his part in all the worst local government legislation, a comment which was later withdrawn. Sir Terence counters such claims by asking, 'How many civil servants have ever resigned on questions of principle? They are political neutrals serving the Government of the day.'[6]

Yet for most people, as the decade wore on and as Mrs Thatcher's position within her own party began to weaken, the credibility of the politicization charge began to fade as well. Take *The Times*'s description of two appointments in November 1989 – Nick Monck, who became second permanent secretary in charge of public expenditure in the Treasury, and Peter Owen, who moved from being deputy secretary in the Department of Environment to the Cabinet Office. The first hailed from Eton and King's College, Cambridge, the other from the Liverpool Institute and Liverpool University. According to *The Times*, both owed their promotion to their 'policy coups', the first on privatization and the other on housing and council finance. The 'policy coups', *The Times* laconically points out, 'refer not to effects of their work on the wider world but its perception within Whitehall, which is all that matters in the promotion stakes'.[7]

The fact is that the evidence for alleged politicization was always slight, inevitably based on rumour. All the obvious promotions during the decade in which Mrs Thatcher was Prime Minister gave little sign of being decided on party political grounds. The Royal Institute of Public Administration (RIPA) working party's careful study of appointments and promotions undertaken in 1985 found no evidence at all of these being made on political grounds. They concluded that 'to some extent the appointment process has become more personalized in the sense that at the top level "catching the eye" of the Prime Minister may now be more important than in the past . . . one ministerial special adviser from another department was asked for his views on the promotability of senior officials in his

department' in sharp contrast with the attempts of the Senior Appointments Selection Committee and 'succession planning' arrangements to
'make a broad and objective survey of a wide field of candidates'.[8]

Even the First Division Association stated in its evidence to the working
party that 'it is style rather than political belief which tends to be considered
important. The style which appears to appeal to the Prime Minister is the
"can do" approach, best characterized by decisiveness and an ability to
get things done'.[9] Nevertheless, there has undoubtedly been a 'greater
involvement of ministers' in what used to be the civil service's preserve,
since it was 'generally accepted . . . that the service itself was the best judge
of ability and should therefore have the decisive voice in selection and
promotion. The service has a well-developed system of annual reporting
on its members right up to the highest levels, and a judgement by a
permanent head about the merits of various candidates for the post rests
not only on a long acquaintance with them, but also on a measured
appreciation of the judgement of others over an even longer period. The
minister in charge of a department, still less the Prime Minister, can never
have such a detailed and comprehensive knowledge of the merits of
claimants for promotion.'[10]

Promotion has clearly not depended on the individual's ideological
commitment during the Thatcher Governments any more than it did in
the preceding years. No one's promotion has been held back or accelerated
because of their political views. A certain style has been relevant. Civil
servants who demonstrate the ability to take decisions and follow them
through were more likely to succeed under the Thatcher Governments
than those who consider all the difficulties and obstacles to such an extent
that action and decision do not take place. 'The emphasis is on subsequent
implementation. Senior civil servants in the past would have considered
that their work was completed once the minister had taken a decision, but
they are now expected to ensure that something happens once the decision
has been taken. This is what the "Next Steps" emphasizes.'[11] It is too early
to assess the influence of John Major on senior appointments, but given
the link with the 'Next Steps', it is likely that the emphasis on decisiveness
will continue.

Policy advice may be the 'golden route to the top', but senior civil
servants are often less than clear about how to travel along the route. In
some parts of the civil service, where there are vacancies at senior levels,
the shortlist for the most senior posts is obvious, simply because only a
very few people are eligible. It is clear 'whose hat is in the ring', but in
other departments the range of choice is wider, and for that reason it may

be difficult to spot the frontrunners. For those aspiring to promotion, there appears to be some uncertainty about the way in which they can put themselves in the way of promotion to Grades 1 and 2. This is not the case with promotion to Grade 3 from Grade 5, which is likely to be available to 'fast-stream' civil servants who enter the service as graduates. It is not so obvious who will be promoted from Grade 3 to Grade 2 because virtually all the Grade 3s will have been on this fast stream and they therefore will have to be sifted out at that stage.

A permanent secretary may be given a strong steer and/or briefing by the Head of the Home Civil Service as to the sort of person required for a particular post. The consultations are very much a 'two-way street' in which the head of the department will explain to the Head of the Home Civil Service the kind of strength he feels he needs in the department. That is, however, only part of the process. After 1981, following Sir Derek Rayner's advice, each department prepared 'succession plans' and 'year plans' for specified posts and individuals on an annual basis, but these are now less extensive than the plans recommended by the Management and Personnel Office in 1983.

Promotion – A Secretive Process

There have been other more subtle changes in the approach to promotions at the senior level. It is claimed that the 'system is less clubby than it was in the past. It is less likely that appointments will be made in Pall Mall clubs. The pressure of work no longer allows for such a leisurely approach. Senior civil servants do meet but in formal meetings of groups of establishment officers to discuss mutually relevant issues.'[12]

Less clubby it may be, but it is still a secretive process in which the grounds for promotion are not clear, and one in which women still face difficulties, despite some recent promotions to deputy secretary level (nine out of forty-eight at the time of writing, autumn 1991). There are no women permanent secretaries in charge of departments; Dame Anne Mueller was Second Permanent Secretary at the Treasury until retirement in 1990.

Lurking, unarticulated prejudice persists, such as being careful not to have 'too many women' at or near the top, and, of course, more than one is too many! In a system which depends so much on the recommendations of departmental permanent secretaries, themselves all male, women are highly likely to suffer from the 'invisibility factor'. No matter how competent, efficient and intellectually able they are, they will simply not be noticed, if the views expressed by Sir Peter Kemp, Project Manager for the 'Next Steps' programme, to the Treasury and Civil Service Select Committee, are at all typical. In response to a question from John Garrett, MP for Norwich South, about recruitment Kemp said, 'I mean that the Civil Service recruits the best people to present themselves, and the best people who present themselves for the job happen to be Oxbridge, male and white.'[13] Sadly, none of the MPs cross-examining him allowed this astonishing statement to go by unchallenged.

Secrecy over the criteria for promotion also applies to another stage, that of performance-related pay for those in Grades 5–7. On the basis of an analysis of reports on their current performance it appears that women perform slightly better than their male colleagues, yet an analysis of the departmental statistics shows that more men than women receive performance pay and receive beneficial pay points. The Treasury refuses to make the statistics available centrally, and the criteria on which the pay awards are made are extremely vague, particularly the concept of 'marketability'. Such behaviour of the Civil Service Management and Pay Division may well conflict with a recent ruling of the European Court, which held that 'where a system is characterized by a total lack of transparency, the burden of proof is on the employer to show that his pay practice is not discriminatory where a female worker establishes, by comparison with a relatively large number of employees, that the average pay of female workers is lower than that of male workers'.[14]

Subtle forms of discrimination still exist, preventing women from reaching the top, and transparency over pay should be accompanied by transparency over criteria for promotion. The discrepancies of the awards of performance-related pay are of course one form of discrimination. Other forms of discrimination apply to the procedures for promotion at senior levels; for example, the system of self-nomination for promotion at assistant secretary level, which operates in some central government departments, always results in fewer women nominating themselves. Being moved to the Treasury is often a sign that a civil servant is being groomed for promotion to the post of under-secretary and then perhaps the most senior post of all, permanent secretary. The Treasury, however, along with some other government departments, has a culture of excessive hours of work, sixty hours a week being typical. A spell in the Treasury as an important career move may be offered to women civil servants in their early thirties, just at the point where family and career considerations conflict most strongly. But above all the secrecy surrounding promotion procedures, and the subjectivity of the judgements involved in the process work together to make it much more likely that chaps will promote and encourage chaps like themselves.[15]

The secretive nature of the latter process certainly emerged from the investigation carried out by the RIPA working party, which produced an account of them 'assembled only with difficulty'.[16] The procedures are 'shrouded in secrecy: only those directly involved in the process know exactly how and why decisions are taken'.[17] The working party offered the following description of the senior promotion practices:

> Appointments and promotions to deputy and permanent secretary posts, Grades 2 and 1 respectively, and transfers between departments for officials in those grades require the approval of the Prime Minister. All proposals for such appointments, promotions and transfers are discussed by the Senior Appointments Selection Committee. The Prime Minister receives the advice of the Head of the Civil Service, not that of the SACS, which formally only advises the Head of the Service. In practice, the Head of the Civil Service is guided by the consensus emerging from this collegiate body. Decisions are taken by an emerging consensus from what is in fact a 'collegiate body'. The Senior Appointments Committee meets once a month as a rule to discuss any vacancies which are likely to occur in the near future, as well as taking a long-term view of staffing requirements. Emergency meetings can be arranged if a sudden vacancy occurs.'[18]

The membership of the Senior Appointments Selection Committee includes permanent secretaries from the most important departments such as the Ministry of Defence, the Department of Trade and Industry, Department of the Environment, Department of Health and Social Security, and one or two specialists, with the Head of the Home Civil Service as the chairman and a member of the staff of the Management and Personnel Office as its secretary. The membership of the committee varies from time to time so that the committee gains a new perspective on appointments. Currently it considers annual appraisals and curriculum vitae, though it appears that full appraisal and promotion reports are no longer carried out.

The department apparently puts forward one or two candidates and the Management and Personnel Office proposes a few candidates on the basis of its annual review of promotable staff in all departments. In these circumstances the departmental permanent secretary becomes a member of the committee if he is not already. Once a decision has been made, the departmental permanent secretary informs the Secretary of State who can, in theory, select another candidate, but rarely does so. Then the Head of the Home Civil Service sends in the recommendation to the Prime Minister. When the Prime Minister and other ministers have to approve appointments they see the standard curriculum vitae of the individuals concerned, but no further background material, such as their annual assessments. In these circumstances, it is understandable that ministers, including the Prime Minister, attempted to find out more themselves about possible candidates.

Promotions to the rank of under secretary (Grade 3 and above) take place within the department and candidates are considered by a departmental management board, consisting of the permanent secretary, second permanent secretaries and deputy secretaries. The Management and Personnel Office is also generally represented at the meetings. The permanent secretary will discuss the vacancy and the proposed appointment with the minister before making a recommendation, but the procedure may be different if the post is a politically sensitive one.

Appointments to the post of principal establishment officer and principal finance officer have to be approved by the Head of the Home Civil Service and the Prime Minister. This rule applies both to promotions and to a sideways move on the part of the individual concerned. The Treasury is consulted on these appointments.

Detailed succession plans and annual assessments were introduced in 1983 on the recommendation of the Management and Personnel Office.[19] The departments regarded such plans as an unnecessary burden at first and groaned about the burden of paperwork involved, according to one former senior civil servant involved in the process. After three or four rounds of preparing such plans, departments apparently settled down to following the new procedures. Succession plans were regarded by the MPO as a valuable management tool, indicating a 'shortlist' of people who, after an annual review of their promotion potential, would be thought qualified or suited to future vacancies. But, in general, plans for individual development are not as well developed as the succession plans. The arrangements for both vary from one department to another with some departments being much more conscientious than others.

With succession plans, senior management looks across the department, comparing the merits of relevant individuals. The heads of departments and the establishment officers also consult with other heads of departments about suitable individuals. The process involves relating senior posts to promotees, especially those with special or scarce skills. It opens up the question of succession for proper consideration. It gives a better information base for the Senior Appointments Committee to work on. The succession plans are, however, extremely confidential and would never be shown to ministers, especially as they are likely to be implemented beyond the timetable of any one administration. One senior civil servant said firmly: 'It would not be appropriate for ministers to be informed about succession plans. They are a management issue, considering posts to be filled on a long-term basis, and would require a detailed knowledge of the future development of the department.'[20] This is itself an interesting comment on the civil service's view of the relationship between the government and the civil service.

One former senior civil servant regarded making succession plans as a 'valuable discipline and an objective procedure which opens up opportunities for women and those with a scientific background, provided only that there are two or more names under consideration. The new system has brought scientists and other specialists into the promotion structure. For the first time, it is clear that they are beginning to look at specialists in a different way, although it is still the case that scientists and other specialists are promoted later in their careers than generalists'.[21] But succession plans are beginning to disappear from the agenda as the agency system develops and more people are brought in from outside.

A further disadvantage of a selection procedure of this kind is that the criteria for promotion are neither clear nor public. As the RIPA working party concluded: 'All appointment and promotion procedures should be published. Openness will enhance the legitimacy of the system in the eyes of the public, politicians and civil servants themselves; will allow constructive debate on ways of improving the civil service's methods of identifying and appointing senior staff; and will also head off arguments for wholesale "politicization."'[22] The working party recommended some kind of external input, in the form of two outside appointees to the panel, or involving outsiders in a continuing scrutiny of the way in which the civil service handles top appointments.

Such steps would certainly help to reassure the public that the top appointments had not been made on political grounds. They do not, however, go far enough in opening up top level appointments. Open advertisement of all senior posts at least within the civil service could well bring certain names to the attention of a Senior Appointments Selection Committee which would not otherwise be considered. Such a system operates for all but the top three positions in the Swedish civil service, which are made by the Government. There, all vacant positions have to be advertised, stating what qualifications they wish the applicant to possess, and applications are invited from within and outside the civil service. The appointing committee does not have to state its reasons for the appointment of the candidate it selects, but it is possible for any one of the rejected candidates to challenge the choice and appeal to the Government against the appointing committee's decisions. In these circumstances the reasons for the choice and all the relevant documents would have to be made available to ensure that there had been no untoward discrimination.

There may be certain difficulties in transposing such an arrangement into the senior levels of the British civil service, especially for permanent secretaries in which ministers naturally take an interest, or for politically sensitive posts. These difficulties could be overcome by consultations with ministers and the departmental permanent secretaries once the shortlist has been established. But both those who are being consulted about the appointment and the selection committee itself should be aware that the appointment could be challenged and must therefore be justified. It is unlikely that the committee's decisions would be challenged very often, but the mere fact that they are open to challenge and that the documentation must be revealed would improve the quality of the decision-making process.

A system of selection of this kind could well increase the opportunity for women to reach the top. They would be able to put their own names forward, thus overcoming the invisibility factor which too often plagues them. Opening up the selection process in this way would be another element in improving the quality of the advice ministers receive by ensuring that the best people reach the top, and are employed there, not only in a managerial role, but also in the traditional role of policy advisers.

The emphasis in the reforms carried out in the civil service over the past twelve years has been on management, on improving the efficiency of public services and, above all, on cutting the costs of providing those services and the numbers of staff involved. Mrs Thatcher was notoriously impatient about advice, although she was impressed with the civil servants whom she felt would assist with the development and then the implementation of policies on which she had already decided. During the Thatcher era, ministers too were increasingly unwilling to listen to civil servants who pointed out the difficulties in pursuing certain policies. That in itself put civil servants seeking promotion in difficulties. Playing down the obstacles and problems in the path of implementing policies would obviously seem to be the wisest course for such civil servants to take.

The Importance of Policy Advice

Despite the vagaries of the Thatcher era, the role of policy advice in the civil service is still a crucial one. In view of her hostility towards the civil service in general, Mrs Thatcher sought to supplement that by building up her own policy unit at No. 10, and was in a position to draw on the idea carried in right-wing think-tanks such as the Centre for Policy Studies. It is too soon to say whether Prime Minister Major will depart from a conventional view of the role of civil servants in giving policy advice.

It is a crucial role, partly because of the difficulties opposition parties face in preparing policy. Well-funded think-tanks exist only on the right. Left-wing think-tanks have been established but their financial resources are slender, although they can draw on a wide range of expertise in the universities, the voluntary sector and the worlds of industry and commerce. Members of Parliament face the financial constraints as well. Their resources for secretarial and research assistance are laughable for a modern Parliament, currently £27,166 per annum, out of which MPs generally pay the going London rate for the salary of a full-time secretary, leaving a few thousand pounds to employ a youthful research assistant.

Overloaded ministers, coming into office with manifesto commitments, ideological beliefs or a certain set of aims and objectives, or perhaps nothing more than personal ambition, find it hard to turn these into coherent policies. Unless they are experienced, they will find themselves at a loss in Cabinet when presented with complex and technical issues proposed by departments other than their own. It is often easy for departments to secure Cabinet agreement on such proposals, given the limited time for explanation and discussion in full Cabinet. If these are the problems which beset ministers in actually dealing with short- to medium-term policy issues, then there is even less time for tired and overworked ministers to consider the longer-term. Cabinet ministers often work a twelve- to fourteen-hour day, attend to the demands of their constituents, perhaps nurse a marginal constituency, *and* answer to Parliament.

Improving Policy Advice

The need for policy advice is clear enough. Improving its quality should be as much part of a programme of reform of the civil service as the managerial reforms of the past twelve years. Freedom of information has a role to play here as well. William Plowden and Tessa Blackstone's description of the operations of the Government's Think-Tank, or Central Policy Review Staff, under Lord Rothschild illustrate the point well:

> The tone was initially set by Rothschild, whose personal network was probably the most extensive of any. An international cast of experts was pressed by him into the service of the CPRS: some became standing members of project teams, others were more intermittently consulted by Rothschild. His scientific background inclined him strongly to the belief that for every subject there were a very few – perhaps only one – generally acknowledged experts, whose advice on that topic was likely to be objectively better than that of other people. The theoretical drawback to this approach in a Whitehall context is that it is often disbarred by the Official Secrets Act; this rarely inhibited Rothschild. There is no evidence that consultation with unlicensed outsiders ever led to unauthorized leaks of information. Later heads of the CPRS were considerably more cautious in this respect, and it is arguable that in these circumstances 15–20 professional staff is too small to do a really effective job.[23]

The value of such widespread consultation is obvious – the opportunity to draw on truly expert advice. Nor is it just a question of access to advice, but also the opportunity for criticism and the exchange of ideas. The ideas and policy analysis offered by civil servants to ministers are subject only to internal scrutiny. A departmental view develops. The critical examination of the analysis offered by one civil servant is scrutinized by another but apparently in a polite and formal manner. Policy analysis should be subject to sustained and informed criticism. The lack of access to information makes that impossible. Some sort of access to background policy papers might be possible under Freedom of Information, but the legislation in other countries protects the advice actually given to ministers by civil servants, and that course would have to be followed here as well. The value of making background factual information and analyses available is that this will make it possible to subject the basic assumptions underlying government policy to informed criticism and therefore improve the quality of policy-making.

Bringing outsiders in to give advice to ministers is increasingly important, and not only to deal with the 'hole in the centre', the lack of a comprehensive view of government policy or of areas of concern which require attention. It is also necessary to provide individual ministers, both Cabinet and junior ministers, with better support. One of the advantages of the way in which the Cabinet system operates in France is that it 'improves the quality and variety of policy advice to the minister. In particular, the integration of advisers who liaise with outside groups and members who can assess policy pressures from the bureaucracy, within one team [rather than] more piecemeal systems of advice'.[24]

Of course, the way in which the Cabinet system operates in France could not be imported wholesale into the British system, but would have to be adapted to it. The former structure differs from the latter in two important respects. Each ministry is composed of a range of sub-departments each dealing with a particular area of policy. The divisions are then subdivided into bureaux, each covering a more limited area of policy. Instead of one or two influential and powerful permanent secretaries, each ministry has about eight to ten influential directors, often specialists, such as scientists or technicians, reporting directly to the minister, and bureaux chiefs. The directors do not share, and may well decline to accept, the Minister's policy assumptions. The dangers of fragmentation and compartmentalization within the departments and the subsequent implications for policy development and coordination is obvious, and exacerbated by the '*corps*' system, that is, the way in which French civil servants are organized into '*corps*' or administrative/professional groups. The cabinets exist to counteract such tendencies.

There is no system of permanent cabinet committees in France, apart from the Defence Council, which is chaired by the President. Since governmental powers are dispersed through the ministries, no question can be settled by a single ministry. They compete with each other, especially over resources. In the face of warring departments, inter-departmental committees, missions and delegations staffed by trusted civil servants have become the vehicle to coordinate government policies, carry out policy studies, and finally set up *ad hoc* ministerial meetings, which are designed to make policy decisions.

All ministers have cabinets; ministers are allowed ten and junior ministers, seven, but ministers often have up to twenty and junior ministers ten. The ministerial cabinets date from the beginning of the Third Republic, with the rules governing them established in 1911. Appointments to the cabinet have always been at the minister's discretion, allowing him to choose and dismiss staff as he sees fit. A high proportion of the members of the cabinet are in fact civil servants, but share the minister's political commitment. Civil servants are free to be active members of political parties, and their political allegiances may well be known within the service. Indeed, one of the civil servants I interviewed often distributed Communist party literature outside his office, and then came into the office for the day's work. No one in the department, ministers or officials, thought that there was anything worthy of note in his behaviour. It is quite possible to campaign actively for another political party, and publicly support policies in opposition to the Government, and yet provide the minister with objective advice.

Others join the cabinet from outside the civil service – young, intelligent high-flyers, who may remain in the civil service after leaving the cabinet. They come from party organizations, think-tanks or from the minister's local base. Civil servants earn their usual salary, but since the minister's cabinet budget is very small, outsiders are paid a small amount, and have to add an independent income, perhaps from the Party organization or other sympathizers, which can bring the risk of corruption in its chain. There is considerable interchange between the permanent civil service and the cabinet; in fact, working in a ministerial cabinet at some point in one's career is considered to be an essential move for those seeking promotion, provided one makes a careful choice. Others simply find the work more interesting and challenging than the general work of the department.

The work of the cabinet varies considerably from one department to another, with some of the functions clearly recognizable as part of the work of a minister's private office in Britain. This is, of course, the cabinet's function in organizing the minister's time, setting priorities and providing the preliminary back-up work and briefing the minister on the week's engagements. The Chef de Cabinet is appointed by the minister and approved by the President and occupies something like the role of a permanent secretary in that he is in charge of the management of the cabinet and acts as an adviser to the minister. The Chef de Cabinet is also primarily responsible for handling relations with the National Assembly, the minister's former constituency (since most ministers are also mayors or local councillors), the Party, as well as links with outside groups, interest groups and the media.

The cabinets are also responsible for giving policy and legal advice and for handling all the significant and sensitive relations for the minister, such as liaising with the Prime Minister's and President's staff and services, inter-ministerial problems and conveying and explaining the minister's wishes to the top permanent civil servants, filling a gap which in the British system would be the task of the permanent secretary. The first stage of the policy-making process involves, not ministers, but the cabinet members from the departments interested in a particular bill. They prepare the technical clauses of the bill, and ministers only come in at a later stage to settle any interdepartmental disputes. They will, in any case, be briefed by cabinet members, and much of the work on a bill will have been completed by that stage. The cabinet is also responsible for supervising the administration, and some carry the supervisory role to extremes, causing resentment amongst the departmental civil servants. Plainly it would be entirely inappropriate for the cabinet to take on this task within the British system. Where implementation is transferred to the executive agencies, supervision will be the responsibility of the department and the National Audit Office, dictated by the pressures of public accountability.

The French system does not always work perfectly and cannot simply be transposed to the British context. It has been considered and proposed by the Treasury and Civil Service Select Committee. Senior civil servants, past and present, have indicated that it would be possible to adapt and integrate the system into Whitehall departments. Other less traditionally minded civil servants would find the presence of a cabinet stimulating and refreshing, giving the departmental civil servants a chance to explore new angles and to test out their ideas on policies.[25].

A cabinet would be composed of sympathetic technical experts, perhaps some brought in on a short-term basis to assist the minister with the introduction of a major change in the minister's policy area. The team should be primarily concerned with policy and the function of the experts involved is to work on policy, but it should contain a political adviser or advisers, and those with administrative experience to ensure the feasibility of the policies being developed. One of its members, as in the French cabinets, should be an expert in the relevant area of policy in the European Community and should maintain constant contact with Brussels so that policy development takes place within that context. Its function, of course, would be to advise and support the minister. The permanent secretary would continue to be responsible for the administration of the department, since the cabinet would not usurp the managerial functions of the civil service.

The way in which the cabinet is integrated into the department would be significant. Its members should be involved in policy formation at every level, and the permanent secretary would be responsible for ensuring that such integration took place. The cabinet should also contain two civil servants who share the same political commitment as the minister. They would presumably select themselves for this task, and with their knowledge of the administrative machinery, they would liaise with the department. They would, in effect, become temporary civil servants like other members of the cabinet. With a change of government, the two temporary civil servants would be free to re-enter the service or join the Opposition Cabinet and continue to advise members of the Shadow Cabinet.

A cabinet system does not automatically ensure good-quality advice. It depends on the selection of advisers, the openness of the advisory system and a willingness on the part of ministers and cabinet members to consider innovative policy ideas. But it does have one significant advantage; it counters one of the limitations of the civil service, which comes out in a comment made by David Henderson, a former chief economist at the Ministry of Aviation, and now head of economics and statistics at OECD: 'I'm not sure that in the British case [the civil service] has been a major influence on economic performance ... [But] the British civil service has something to answer for in its closed nature and the way it has not reacted to evidence.'[26] It is only by exposing ideas and policy analysis to external criticism that there will be any chance of progress. Ultimately, of course, ministers have to be both intellectually and personally capable of drawing together a team of advisers, inspiring them to work out relevant policies and be willing to take advice. A cabinet system will not save a weak minister but it could strengthen the hand of one with the requisite qualities.

It has been forcefully argued that support for ministers in policy-making is not enough to aid the smooth and effective running of government. Lady Sharp was amongst the first to observe that 'there was a gap in the machinery of government at the centre. Should there be a Prime Minister's Department? Or a staff to serve the Prime Minister and Cabinet Ministers?'[27]

Lady Sharp's views were shared by a small group of former civil servants, whose task was to review the machinery of central government for Mr Heath. They eventually recommended an 'Office of the Prime Minister and the Cabinet', which would have as its objectives the 'coordination, planning, research and study, management and organization of services at government levels' and above all, the 'crucial task of enabling the Government to identify its main objectives, to relate individual decisions to their wider context and, in doing so, to coordinate its own activities'.[28] Others, including Sir Richard Clarke, Sir Burke Trend and Sir William Armstrong, propounded similar advice. All concluded that 'there was no central staff whose task it was to help ministers to develop a strategy for the Government as a whole, to guide the Cabinet's thinking about Government as opposed to departmental priorities, and to ensure that the actions of individual ministers were consistent with each other'.[29]

The Central Policy Review Staff

When the Conservatives won the election with Mr Heath in June 1970, one of the first tasks was to establish the Central Policy Review Staff under the leadership of Lord Rothschild. The CPRS was to stay in existence from November 1970 until 1983, when Mrs Thatcher announced its abolition after the General Election in June of that year. The think-tank had its heyday during the time of Lord Rothschild, but its career was turbulent even then and throughout its subsequent history. Its function and method were set out in a kind of unofficial charter prepared by Mr (now Sir) Robert Wade-Gery:

Sabotage the over-smooth functioning of the machinery of Government.

Provide a Central Department which has no departmental axe to grind but does not have overt policy status and which can attempt a synoptic view of policy.

Provide a central reinforcement for those civil servants in Whitehall who are trying to retain their creativity and not be totally submerged in the bureaucracy.

Try to devise a more rational system of decision-making between competing programmes.

Advise the Cabinet collectively, and the Prime Minister, on major issues of policy relating to Government's strategy.

Focus the attention of ministers on the right questions to ask about their own colleagues' businesses.

Bring in ideas from the outside world.[30]

The 'think-tank' was certainly able to work on that basis until 1973, when the country was hit by the oil crisis and the ensuing political crisis which led to the election of a Labour Government in February 1974. Lord Rothschild was followed by Sir Kenneth Berrill after the second election of that year, in October, 1974.

Berrill initiated and then accepted the task of carrying out the infamous Review of Overseas Representation, which was to demand so much of the think-tank's time during the latter part of the 1970s. Later he spoke of it as an 'own goal. It was one of those cases where, when asked to do a piece of work, frankly, as Head of the think-tank, I should have found a reason for not doing it.'[31]

The terms of reference for the think-tank called for a review of the nature and extent of Britain's overseas interests and commitments, covering every aspect of the work of overseas representation. The Diplomatic Service worked on rubbishing the whole report long before it appeared, itself an interesting cause for suspicion. Their fears were by no means justified when the report was published in August 1977, for it recommended a smaller, less specialized, less hospitable Diplomatic Service with fewer diplomats and more home civil servants, instead of the wholesale abolition of the Foreign and Commonwealth Office rumoured in baseless press reports. Looking back on the whole episode, Blackstone and Plowden argue, with the coolness of hindsight, that 'no one could claim that the Review of Overseas Representation was the CPRS's greatest success. Mistakes were made in the handling of the study and the presentation of the report. But the episode probably did no lasting damage. The CPRS soon recovered from the blow to its morale at the time and went on to do a number of successful studies in other areas under Berrill and then Ibbs.'[32]

The work of the CPRS, however valuable it may have been, ended with *The Economist*'s leak of its study of long-term public spending in September 1982, at the beginning of the party conference season. The study was basically an examination of a range of economic scenarios together with tax and public spending implications. At the Cabinet's request the CPRS looked at a variety of ways of cutting public spending on education, social security, the National Health Service and defence. *The Economist* was the first to leak the report on 18 September, but it was quickly taken up by the rest of the media, provoking headlines about the Government's 'hidden agenda'. The Opposition naturally took up the cudgels on behalf of the National Health Service in particular, harrying the Government about their secret plans in the run-up to the election. Not surprisingly, this and other damaging leaks, such as the possible fragmentation of state monopolies, sealed the think-tank's death warrant. It was abolished after the June election in 1983, and Mrs Thatcher began to build up the No. 10 Policy Unit.

Whatever merits a central think-tank may have, the public spending leak well illustrates the severe difficulties facing governments of any political persuasion which wish to undertake a radical review of major programmes of public spending. The government of the day may well decide to reject the entire contents of such a report; it may be an entirely open-minded review, but the mere fact that such a review is being undertaken arouses public suspicion and hostility and gives all the vested interests a chance to marshal their arguments and drum up support. Of course, if the reviews were never leaked, the government might be able to take a more rational long-term view, but only a foolish government would expect a think-tank (or any other part of the civil service) to be leak-proof. There are only two options – think-tanks operating quite independently of the government or any political party, from which the government of the day can distance itself without any difficulty or embarrassment; or an entirely different approach to policy-making which is outlined below. Only independent think-tanks can take a radical approach and 'think the unthinkable'. Despite these limitations, a think-tank at the centre of government would still be able to fulfil important and useful functions.

A New Central Policy Unit

Governments, particularly from mid-term onwards, begin to lose any sense of an overall, coherent direction. Ministers increasingly come to take a departmental view, responding to their own clients and pressure groups. They fail to consider, or even have the time and necessary information should they wish to take an overall view, the way in which their own pet projects may clash with more fundamental aims or with another department's plans. It is all too easy for sectional interests to dominate collective interests and governments may and often do lose sight of reality as the period of office progresses, and senior politicians become increasingly insulated from the ordinary life of the community. Beleaguered politicians, facing serious economic or political problems, are unwilling to face up to reality; they become more concerned about preserving their own position or realizing personal ambitions. The sheer pressures upon them encourages too much attention to short-term problems. In this context, it may very well be hard for a central policy unit to succeed, but without its presence and any such attempt to draw the government together and to facilitate collective decision-making, the problems a government faces will undoubtedly be intensified. Ministers will have to be encouraged to see the central unit's work as enabling them to overcome these problems, which, in turn, will require special personal skills on the part of at least some members of the unit.

The role of the central policy unit is to coordinate policy, to ensure that manifesto commitments are fulfilled and to give, as Plowden and Blackstone have pointed out, non-departmental advice. To some extent these insights can be provided by the ministerial cabinets. But another element is required: briefing ministers adequately for taking collective decisions in Cabinet, a task which it is difficult for the departments to carry out. Ministerial Cabinet members may be able to consult with each other, forming an informal, interdepartmental network, but loyalty to their own ministers may stand in the way of full consultation. The CPRS typically provided all Cabinet ministers with a briefing for collective decisions, covering the basic facts of the existing situation, the effectiveness of existing policies, the expected effects of the new proposals, unintended and long-term effects, and the true costs of implementation. In the new structure of the civil service, both the central think-tank and the ministerial cabinets should consult fully with the chief executives and senior staff of the executive agencies about the feasibility of the proposed policies and the possible consequences as well as costs. Speed of implementation and coordination of implementation between the agencies would also have to be considered by both policy-making bodies.

Finding the right staff is vital. A central think-tank requires a careful mix of civil servants and outsiders – generally bright young people with various specialist skills. All the accounts of members of the CPRS suggest that Lord Rothschild was the best Chairman and that his assiduous use of such a wide range of brilliant contacts enormously benefited the think-tank. The proper use of networks is something which political parties should learn. They often fail to do so in Opposition, but in Government it is crucial. In Government, it is not something which ministers can easily undertake for themselves. The chairman of the think-tank or better, a central policy unit, should be able to carry out that work, and an 'unusual, unorthodox, brilliant man', a 'twentieth-century original', not afraid to tell the truth or to tease out the answers, would be an ideal choice for any government, but hard to find. In the end, however, not even the CPRS under Lord Rothschild could save Edward Heath from the ignominious and unexpected (to the Labour Party leadership) defeat, arising from the panic caused by the miners' strike and the economic crisis of the oil price hike in late 1973.

When Mrs Thatcher abolished the CPRS in 1983, she began to build up a policy unit at No. 10. The move attracted Parliamentary attention at the time, and the build-up in the total running costs at No. 10 was noted by the Opposition: £2.8 million in 1983–4. It was also interpreted as a symbol of the Prime Minister's authoritarian approach to her Cabinet, although in fact the Policy Unit was created by Harold Wilson in 1974. It was its development, together with the abolition of the CPRS that had served all the Cabinet, which gave rise to these suspicions. David Willetts, once a member of the Prime Minister's Policy Unit, set out the 'four crucial reasons' for her decision to kill off the CPRS and rely on her own advisers:

First, this Prime Minister is better aware than most that a strategy is nothing without the right tactical decision. The strategic direction of her Government has been clear from the start – the reduction of inflation, extending the operation of the markets, and allowing greater scope for personal responsibility and choice. The challenge is to ensure that the day-to-day decisions coming before ministers fit in with these strategic objectives. Yet the CPRS seemed to become more donnish and detached from hard day-to-day decisions.[33]

Whilst he was a member of it, it consisted of eight or nine people, and covered all aspects of domestic policy, aiming to discuss any major issue or any paper coming in from a department before the Prime Minister considered it. In that sense, it was designed entirely to serve the Prime Minister. Each paper was analysed entirely from the Prime Minister's point of view:

When a department puts a paper to the Prime Minister the relevant member of the Unit can ask himself some basic questions such as: Is there a less interventionist solution which has not been properly considered or has been wrongly rejected? Is there a less expensive option? Are the arguments consistent? What is the evidence to back them up? Are there relevant facts which the Prime Minister needs to know?[34]

These questions obviously represent Mrs Thatcher's ideological stance, but it illustrates the fact that the Policy Unit has always existed to advise the Prime Minister of the day.

It had other functions as well, which David Willetts identified and listed in his account of it as a 'small, creative think-tank', on the lookout for new policy ideas and angles, existing to deal with 'important issues not thrown up by the chance divisions of Whitehall'; and willing to put forward 'free-standing think pieces'.[35] The Unit also operated as a 'grand suggestions box'. Apart from the production of ideas and advice, it was there to smooth relations between No. 10 and the departments and ministers or bring in outsiders who have 'visited the real world, seen it unadorned and heard it uninhibited'[36] for a non-Whitehall perspective.

All of this sounds harmless enough. Indeed, it is just what one would expect any sensible Prime Minister to do. But any attempt on the part of the Prime Minister to surround themselves with their own advisers is regarded as a 'dangerous step towards presidential government' as David Willetts put it. He rightly points out that any other Western leader would expect to have even more direct official support. Such objectives reflect the British cult of amateurism. They could, however, signify a glimmering of a more fundamental problem: that the circle of advisers may not lubricate relations between the Prime Minister and other ministers but serve only to insulate the Prime Minister from his or her colleagues. Worse still, if the Government of the day is steering its way through stormy waters, the circle may reflect and confirm incipient paranoia on the part of the Prime Minister. That is a real and constant danger which can undermine the coherence of the Government's policies, and is more important than a so-called presidential style.

Making a re-established CPRS and the Prime Minister's policy unit work together constructively would be difficult, but not impossible, provided the chairman of the think-tank had open access to the Prime Minister (as indeed they have done in the past). The chairman of the think-tank and the head of the No. 10 Policy Unit would obviously have to meet on a weekly basis and *inter alia* jointly discuss the advisory work undertaken by the think-tank. Neither are suitable bodies to undertake that radical review of existing Government policies and programmes. Independent think-tanks have already been proposed as suitable bodies to carry out that degree of fresh thinking about public policy. But left-of-centre think-tanks have great difficulty in attracting adequate funds in Britain, which limits full and serious consideration of the available alternatives to current practices.

A much more radical approach would be to look at the whole relationship between Parliament and Government on the process of policy-making. The Swedish system of policy-making provides for the Government of the day to take the initiative. Since participation in the process is disseminated widely and publicly, this enables the Government to draw upon all the available expertise and then to build up a consensus for the changes which the Government finally decides to introduce.

The Government takes the first step when it appoints an official committee or commission (often called 'royal commissions') to examine a particular area of policy. It issues guidelines for their work and will ultimately determine whether or not the proposals of the official committees are to be turned into Government bills. Before that stage is reached, however, thorough consultation takes place within government itself. Government policy is coordinated through a series of meetings apart from the weekly Cabinet meeting. The latter is usually followed by a 'general drafting session', in which various policy and political issues are discussed on the basis of a formal agenda. Ministers notify the Cabinet Office in advance of the issues they wish to raise, but apart from that, there are no minutes nor are votes taken. Government ministers usually meet together for lunch on a daily basis, which gives more opportunity for informal discussion. These play a significant part in the policy-making process. Under secretaries of state (political appointees) also meet regularly and seek to coordinate policy.

The government sets up long-term working parties to allow for discussions of issues which affect more than one department, such as those relating to information technology or regional policy. Whatever the issue, any decisions affecting more than one ministry must be drafted on a joint basis. In other words, an elaborate machinery exists to ensure that policy is coordinated and that the Cabinet does, as it constitutionally must, take collective decisions. Once the Government has taken a conclusion that a particular policy area must be investigated with a view to reform and legislation, a commission is established.

There can be as many as 300 to 350 of such commissions sitting in any one year, appointed when a reform of any kind is being considered. It is staffed by a secretariat which is often led by civil servants from the department concerned, and is composed of representatives from the various parliamentary parties, civil servants, ministerial representatives, representatives from business (SAF) and labour (ILO and TCO), experts and other interested parties who may be seriously affected by the proposed reforms. Both the initial proposal from the Government and the guidelines the Government issues are subject to comment and criticism. When these are finally agreed, the commission begins its work. Its final report is then subject to a new 'remiss' procedure in which all the public and private organizations likely to be affected by the proposals, including the agencies responsible for administering the current and new policies, are consulted once more. If the reports and subsequent comments are largely favourable, the bill is included in the Prime Minister's announcement of the legislative programme at the beginning of the parliamentary year. The commissions normally report within the parliamentary year and tend to be dominated by the Government party.

The process of consultation is thorough and is designed to establish a consensus. That and the standing committees (equivalent to select committees) occupy the time of Members of Parliament, almost all of whom are involved in a committee or a commission. It is obviously a radically different approach from British governmental and parliamentary procedures. However, one aspect of parliamentary procedure in Britain could be adapted to allow for public consultation and expert evidence to be taken into account before a bill reaches its final stages. It is possible to turn the standing committee stage into a select committee under current procedures and receive evidence on the implications of the bill, rather than the line by line, amendment by amendment, clause by clause debate in standing committees, much of which makes no difference at all to the final outcome. It would be a useful adaptation of the current framework, but it would not bring about a thorough sifting of policy proposals in a pre-legislative stage.

The latter would be too much to expect in the British context. First of all, none of the political parties will give up the ability, once in government, to get almost any legislation they wish through Parliament unscathed. Secondly, radical proposals of this kind meet the typically British conservative response that moving towards a consensus as opposed to an adversarial form of government is 'not part of the British culture'. The trouble with this knee-jerk reaction is that it does not recognize that a certain set of practices do not constitute a 'culture', nor is 'culture' something fixed and immutable. Not only could the above proposals be seen as a much wider application of procedures which are already available, but they could also be regarded as a development of the select committee system which has worked successfully since 1979.

Notes

[1] D. Wass, 'The Public Service in Modern Society', *Public Administration*, Spring 1983, Vol. 61, p. 14.
[2] Cabinet Office, Management and Personnel Office, 'Civil Service Management Development in the 1980s', 1983, pp. 40–1, para. 8.6 (a).
[3] J. Callaghan, 'Civil Servants and Ministers', Seventh Report, Minutes of Evidence, Q. 725–8.
[4] W. Wallace, Memorandum for the Liberal Party in 1985 and reported in the *Guardian*, 6 June 1985.
[5] D. Owen, *Political Quarterly*, 1984, Vol. 55, No. 1, pp. 17–22.
[6] T. Heiser, 'A New Breed Emerges in the Corridors of Power', *Financial Times*, 30 January 1990.
[7] *The Times*, 27 November 1989.
[8] 'Top Jobs in Whitehall, Appointments and Promotions in the Senior Civil Service', 1987, p. 43.
[9] ibid., p. 44.
[10] D. Wass, 'The Civil Service at the Crossroads', *Political Quarterly*, July/September 1988, p. 231.
[11] interview with author.
[12] private information.
[13] P. Kemp, Treasury and Civil Service Select Committee, Eighth Report, 'Progress in the Next Steps Initiative', 1989–90, HC 481, p. 53.

[14] 'Law report in the Equal Opportunities Review', No. 29, January/February 1990.

[15] private source.

[16] 'Top Jobs in Whitehall, Appointments and Promotions in the Senior Civil Service', 1987, p. 9.

[17] ibid., p. 25.

[18] ibid., p. 26.

[19] MPO Report, 1983.

[20] private information.

[21] private information.

[22] op. cit., 'Top Jobs in Whitehall', p. 53.

[23] W. Plowden and T. Blackstone, *Inside the Think Tank, Advising the Cabinet 1971–1983*, 1988, pp. 34–5.

[24] op. cit., 'Top Jobs in Whitehall', p. 74.

[25] based on interviews with the author.

[26] in P. Hennessy, 'A Conditional Discharge for Mandarins', *Independent*, 30 November 1987.

[27] E. Sharp, Letter to William Plowden, 3 September 1982, in W. Plowden and T. Blackstone, *Inside the Think Tank, Advising the Cabinet 1971–83*, p. 7.

[28] Machinery of Government Group, First Report to Mr Heath, 1969, in W. Plowden and T. Blackstone, *Inside the Think Tank*, pp. 7–8.

[29] ibid. pp. 9–10.

[30] in P. Hennessy, *Whitehall*, 1989, p. 226.

[31] conversation with Sir Kenneth Berrill, 'Routine Punctuated by Orgies', BBC Radio 3, 14 October 1983.

[32] op. cit., W. Plowden and T. Blackstone, p. 177.

[33] D. Willetts, 'The Role of the Prime Minister's Policy Unit', *Public Administration*, Winter 1987, Vol. 65, p. 445.

[34] ibid., p. 451.

[35] ibid., pp. 450–51.

[36] ibid.

FIVE

Civil Service Ethics

Top civil servants have begun to talk about ethics, both in public and in private. The turbulent events of the 1980s – removing trade unions rights at GCHQ, with a blatant disregard for internationally recognized human rights; the Ponting affair; a twenty-three-year-old clerk, Sarah Tisdall's decision to give the *Guardian* photocopies of two documents detailing the date on which the Cruise missiles would arrive at Greenham and what plans had been made to deal with the Greenham Common women, and her subsequent six-month imprisonment; Westland; and the amazing saga of the Government's pursuit of Peter Wright through the world's courts, to name but some of the key cases, have all played a part in forcing the issue of public service ethics on their attention.

The Ponting Affair

The issue of public service ethics first arose as a result of the Ponting affair. Clive Ponting, Assistant Secretary in the Ministry of Defence as head of Defence Secretariat 15, the legal division of the Ministry, leaked information about the sinking of the *General Belgrano*, which indicated that the ship was not the threat to British forces the public had been led to believe. The prosecution, trial and subsequent acquittal of Clive Ponting for passing on these documents and reporting the matter to Tam Dalyell, MP for Linlithgow, served to focus attention on the duty of the civil servant to the Government of the day, and on his duties as a public servant.

The reasons for Clive Ponting's action derived from his concern at the way ministers were flouting constitutional convention by hiding information from Parliament. His case is an illustration of the extreme situation in which a civil servant comes into conflict with ministers and there is no constitutional solution to hand. Other governments have recognized means of handling the whistle-blower and indeed have sought to provide protection for whistle-blowing both in the public and the private sector. Neither the Government, the judge nor the Head of the Home Civil service believed Clive Ponting's action was in any way justifiable. And that view was privately endorsed in other quarters as well. One former Labour minister remarked that one would not wish to have a Clive Ponting in one's private office – a reflection of Sir Robert Armstrong's words to the Treasury and Civil Service Select Committee that 'it is very important for a minister to be able to trust his civil servants and to be able to have confidence in them'.[1]

In February 1985 Sir Robert Armstrong faced the Select Committee shortly after issuing his now famous Memorandum on the Duties and Responsibilities of Civil Servants in Relation to Ministers. It tersely restates the traditional position: 'Civil servants are servants of the Crown. For all practical purposes the Crown in this context means and is represented by the Government of the day ... The civil service as such has no constitutional personality or responsibility separate from the duly elected Government of the day. It is there to provide the Government of the day with advice on the formulation of the policies of the Government, to assist in carrying out the decisions of the Government, and to manage and deliver the services for which the Government is responsible. Some civil servants are also involved, as a proper part of their duties, in the processes of presentation of Government policies and decisions.'[2] In his response to the Select Committee's cross-examination, he said that in the extremely unlikely event of a civil servant being told, for example, by a minister to lie to a Commons Select Committee, that 'the civil servant would have to go and talk to his permanent secretary in the first instance and share his problem with him and then the permanent secretary would have to talk to the minister'.[3]

Peter Jay once paraphrased Sir Robert's restatement in the following words:

> The civil service has no constitutional personality or responsibility separate from the Government of the day;
>
> a civil servant's duty is first and foremost to his minister and this duty is unconditional;
>
> if this duty raises a fundamental issue of confidence or engenders an opposition so profound that the civil servant cannot consciously

administer it, he should consult a superior officer or in the last resort the permanent head of department;

the permanent head may consult the Head of the Home Civil Service [Sir Robert himself]; and

thereafter, the civil servant must do as he is told or resign – and even then he must preserve official confidences.[4]

This bald version of Sir Robert Armstrong's statement throws the question of its adequacy into sharp relief. For Clive Ponting, it appeared during the trial, had been required to give false and or misleading answers to the large number of parliamentary questions tabled by the indefatigable Labour MP, Tam Dalyell. Ponting did not apparently consider consulting anyone else in his department, but his anger was roused by Michael Heseltine's actions after the Prime Minister wrote to Denzil Davies MP, then the Opposition Spokesman on Defence, admitting for the first time that the *Belgrano* had been sighted on 1 May. Ponting then drafted replies to Dalyell's parliamentary questions, which Heseltine refused to use. Ponting later stated that 'he had never come across anything so blatant in my fifteen years in the civil service. It was a deliberate attempt to conceal information which could reveal that ministers had gravely misled Parliament for the previous two years.'[5]

Ponting then took the astonishing step of sending an anonymous letter to Tam Dalyell, which blamed John Stanley, the then Minister of State for the Armed Forces, for the fact that Dalyell had not received a proper answer and suggesting further questions which he should ask. Later he leaked a memorandum about the sinking of the *Belgrano* and the draft of his replies to Dalyell's questions to the MP.

Ponting was prosecuted under the Official Secrets Act, Section 2, but was acquitted. The judge, in his summing up, clearly identified the policies of the State with those of the Government of the day, and then went on, quite wrongly, to identify the 'interests of the State' with the 'policies of the State', and then argued that 'the policies of the State mean the policies laid down for it by its recognized organs of government and authority', allowing no scope for any kind of 'public interest' defence.[6] In other words, the interests of the State are whatever the Government of the day says they are, a dangerous view indeed, and one which is plainly 'morally bankrupt'. But the judge's view was to be echoed in the Code of Ethics provided shortly afterwards by the then Head of the Home Civil Service, Sir Robert Armstrong. Both the judge's summing up and Sir Robert

Armstrong's Memorandum, outlined above, suffer from the lack of a proper concept of the State, a valuable asset, as Professor Ridley, Professor of Political Theory and Institutions, University of Liverpool, argues.

Elsewhere in the world civil servants are the servants of the state. They have a clear concept of what that implies. Obedience to the democratically elected government is enjoined on them everywhere, but they are quite capable of distinguishing between the two, of recognizing that the Government of the day may not be pursuing the interest of the State even if they serve it loyally; and ... transposing the words of Sir Thomas More, it will at least make sense to them to say, "I am the government's good servant, but I am the state's servant first."[7]

Armstrong derived his Memorandum from the statement made to the Tomlin Commission by Sir Warren Fisher in 1930, and a statement on ministerial responsibility made by Sir Edward Bridges in 1954, but which was not widely disseminated at the time. It can be seen as part of a long tradition and, indeed, Sir Robert Armstrong saw it in those terms:

> When Queen Elizabeth I appointed Sir William Cecil to be her Secretary of State in 1558, she said: 'This judgement I have of you, that you will not be corrupted by any manner of gift and that you will be faithful to the State, and that without respect of my private will, you will give me the counsel that you think best.'
>
> I think that summed it up pretty well. I think that is what we still expect of our civil service and I think that's what we still get out of it. And I have every confidence that it will continue to provide good public service, an outstanding public service on that basis.[8]

But the matter did not rest there. This was hardly surprising in view of the jury's rejection of the judge's interpretation of Clive Ponting's duty. Armstrong's Memorandum, with its bald statement of duty without any caveats, came under further pressure during the Westland affair and the apparently impossible position in which Miss Bowe was placed, and his own behaviour during the Peter Wright trial, in which he admitted to being 'economical with the truth'. Against this background and with its own anxieties to consider, the First Division Association presented its proposals for a code of ethics.

The First Division Association Code of Ethics

Even proposing a code of ethics meant a direct rejection of the Establishment Officers' Guide for the Civil Service which explicitly rejects the need for such a code. The code itself sets out the agreed duties of a civil servant, but adds civil servants should avoid maladministration, 'which includes such matters as misleading members of the public as to their rights, and administering the law in a manner which causes the public to be deprived of their rights, which in some cases would also be unlawful'.[9]

In addition, 'it is part of the duty of civil servants in some posts to assist their minister in presenting government policies and decisions. Civil servants should ensure that ministers are supplied with all relevant information and that the material they provide does not suppress, delay or misuse information or select it in a way which would advance particular social, economic or political points of view.

'Civil servants and ministers should follow the existing guidelines on the integrity of Government statistics which stress among other things the clear separation of statistics from ministerial comment when they are being made available to the public ... Should civil servants consider that they are being asked to assist ministers in misleading or lying to Parliament or the public they should so advise the minister or a senior official in writing, placing a copy of the advice on the registered file or some other permanent record. If the requirement is not withdrawn the matter should be reported in writing to the permanent head of the department.'[10]

Finally, the code alludes to the constitutional position and what further action civil servants should be able to take if they are required to act unethically. The code states: 'Ministers are accountable to Parliament, and Parliament should call ministers to account for misleading it or the public, or for requiring civil servants to act unethically. A civil servant who considers that he or she has been required to act in this way shall have the right, if a senior official or the permanent head of department have not been able to resolve the matter, to bring it before a body or person appointed for that purpose. This body or person, which might be a select committee of Parliament or an ombudsman, should have the right to ask for statements from ministers and civil servants and should have the right to make a report to Parliament of its findings.'[11]

The then General Secretary of the FDA, John Ward, pointed out that 'the FDA draft code was designed to give a degree of liberalization and, most important, was to be set in the context of the repeal of Section 2 of the Official Secrets Act and the introduction of a Freedom of Information Act. In other words our draft took account of the problems highlighted by recent events and looks forward. Sir Robert's looks backwards.'[12]

In other respects, the FDA document is not as radical as all that. Civil servants are described as 'servants of the Queen in Parliament. Executive government as a function of the Crown is carried out by ministers who are accountable to Parliament. Civil servants therefore owe to ministers the duty to serve them loyally and to the best of our ability.'[3]

The 'independent' status of the career civil service is one of the fundamental issues in the debate about the Armstrong Memorandum. The FDA at the time considered proposing an independent status for the civil service, in which the service would no longer be regarded as employed by the Crown, but by an independent commission. It was an attempt to deal with the distinction between the duty to the state and the duty to the Government of the day in the absence of a proper concept of the State. The FDA decided that, since such a fundamental change in the status of the civil service would require new Orders in Council, it was inappropriate to include this in the code of ethics.

Since then, the First Division Association has continued to argue for a code, and stressed the need for protection for civil servants against improper ministerial instructions. And at the same time, senior civil servants have continued to reject such a code as being unnecessary. Sir Michael Quinlan, Permanent Secretary at the Ministry of Defence, for example, turned his mind to the question of civil service ethics and found that the problems simply do not exist. If they did, then the existing system of appeal up to and including the Head of the Home Civil Service would suffice to cope. No one has, however, turned to Sir Robin Butler for sympathy and support, although it is, of course, entirely disingenuous to suppose that a young, ambitious civil servant ever would, since he or she would obviously put their promotion prospects at risk in some way.

For the rest, a civil servant's duties are entirely relative. Quinlan illustrated this with a simple example of relative truth in public life:

Consider the question 'Is the Prime Minister doing a good job?' posed publicly to a Cabinet Minister, an Opposition frontbencher, a civil servant and a media commentator. For three of those four, the answer is quite properly role-determined: the Cabinet Minister has to say 'Yes', the Opposition frontbencher to say 'No', the civil servant to decline to answer. Only the media commentator is free [if his editor is content, perhaps] to express what he really thinks; but it would be superficial to the point of silliness to suppose that that makes him or his calling more moral than others. Anyone who seeks to sit in judgement upon the behaviour of people in working roles is simply being foolish if he does so without reference to the proper necessities of their responsibilities.[14]

The trouble with this example and the supposed relativism to which it gives rise is that it is too superficial. Most people would concede the point Quinlan makes, though many answering the question would find more subtle, and at the same time more truthful, ways of answering the question, by praising the one or two qualities they genuinely admired, or some event which they believed the Prime Minister handled well, leaving the rest unsaid. Be that as it may, the duties in connection with a particular role must be seen in the context of wider and deeper ethical principles with which the more limited duties of one's role may clash. It would otherwise be possible to claim in all circumstances that one was simply obeying orders.

The recognition of explicit duties arising from the nature of one's role as a civil servant is a small price to pay for 'above-average job security, admission to confidence, work of great interest and the opportunity to rise to high position within the state structure, albeit for unspectacular material reward. Our job is to offer career-long service to the best of our ability, and irrespective of personal liking or political inclination, to whomever the electorate chooses to put at the head of the nation's affairs'.[15] In return, the senior civil servant provides 'knowledge of particular areas of public business, and of how to operate the complex mechanisms of Government, in advising and supporting elected politicians who – because of the other demands of their own roles – cannot always know enough about these matters to manage without expert help, and who certainly cannot, unaided, cope with the volume of work.'[16]

To be fair to Sir Michael, he does recognize the possibility of clashes between one's duty as a civil servant and fundamental ethical principles, but insists that such cases are rare. 'Hard cases make bad law; catering to the far-fetched or the very rare can import features of much greater and more probable disadvantage than the hypothesis guarded against.'[17] But when Peter Hennessy asked if Suez was a hypothesis, or GCHQ, or Westland, not to mention, Ponting, Wright and Wallace (all of which have occurred since Sir Michael joined in 1954), he replied, 'That's not a long list for an organization of over half a million people over a period of forty years. We're still talking of a very few cases.'[18]

The list is undoubtedly longer than that, but such cases are not the only issues to be considered. Attention should also be paid to the fact that over recent years, many civil servants have allegedly felt that their principles have been traduced by the manner in which they have been expected to carry out their work. These problems have been explored by two journalists: first by Hugo Young and later by Melanie Phillips. They are also problems to which the FDA drew attention in its evidence to the Royal Institute of Public Administration working party.

One of the problems lies in the nature of the advice many civil servants feel they have to give. 'They have had to instil in themselves enthusiasm: a commodity which can "colour judgements and lead to unwise decisions". As a result, I think I know more civil servants than before who speak with a kind of despairing cynicism of the policies they are assigned to carry out, while devoting to that task an often manic energy which they hope will be duly noted in high places.'[19] He has the impression that officials give the advice they reckon the Government wants to hear.

The FDA evidence to the RIPA working group in 1985 was much in line with Hugo Young's assessment. The FDA said:

> If [civil servants] think that ministers are looking for action rather than discussion of or advice on alternative approaches they may give more emphasis to implementing ministerial policy without asking questions instead of giving frank and objective advice ... Certainly civil servants must actively assist the execution of Government policy but in advance of a minister's deciding on a particular course of action it would be a serious dereliction of duty for a civil servant to give less than the fullest advice on the basis of all available information, even if that advice does not coincide with known or perceived ministerial wishes. To the extent that the most senior officials trim advice or fail to question policies there will be an impact on the behaviour of more senior staff, with a tendency to 'aim off' in order to meet the assumed prejudices on ministers.[20]

Another civil servant told the working group in February 1985: 'I sometimes think I see advice going to ministers which is suppressing arguments because it is known that ministers will not want them, and that for me is the great betrayal of the civil service.'[21]

Other concerns have surfaced as well. Any government which has been in power for a long time and which has a strong ideology might well overlook the political neutrality of the civil service. Long before the 1987 General Election, a number of civil servants complained that Government ministers insisted that they should price Labour's policy documents and discussion documents (and indeed TUC or documents produced by the Fabian Society as well) on the basis that all commitments or alleged commitments were supposed to be fulfilled in the first year of office, an assumption made not by the civil servants, but by the ministers' political advisers. Pricing a manifesto shortly before an election is standard practice, but pricing a policy document well outside an election period was considered by civil servants to be plainly political work. The work was demanded from assistant secretaries, cogs of the policy machine, important thinkers around Whitehall. The results of their work were fed back to ministers' political advisers.

The official view taken of this complaint within Whitehall was that the information provided was no more than would be given in answer to a parliamentary question. But in the case of costing Labour's programme, the questions civil servants were asked to answer were not clear and certainly bore no relation to the assumptions on which the Labour Party regarded its policy as being based. The use of civil servants to carry out this work was certainly subject to an official complaint from the Labour Party, from the Rt Hon. Roy Hattersley, then the Party's Shadow Chancellor. But the position taken by some senior civil servants was that it is for the political advisers to interpret and to make judgements about the information civil servants involved in this work felt that they were being asked to feed the Party machine, and that they should not be asked to undertake political work at all.

The Government, however, did not learn from the unrest caused in the civil service by making such demands before the 1987 election. Since then civil servants have once again complained that they have been asked to carry out such work, no doubt in preparation for the 1992 election. Civil servants in seven Government departments complained that they were being asked to carry out this kind of political work, designed to feed Conservative central office, and that such work appeared to be sanctioned at senior levels of the civil service.[22] Neither is this the only way in which civil servants have felt that they were being pushed into actions which they believe compromise their political neutrality. Again Hugo Young points out that 'there have been well-publicized instances of civil service information officers seeking to draw a more rigorous line than ministers want them to between official truth and party propaganda. They have sometimes had a hard time.'[23] Hugo Young looks for a restoration of 'institutionalized scepticism' on the part of the civil service, and a renewed recognition of the value of public service.

Melanie Phillips published an article in the *Guardian* in January 1991 entitled 'Private Lies and Public Servants', based on a number of interviews with civil servants, all but one of whom spoke to her on condition that their identities would not be disclosed. Phillips cites the example of one former Government statistician who resigned after an unhappy period in which he was told to produce a set of politically sensitive figures biased towards Government policy. He told the *Guardian* that, although the

Government Statistical Service is an independent body, 'we had instructions to put out in press notices the good news, put out the things that present Government policies in the best light ... It's a deliberate intention to mislead and deceive'.[24]

The article was immediately and fiercely rejected by Sir Robin Butler in a letter to the *Guardian*. In it, he correctly points out that ministers are entitled to make the best of their case; and Parliament and the Opposition test that case. Civil servants should not be asked to take political sides or to distort the truth, but 'in these highly charged circumstances it would be extraordinary if from time to time difficult questions did not arise about what are the proper limits to the help which civil servants can give'. The case may well have been overstated but Sir Robin puts his finger on the problem. It is certainly one which his predecessors recognized. Sir Douglas Wass claimed that 'deviousness is a more common failing. Most civil servants will have come across the minister who, seeking to present himself in the most favourable light, colours his statements by judicious omission and by the use of words which are misleading without being untrue.'[25]

It is hard to tell just how far have ministers overstepped the limits or put too much of a gloss on government statistics. Certainly the Royal Statistical Society was sufficiently concerned to carry out its own investigation and to publish a working party report in July 1990 entitled *Official Statistics: Counting with Confidence*, expressing concern at the inadequacies of Government statistics. The working party itself arose out of 'unease' about the 'quality and adequacy of certain [governmental] statistical publications'. Indeed, the report noted that 'the widespread view that there is concern is, in itself, cause for concern.'[26] The source of many of the problems facing the government's statistical service is the Rayner review of 1980, which was 'directed primarily towards the cutting of costs and did not assess the consequential reduction of coverage and quality'.[27]

No evidence of a lack of integrity on the part of the government statisticians was found by the working party, but important recommendations were made. These include the establishment of a central statistical service to undertake the work of data definition, collection, processing, primary analysis and publications. The Head of Government Statistical Service should be responsible for all the operational and personnel aspects of the service and should direct a service which is clearly 'autonomous and free from any possible political interference'.[28] The necessary constitutional safeguards for the Government Statistical Service should be set out in a Statistics Act. The latter should also establish a

National Statistical Commission to advise on the objectivity, integrity, timeliness and scope of UK official statistics. Implementing these and other recommendations of the working party would only be considered revolutionary in Britain. They would merely bring the British Government Statistical Service in line with autonomous service provided in most advanced countries.

But by the autumn of 1991, attention was being given to the appointment of a new Head of the Government Statistical Service to replace Sir Jack Hibbert on his retirement. The working party pointed out that the Head of the Service should have the responsibility for 'questions of methodology, definitions, scope and timing of publications and the release of data to the ESRC Data Archive', because this would 'strengthen the perceived independence of government statisticians, and the line of professional responsibility to the Head of the Service on technical and methodological matters, and would be a major factor in allaying public concern over the question of political interference'.[29] Plainly an eminent statistician would have to be appointed to fulfil these requirements. But the Government at first insisted that a manager should be appointed to head up the service instead of a statistician, but the ensuing public outcry forced the Government to rewrite the job description, and to call on external advisers, such as Sir David Cox, Warden of Nuffield College, to assist with making the appointment. No decision over the appointment was made by November 1991.

It is, of course, extremely difficult in the circumstances to obtain hard evidence that many civil servants have been put under the kind of pressure described above. But the events of the past twelve years, from the abolition of the trade unions at GCHQ to blaming junior officials for the Government's failure to heed warnings about extensive fraud in the Bank of Credit and Commerce International, the disquiet expressed in the City and the disquiet expressed by leading journalists, civil servants and politicians, all suggest that the subtle pressures do exist sometimes in some quarters.

A 'Genetic Code of Conduct'

Civil servants, it seems, are clear enough about where their duties lie. Indeed, if Peter Hennessy is to be believed, 'mandarins' inherit a 'genetic code of conduct', which he set out beautifully in his GCHQ lecture in June 1989. Few would disagree with the main items of ethical conduct for the British civil servant, which he spelt out there. These included probity; care for the evidence and respect for reason; a willingness to speak truth unto power (that is, ministers) and a readiness to carry out instructions to the contrary if they override you; an appreciation of the wider public interest in the sense that the prospects of all of us can be harmed if central government policy is made without due care and attention; equity and fairness in the treatment of the public, which means that the 'pensioner in Orkney' gets the same treatment as any other pensioner and the unemployed and angry teenager in Skelmersdale has the same entitlement to careful, reliable individual treatment as the same sort of teenager in Windsor.[30]

For many civil servants the sense of public duty is an integral part of their working life, as distinct from their private lives, summed up by Sir William Armstrong in his admission to Chapman: 'I am accountable to my own ideal of a civil servant.'[31] These values and attitudes are crucially important in a democratic society which depends on powerful bureaucratic machines, especially when they are structured in the way ours is. It would, however, be unwise to rely on their continued existence if politicians seek to create a society, as Mrs Thatcher did, in which the values it admires and rewards militate against the commitment to public service.

To the 'genetic code' outlined above, Hennessy adds three 'flying buttresses crucial to keeping our civil service a constitutional body under the control of ethical people', that is: a 'constant and careful concern for the law; a constant concern for Parliament, its needs and procedures – no lying or misleading; a constant concern for democracy – even the milder forms of destabilization are out'.[32]

These three are also entirely unexceptionable and acceptable. But a civil servant pursuing any of these could well clash with the demands ministers make upon them. The simple view of ministerial accountability is, of course, that the 'flying buttresses' Hennessy outlines are irrelevant because 'the British system places limitations on the minister's powers to issue commands. First they must be within the law. Civil servants, like all other citizens, are obliged to act within the law, and this includes acts followed at the behest of the minister. It follows, therefore, that commands that are contrary to the law are not commands that the minister is entitled to issue.

'Secondly, ministers are accountable to Parliament for their actions. They are required to answer to Parliament for anything that is done in their name. Arbitrary ministerial commands are unlikely to be a problem as long as they are thus subjected to scrutiny and the glare of parliamentary publicity.

'Thirdly, there is the traditional principle of the collective responsibility of Cabinet. The Government is held collectively responsible for the policies and decisions at which it arrives. This imposes strict limits on the power of any individual minister to issue commands to civil servants that are contrary to the collective decisions of the cabinet.'[33]

To be fair to the authors they realize that this breathtakingly simple structure of the principles of accountability has been subject to all kinds of stresses and strains over recent years. But it is an account which ministers articulate whenever it suits them. It does depend on the notion that ministers act like 'gentlemen' collectively, if not individually. The Westland affair, the 'cover-up' in connection with the sinking of the *Belgrano* and the payment of 'sweeteners' to British Aerospace might give pause for thought.

The Whistle-blower

Against the background of disquieting ministerial decisions and the pressures civil servants have faced over recent years, the question arises not only of the kind of behaviour expected of civil servants, but, with greater clarity than ever before, of the kind of institutions and styles of government which would enable them to carry out their work in the desired manner. If, on the other hand, civil servants are being asked to carry out tasks, which, being people of character and intelligence (presumably the kind of people the government wishes to have as civil servants), they feel impugns their integrity or obliges them to give the answers ministers want to hear, then the government may fail to get the result it wants. It may and indeed has ended up with whistle-blowers.

The actions of whistle-blowers arouse extraordinary hostility. It is an extreme course of action, involving breaking trust with former colleagues and with employers. Constantly 'going public' on the activities of any organization could not be the basis on which any of them operate, and in government, even more so, because of the involvement of issues national security or international negotiations (which, of course, governments conduct in secret), quite apart from the issue of trust between ministers and civil servants. All of these considerations underline the point that whistle-blowing is an extreme response and one which the whistle-blower has to be sure is not based on any kind of misunderstanding or misinformation.

In this country whistle-blowing is not likely to be concerned with corruption but with matters which cannot easily be taken to law, such as lying to Parliament, or concealing wasteful spending. At this point a civil servant may consider that he has a duty to reveal what the Government is actually doing. The problem is defining that duty, which the jury in the

Ponting case seemed to recognize. 'It is,' as Bernard Williams put it in an article on 'Whistleblowing in the Public Service', 'essential to democratic government ... and indeed to any decent government, that there should be some concept of the standing interest of the public that exist whoever the government may be and whatever the government may want.'[34] Such a concept could even be expressed in a code of ethics, as indeed is the case in the United States, which demands 'loyalty to the highest moral principle and to country above loyalty to persons, party or government department'. That may not be the most appropriate expression of the underlying principle, but the point remains that obedience and trust has to be earned, and cannot be granted unreservedly to any government regardless of its behaviour. The excessive secretiveness of British Government, and the demands the Government has made of civil servants from time to time, creates the dilemmas and leads to the actions of the whistle-blower.

In his Memorandum to the Treasury and Civil Service Select Committee when the Committee examined the duties and responsibilities of civil servants and ministers, Richard Holme asserted that 'Many of the dilemmas faced by individual civil servants would disappear if it was clear that in most cases official information was legitimately accessible to the press and public. There would be far less conflict between a civil servant's perception of his "public" or "civic" duty and his official obligations.'[35] This is the fundamental point. Ministers are not truly accountable to Parliament so long as they are in control of the information Parliament receives and can suppress information, misrepresent the facts, give a partial and therefore misleading account of the truth, or provide selective statistics to present the Government's 'successes' in the best possible light. Members of Parliament have to be satisfied with such crumbs of information as ministers toss in their direction in their attempts to call the executive to account, since they have no more access to information than any member of the public (apart from a few exceptions, such as members of the Select Committee of Defence, entrusted with access to confidential information on defence on the understanding that it remains confidential, or members of the Shadow Cabinet being given information on Privy Council terms).

The temptation Government ministers face suggests that a code of ethics for civil servants is only part of the story. The requirement for a ministerial code of ethics was spelt out by Peter Kellner in his submission to the same Treasury and Civil Service Select Committee. He set out proposals for a Code for Ministers, which included a rule to the effect that they should act in accordance with Britain's obligations under the Charter of the

United Nations and the European Convention on Human Rights; obey the laws of the United Kingdom; act in a manner consistent with the decisions of Parliament; with the decisions of Cabinet; and, where relevant, consistently with the policies of their Secretaries of State. Ministers should not lie; nor wilfully conceal information that it is reasonable for Parliament and the people to possess; and should only give civil servants 'proper instructions'. In cases of dispute the matter should be referred to some suitable independent machinery, and in the last resort to the courts, where ministers would have to prove that their actions were 'in the national interest' if they claim to have acted on those grounds. Clear rules would have to be devised to ensure that 'proper instructions' were issued, and they would be tested through some independent machinery. Peter Kellner concludes, in my view rightly, that the 'existence of some form of independent machinery, and the right of officials to use it, is likely to encourage ministers and officials to observe the rules and to seek to resolve disputes with the minimum of fuss or disturbance to the progress of the government's legitimate business'.[36]

Both Holme's and Kellner's submissions are valuable because they recognize more clearly than most that the problems arise out of the relationships between ministers and civil servants, and that attention must focus on what ministers ask civil servants to do, or indeed, what impression civil servants receive, rightly or wrongly, of ministerial expectations of them. In this connection, it must first of all be recognized that freedom of information legislation will by no means remove all the dilemmas facing civil servants. Information is power, particularly in a modern society. The battle over access to information will be a continuing one, even if the two sides are more evenly matched through the introduction of freedom of information legislation. The experience in most countries which have the right of public access to information on their statute books is that governments and their bureaucracies will always seek to control or limit access, and with good reason from their point of view. Government and bureaucracies will seek to cover up embarrassing mistakes, though that may be the least worrying of the attempts to limit access from the public's point of view. For the civil servant it may mean that the dilemmas are less frequent, but they could still occur. The civil servant will have to seek guidance on what action he should take if the Government is unjustifiably concealing information from the public, or distorting it. The FDA code does not and cannot provide moral guidance on this point, simply guidance on the action the civil servant should take to inform others of the problem, and in the last resort, steps to provide him with an independent 'tribunal'.

The United States realized that, even within the context of the right of public access to a wide range of information, conflicts between government and the bureaucracy over such access will still occur. The Office of the Special Counsel was established on 1 January 1979 by the Reorganization Plan of 1978 that followed the Watergate scandals, and its duties and responsibilities were spelt out under the Civil Service Reform Act, 1979. Its responsibilities are 'to establish procedures to ensure that allegations of wrongdoings are properly investigated in the executive branch and to protect from reprisals those employees who disclose information about agency wrongdoings'.[37] The Special Counsel could receive and investigate any allegation of a prohibited personnel practice, reprisal actions against the whistle-blower, to find out whether there were reasonable grounds for the allegation whilst protecting the anonymity of the whistle-blower. Corrective action could be recommended by the Special Counsel, and if the action was not taken within a specified time, the Special Counsel could ask the Merit System Protection Board to look into it. The Merit Board can then demote, dismiss or disbar the person concerned from the civil service, and impose a fine of up to $1000.

But the Office of Special Counsel was immediately faced with enormous difficulties; the first Special Counsel resigned eleven months later and its budget was halved for the fiscal year 1980. The first report of the General Accounting Office, published in December 1980, stressed how important it was that the role of the Special Counsel be understood by Federal employees.

'The eventual success of the whistle-blowing legislation may be directly attributed to how the Special Counsel's office is perceived and accepted by Federal employees. Therefore, it is necessary for Federal employees to have confidence in reporting mismanagement and illegal activities to a Special Counsel that can be removed only by the President for inefficiency, neglect of duty, or malfeasance in office. Without this assurance of independence, Federal employees may not have the necessary confidence to report mismanagement and illegal activities.'[38]

The tone of the General Accounting Office's report is noteworthy. Its concern is with the protection of the whistle-blower without any hint or merest suggestion of distaste for the activity. It is, however, one of the most threatening forms of dissent, which unsurprisingly gives rise to great hostility and a determination to retaliate by the organization concerned, using tactics such as bureaucratic isolation, character assassination, and (where possible) dismissal. Hence the need for protection. By 1985, the situation showed little sign of improvement. The GAO report for that year commented; 'In its six-year history OSC has been the object of criticism from Federal employee representatives, GAO, and the Congress. The Office of Special Counsel has been described as administratively inept, ineffective in prosecuting violations, and of little benefit to Federal employee complainants such as whistle-blowers alleging management reprisals for their disclosures.'[39] As a result, only a small proportion of complaints, one in a hundred in fact, by Federal employees have been upheld with disciplinary action.

There are real difficulties associated with the Office of Special Counsel and whistle-blower protection. They fall into two groups. 'A major part of these difficulties also stems from a fundamental disagreement as to how far public officials can be trusted on their own and a pragmatic dispute as to the possibility of defining clear, unassailable legal criteria to guide official decision-making and extra legal machinery for calling officials to account over disputed decisions.'[40]

A close study of the Office of Special Counsel before setting up any such independent appeal tribunal for British civil servants is obviously essential. But the availability of such an office would be an important contribution to ensuring ethical behaviour in the relations between civil servants and ministers, and preferably one which would be able to offer advice and mediation as well as serve as a final court of appeal once the whistle-blower has blown the whistle.

A New Code of Conduct

Both an ombudsman and a code of some kind are an essential step forward in the development of the civil service and a means of clarifying the relationship between ministers and civil servants. The need for such a code has been recognized by many other countries, notably the United States, following the Watergate scandal, and also by both Canada and Australia, which follow the 'Westminster' model. There is still resistance to the idea in Britain, partly because Britain is the only one of two major countries of the modern world 'with so-called unwritten constitutions', the other being Saudi Arabia (which might give food for thought). Indeed, as Professor Chapman points out, 'Britain is the only country in which the unwritten elements of its constitution have so much day-to-day relevance for the conduct of its officials. Unlike most other countries the United Kingdom has no Civil Service Act. There is no fundamental legal document to which

officials can refer which contains a statement of their organization and
their responsibilities. Particular Government departments may similarly
lack such basic documents. Indeed departments can be created or abolished
virtually overnight by Order in Council.'[41]

It is not only departments that can disappear overnight by Order in
Council, but also what many would consider to be basic human rights,
such as the right to belong to a trade union, as was shown when the
Government removed this right from civil servants at GCHQ in 1985.
Orders in Council cannot be voted upon in Parliament, so the Government
could simply present the decision to Parliament as a *fait accompli* at which
Parliament could protest but which it could not overturn. The decision
has had enduring effects on the morale of the civil service, and suggests
that, apart from a code of ethics, legislation setting out in full the framework
in which civil servants operate might well be preferable to the under-
standings and conventions currently surrounding their work, which can
lead to a variety of opinions about what is constitutionally correct in certain
circumstances.

Political neutrality and ministerial accountability provide the framework
in which civil servants could clearly identify their role within the system
and facilitate the development of the practices, assumptions and under-
standings which regulate their working life. Some of these have been more
explicitly developed into codes, covering one aspect of civil service life.
Estacode, which was drawn up during the Second World War and promulgated soon afterwards, deals specifically with potential areas of conflict,
providing first a code for individual civil servants, a guide for the departmental establishment officer, departmental rules and disciplinary rules.
Examples of these rules for individual civil servants cover accepting invitations and returning hospitality. They state: 'There is no objection to the
acceptance of, for example, an invitation to the annual dinner of a large
trade association or similar body with which a department is much in day-
to-day contact; or of working lunches (provided the frequency is reasonable)
in the course of official visits'; and remind civil servants of the usual
conventions of returning hospitality: 'The isolated acceptance of, for
example, a meal, would not offend the rule whereas acceptance of frequent
or regular invitations to lunch or dinner on a wholly one-sided basis even
on a small scale might give rise to a breach of the standard of conduct
required.'

Civil servants should refer any problems to the Establishments Officer,
who has the Guide to assist him. Departments may have special rules
because of their particular circumstances, such as the Department of the

Environment, whose staff are involved in the placing, supervision or overall control of contracts, and must therefore take special care to avoid any appearance of evil.

What is interesting is the preamble to Estacode, which states: 'It [has] never been thought necessary to lay down a precise code of conduct because civil servants jealously maintain their professional standards. In practice, the distinctive character of the British Civil Service depends largely on the existence and maintenance of a general code of conduct which, although to some extent intangible and unwritten is of very real importance.' Estacode itself was the predecessor of the current Pay and Conditions of Service Code and the Establishment Officers' Guide. (Estacode was not, of course, a publicly available document, any more than its successors are. The definitions it contained of administrative secrecy are tough indeed. It set out the implications of the Official Secrets Acts of 1911 and 1920 for the civil servant in no uncertain terms. Under these Acts, it stated, 'it is an offence for an officer to disclose to an unauthorized person, either orally or in writing, any information he has acquired through his official duties unless he has received official permission'. It transpires that these cover 'material published in a speech, lecture, radio or television broadcast, in the Press or in book form; they cover non-secret as well as secret information, and apply not only during an officer's employment but also when he has retired or left the service'. The civil servant is not allowed to reveal information through any of these channels.)

The sentiment underlying the preamble to Estacode has been put under increasing strain, because recent events such as the Ponting case have 'focused attention on an area of growing sensitivity for civil servants. In the past, ministerial accountability to Parliament was of a higher order of generality. The reforms of the parliamentary committee system within the last ten years have meant that representative committees, having authority from Parliament, can probe into minute details of administration across a very broad spectrum ... One of the effects is to greatly increase the opportunities for public knowledge of anomalies between details of administration and ministerial statements.'[42]

The problem is that it is not a question of the minutiae of administration but of substantial policy issues, which civil servants have to handle on their ministers' behalf, and the vital issues of the conduct of a war with which Clive Ponting dealt. Faced with ministers who apparently decide intentionally to mislead or misinform Parliament, the civil servant plainly has to decide where his duty lies – to the public through Parliament or to his minister. The changed circumstances mean the assumptions of the past are no longer adequate.

There are two other important areas of ethical concern: the discretion civil servants have in implementing the law, when of course laws, regulations and orders cannot cover every variation in circumstances. The public should have right of access to all matters relevant to administrative decisions and a more effective means of redress through administrative courts and an ombudsman with proper powers. That is only part of the story. There cannot be appeals against every decision depending on a civil servant's discretionary judgement, so taking proper care over decisions of this kind and balancing the interests of the individual against the national interest are an important part of any civil service ethic.

The standards applied to the civil service have increasingly been confined to judging its efficiency, economy and effectiveness. Although public services have to be delivered efficiently and economically, judging them solely in these terms may overlook other qualities of the proper delivery of services. Efficiency refers to the extent to which maximum output is achieved in relation to given costs or inputs; effectiveness has to do with the extent to which the overall goals of the policy in question are achieved. Distinguishing between effectiveness and efficiency is important from the point of view of the ethics of the profession, since the two aims can pull in opposite directions, particularly if civil servants are motivated to achieve the latter goals by performance targets and performance-related pay. These could be judged on simple throughput measurements, for example, and discourage the civil servant from providing an effective service, because of the constraints of the performance indicators. Others may be prevented from offering the assistance they know the public needs because of administrative rules which channel assistance under certain conditions, such as the rules for the administration of the Social Fund and the judgements which they are required to make concerning need and the ability to pay back loans. Conflicts of this kind are built into the work of civil servants undertaking administrative tasks. Plainly, management has to exercise care in determining the content of efficiency goals so that these do not conflict with the overall aim of effective public services. Equally, the individual civil servant must face a choice between efficiency and effectiveness from time to time and must make an ethical choice.

The pressures under which civil servants are now expected to deliver services, their discretionary decision-making powers and their access to confidential information, provide considerable scope for unethical conduct. 'Through administrative discretion, bureaucrats participate in the governing process of our society; but to govern in a democratic society without being responsible to the electorate raises a serious ethical question for bureaucrats.'[43]

The right of public access to information and appeal against administrative decisions which the citizen believes were unreasonable, circumscribe the actions of civil servants but do not provide an answer to the questions concerning his own behaviour. The First Division Association's Code is a significant beginning to tackling the question of civil service ethics. Merely having a code and referring to it is not enough; that will not make civil servants behave ethically in their work. Teaching ethics, that is, discussing the sort of problems civil servants may encounter, as part of their training, may make a code much more of a reality, though neither a code nor teaching can ensure ethical behaviour. The mere existence of a code, however, 'enhances one's sensitivity' and will 'assist public servants, as trustees of the public, to maintain a high standard of performance and to commit themselves to uphold the public good'.[44] But the lesson of the last decade or so is that the code of ethics for civil servants must be balanced by integrity on the part of ministers.

Notes

[1] R. Armstrong, 'Civil Servants and Ministers: Duties and Responsibilities', Vol. 2, p. 23. 1985–6, Treasury and Civil Service Committee Report, HC92.

[2] R. Armstrong, ibid.

[3] R. Armstrong, ibid. p. 19.

[4] P. Jay, 'Pontius or Ponting: Public Duty and Public Interest in Secrecy and Disclosure', *Politics, Ethics and Public Service*, 1985, p. 76.

[5] C. Ponting, *The Right to Know: The Inside Story of the Belgrano*, Sphere, 1985, p. 101.

[6] The text of the judge's summing up on Friday, 5 February 1985 is given in *The Ponting Affair*, Richard Norton-Taylor, London, 1985, pp. 101–111, and these excerpts are from p. 103.

[7] F.F. Ridley, 'Political Neutrality and the British Civil Service', *Politics, Ethics and Public Service*, 1985, p. 34.

[8] R. Armstrong, 'The Vanishing Mandarins', interview with Hugo Young, BBC Radio 4, 13 February 1985.

[9] FDA News, March 1985.

[10] ibid.

[11] ibid.

[12] J. Ward, 'Sir Robert's "Code"', *FDA News*, March 1985, p. 3.

[13] FDA News, March 1985.

[14] M. Quinlan, 'Ethics in the Public Service', *FDA News*, September 1990, p. 5.

[15] ibid., p. 6.

[16] ibid.

[17] ibid., p. 7.

[18] P. Hennessy, 'Whitehall Watch', *Independent*, 10 September 1990.

[19] H. Young, GCHQ Lecture, First Division Association, 19 March 1990, published in *FDA News*, 'The Decline of Public Service', May 1990, p. 14.

[20] 'Top Jobs in Whitehall', op. cit., p. 46.

[21] ibid.

[22] private source.

[23] H. Young, op. cit. p. 15.

[24] in M. Phillips, 'Private Lies and Public Servants', *Guardian*, January 1991.

[25] Sir Robin Butler, letter to *Guardian*, 14 January 1991.

[26] *Official Statistics: Counting on Confidence*, report by the Royal Statistical Society, 1990, p. 4.

[27] ibid.

[28] ibid., p. 13.

[29] ibid., p. 7.

[30] P. Hennessy, 'The Ethic of the Profession', GCHQ Memorial Lecture, in *The Bulletin*, 1989, p. 103.

[31] R.A. Chapman, *The Higher Civil Service in Britain*, Constable, 1970, p. 141.

[32] P. Hennessy, 'Genetic Code of Conduct Inherited by Mandarins', *Independent*, 5 June 1989.

[33] M. R. Davies and A. Doig, 'Public Service Ethics in the United Kingdom', in K. Kernaghan and O. P. Dwivedi (eds), *Ethics in the Public Service: Comparative Perspectives*, 1983, p. 50.

[34] B. Williams, J. Stevenson, F. Ridley, 'Whistleblowing in the public service' in 'Politics, Ethics and Public Service', RIPA, 1985, p. 43.

[35] R. Holme, Treasury and Civil Service Select Committee, Seventh Report, Civil Servants and Ministers: Duties and Responsibilities, 1985-6, Vol. 2, Appendix 19, p. 330.

[36] ibid., P. Kellner, Appendix 18, pp. 327-8.

[37] US Civil Service Reform Act, 1979.

[38] US General Accounting Office Report, 1985.

[39] US General Accounting Office Report, 1985, p. 6.

[40] G. Caiden and J. Truelson, 'Whistleblower Protection', *Australian Journal of Public Administration*, 1988, Vol. 47, p. 125.

[41] R. Chapman, *Ethics in the British Civil Service*, Routledge, 1988, p. 295.

[42] op. cit., R. Chapman, p. 296.

[43] J.A. Rohr, *Ethics for Bureaucrats: An Essay on Law and Values*, 1978, p. 15.

[44] K. Kerhagnan and O.P. Dwivedi (eds), *Ethics in the Public Service: Comparative Perspectives*, 1983, p. 5.

SIX

Ministerial Accountability

The whole issue of ministerial accountability has come to the fore over recent years. That was inevitable given the well-publicized cases in which civil servants were found to be responsible for 'leaking' information to Members of Parliament or in which they reluctantly did so at the request of their ministers. It was reinforced by the Government's decision through the Financial Management Initiative and then the 'Next Steps' programme to devolve responsibility within departments and then to agencies. At the same time, the Government has sought to retain the traditional concept of ministerial accountability – or rather to insist that nothing has happened since 1979 to make any reconsideration necessary.

> Ministers still remain responsible in the sense that they are liable to report upon the activities of the Government department of which they are a political head to the Crown, to the Prime Minister and Cabinet and to Parliament. Civil servants remain non-political in the sense that they normally receive their appointments independently of ministers, that they are not allowed an overt political allegiance, and that they are not required to perform politically on the floor of either Houses of Parliament. Civil servants are required to appear before parliamentary committees, but they are still neither publicly responsible for the advice they have given to ministers, nor for the efficiency with which they carry out their work.[1]

This division of responsibilities, the 'line which separates the politically committed and publicly responsible minister from the politically neutral permanent official is drawn at a particularly high level in Britain. In practically no other country is there so little change in the administrative apparatus when a new Government takes office'.[2] In theory, therefore, the minister is accountable for a wider range of activities than counterparts in other Western democracies. The minister can be called to account by Parliament for the way in which civil servants administer Government policy and for the policies introduced by his or her department and approved by Cabinet.

In the Armstrong Memorandum the Government simply restated the traditional doctrine of ministerial responsibility, a key concept in constitutional orthodoxy. Many have questioned its applicability to the realities of modern government, but successive governments have reaffirmed the doctrine; as with the Armstrong Memorandum and in the 'Osmotherly Rules', which set out the guidelines for civil servants when they give evidence to select committees.

Osmotherly Rules

These appear to be anodyne enough when they remind civil servants in the section on the 'Provision of Evidence' that the 'general principle to be followed is that it is the duty of officials to be as helpful as possible to the Committees, and that any withholding of information should be limited to reservations that are necessary in the interests of good government or to safeguard national security'.[3] But then the restrictions on the release of information appear, covering advice to ministers, information about interdepartmental discussions on policy issues or about Cabinet committees; the private affairs of individuals or organizations about which ministers have received confidential information; sensitive commercial information; advice given by a Law Officer of the Crown; or matters which are or may become the subject of negotiations between the Government and other countries, including the European Community.

The rules plainly limit the value of the select committees as investigatory committees, calling the Government to account. Their existence and application could also explain why one former senior civil servant claimed that the committees never uncovered the final third of the relevant information, which he attributed to the failure of MPs to pursue a line of questioning, but is surely a failure in which the Osmotherly Rules play a significant role. Their purpose is, of course, to shield ministers, not to speak on their on behalf or on the department's behalf. The Osmotherly Rules are, in other words, just another manifestation of the traditional doctrine of ministerial responsibility.

This is essentially a nineteenth-century notion, and one which cannot easily be stretched to cover the growth and complexity of modern government. The nineteenth-century idea persisted into the twentieth century in Herbert Morrison's assertion that it is 'a firm parliamentary rule and tradition that a minister is accountable to Parliament for anything he or his department does or for anything he has powers to do, whether he does it or not. That is to say, if the action or possible action is within the field of ministerial power or competence the minister is answerable to Parliament.'[4] Even if we take this statement at its face value, problems arise in applying this doctrine to a situation in which responsibility for a particular policy is spread over several government departments or has been delegated to an executive agency or a quango. Then there is the sheer size of government departments and the volume of the business they conduct, making it quite impossible for ministers to know what is going on in their own departments. Last year, the Secretary of State for Northern Ireland talked about the 'very wide canvas' his department covered and pointed out that 'you could not know exactly what was going on everywhere'.

What kind of responsibility can a minister then have? The Efficiency Unit's 1988 Report questioned ministers about the problems of 'big government' and found that they accepted the responsibility for both the policy and management of their departments, but 'they said in practice they were so overloaded that they looked to their permanent secretaries to do the management. A few said candidly that they did not have the skills to manage their departments. The Government has accepted the recommendation of the Third Report of the Treasury and Civil Service Select Committee [1982] that the relationship between ministers and the permanent secretaries on the management of departments should be clarified, but has not yet acted upon it.'[5]

Ministers are therefore accountable in the sense that they must explain and justify their policies to Parliament through the debates, ministerial statements, parliamentary questions; respond to adjournment debates, and give evidence to select committees. 'Accountable' here means 'answerable' – to Parliament. A minister's responsibilities further extend to ensuring that the department uses its resources economically, efficiently and effectively. It is his or her responsibility to see to it that the department has the systems, procedures, organization and staffing necessary for it to be well managed. In this the role should be construed as 'Chairman of the Board' rather than Chief Executive. The demands on ministers are too great for them to take over the detailed running of their department, but they must make sure that the systems are in place. Even that interpretation of ministerial responsibility may be unrealistic, given the short tenure of office in a particular department, and the fact that the lack of suitable systems may be difficult to discover if there are no immediate clues.

Collective Responsibility

The line of responsibility from a department through its minister to Parliament seems clear enough. Yet it is muddled by another fundamental constitutional doctrine: collective responsibility. Ministers are not only individually responsible to Parliament, but collectively so. This can be advantageous since it frequently provides a shield for an individual minister, until that is, a minister makes so many mistakes that his or her position becomes indefensible and they are obliged to resign.

Collective responsibility comes into play when the issues involve the Government's major policy decisions, such as the Government's handling of macroeconomic policy. Ministers cannot deny responsibility for actions resulting from the 'decisions of Government' and are expected to support and defend the actions and decisions of other ministers and of the Government as a whole. Over recent years though, there has been more scope for dissent from Government policy, and ministers have remained in office whilst criticizing it, but this is always a risky business and a matter of fine judgement, since too much dissent might lead to a disagreeable reshuffling of ministerial posts or loss of office. Ministers have therefore often made their disagreement clear with carefully coded messages.

Collective responsibility does not override or contradict the accountability of individual ministers for their own departments. Central government is a kind of federation of separate and often competing departments with their own ministers and their own policies, which easily lapses into independent action rather than the coordinated approach essential for the development of policy.

Collective responsibility has not only been subject to strains arising from the fact that ministers have felt freer to express their disagreement with Government policy, but also be the concentration of power in the hands of the Prime Minister. This was particularly true during Mrs Thatcher's premiership. The then Prime Minister preferred to avoid Cabinet discussion by an increasingly personalized and centralized system of decision-making. The number of Cabinet committees increased 'like rabbits' in the words of one former Cabinet minister. These were often *ad hoc* committees, chaired by the Prime Minister or a faithful minister, set up to consider important policy changes. The Prime Minister built up her own Policy Unit at No. 10, which enabled her to deal with details of departmental policy. Such action tended to undermine the familiar concepts of individual ministerial responsibility and the collective responsibility of the Cabinet.

It remains to be seen whether the present Prime Minister, John Major, will continue or resuscitate such practices or whether any future Prime Minister will. The point is, however, that such possibilities exist, and it is only the personal style of future Prime Ministers which will prevent such a concentration of power. The Armstrong Memorandum, set out above, does not take account of any of these developments. Perhaps, to be fair it could not, since that could have been construed as implicit political criticism. But the developments themselves make the traditional doctrine irrelevant and inadequate for its original task of making those in power accountable to the people who put them there.

Events since 1979, such as the Ponting case and the Westland affair, have sharpened the debate over whether ministerial accountability is a myth or not. Leaving aside for the moment the question of whether or not Clive Ponting's actions were justified, the incident clearly raises the question of the content to be given to the notion of accountability if ministers, at best, control the information given to Parliament or, at worst, misrepresent it. Misrepresenting the facts is certainly what happened in the Westland affair.

The Westland Affair and Ministerial Accountability

The issues raised by the Westland affair illustrate the emptiness of the conventions surrounding ministerial accountability. The affair arose from a small west country aircraft company, manufacturing military helicopters. The company was in difficulties, and between autumn 1984 and autumn 1985, attempts were made to rescue it through the normal Whitehall channels and cooperation between the ministers of the various departments. But in late 1985, ministers began to wrangle over the merits of the rival rescue plans, with internal disputes over the way in which the issue should be handled bubbling away beneath the surface. Finally, the dispute erupted on to the nation's television screens when Michael Heseltine, then Secretary of State for Defence, stormed out of the Cabinet meeting on 9 January 1986, and announced his resignation at an impromptu press conference.

The details of the dispute over the company itself are less important than the implications of the whole affair for the workings of Cabinet government, but it is impossible to make sense of the latter without knowing something of the former. The company's financial position was giving cause for concern at the Department of Trade and Industry and the Ministry of Defence in the autumn of 1984. By the summer of 1985, the Government was considering the use of public funds to prop up the company, with the obvious ideological difficulties for Mrs Thatcher and her ministers. The company itself approached the Bank of England, and with the Bank's help appointed Sir John Cuckney, a well-known trouble-shooter, as Chairman in June 1986. He advised the Government that the American United Technologies Corporation, which included Sikorsky, the American helicopter manufacturer, would be willing to take a large minority shareholding in the company. Leon Brittan, now Sir Leon Brittan and Vice President of the Commission of the European Community, became Secretary of State for Trade and Industry in September and informed the Prime Minister shortly afterwards of the Sikorsky interest in a minority shareholding, but suggested that the company should be encouraged to look for a European partner. Michael Heseltine was determined to find a European solution, and was given permission by the Prime Minister to 'explore further the possibility of an alternative association with Aerospatiale, MBB, and Augusta, becoming available for consideration by the Board of Westland'.[6]

Michael Heseltine took up the challenge with a single-minded, almost obsessive enthusiasm. He fixed a meeting of the national armaments directors of the French, Italian, West German and British Governments, who then recommended to their Governments that their military requirements should be fulfilled by helicopters designed and manufactured in Britain. That set the Ministry of Defence against the Department of Trade and Industry, leading finally to the showdown in January 1986.

The Prime Minister favoured the American solution and proceeded to stack yet another informal Cabinet committee against Michael Heseltine and the European solution. Claims and counterclaims were made in the media about the outcome of the December meeting of the *ad hoc* committee, but the Prime Minister insisted in her statement to the House of Commons on 15 January that the majority of ministers present favoured rejecting the decision of the national armaments directors, leaving Westland free to reach its own decision.[7] The issue had also been discussed at a meeting of the Economic Committee on 9 December 1985, attended by Cabinet ministers, of course, but also and exceptionally, by Sir John Cuckney and Mr Marcus Agius, a director of Lazard's, Westland's financial advisers, to explain their company's position.

The meeting concluded, according to the Prime Minister's statement to the House of Commons, that 'unless a viable European package' could be found by 13 December, the Government would make it clear that the 'country would not be bound by the recommendation of the national armaments directors'. A further meeting of the Economic Committee, a formal Cabinet Committee, was arranged for 9 December, Mrs Thatcher informed the House, in view of the strength of feeling expressed by a minority of ministers, including Michael Heseltine.

That was the Prime Minister's account of events. Heseltine claimed that the meeting ended with a clear statement that the Economic Committee would meet again on Friday, 13 December at 3 p.m. when the Stock Exchange closed. He was astonished when the meeting was cancelled; but according to the Prime Minister, there would only have been another meeting before 4 p.m., 'if unforeseen developments required one' (which they did not). No reconciliation of the accounts of these two events could be found, and that, as much as anything, lay behind Michael Heseltine's resignation.

The row became public after a meeting of the full Cabinet in which Heseltine was not allowed to put his case to the collective judgement of his colleagues. He made the Cabinet's decision on Westland appear 'less authoritative than others' to the media. Both Downing Street and the Department of Trade and Industry used the lobby system extensively for unattributable press briefings to support the Prime Minister's approach to the Westland issue. That went on throughout late December and early January. Then Michael Heseltine put the cat among the pigeons by writing to Horne, Managing Director of Lloyds Merchant Bank, an adviser to the European Consortium that was trying to rescue Westland. It included material which the Ministry of Defence had proposed for an earlier draft of a letter from Mrs Thatcher to Sir John Cuckney, but which the Prime Minister had rejected. 'It is clear,' the Defence Select Committee concluded, that 'this letter was solicited by officials of the Ministry of Defence as a device for making [this material] public.'[8] Plainly, the letter was not cleared with the Prime Minister or relevant Cabinet colleagues. 'The effect of such a letter upon the Prime Minister and the Secretary of State for Trade and Industry can have been nothing short of incendiary',[9] especially as both Horne's letter and Heseltine's reply were published on the same day.

This exchange of letters led to frenzied activity over the weekend on the part of Downing Street. The Prime Minister realized that Heseltine's letter had not been sent to the Solicitor-General for his approval. Leon Brittan, as Secretary of State for Trade and Industry and the sponsoring Minister for Westland, received a message from Downing Street, suggesting that 'he should ask the Solicitor-General to consider ... the Defence Secretary's letter and given his opinion on whether it was accurate and consistent with my own letter to Sir John Cuckney'.[10]

It then emerged that the Solicitor-General did consider that there were 'material inaccuracies', and, as soon as the Secretary of State for Trade realized this, he informed Mrs Thatcher. It was decided that Michael Heseltine should be informed of this by a letter from the Solicitor-General – and that letter was subsequently leaked to the press on Monday, 6 January 1986. The extent to which Downing Street and the Prime Minister were involved in authorizing both the disclosure of the letter and the method of its disclosure was still unclear after all the debates in Parliament and the inquiries launched by Sir Robert Armstrong, the Cabinet Secretary, and the Defence and Treasury and Civil Service Select Committees.

Colette Bowe, Head of Information at the Department of Trade and Industry, after great hesitation and having attempted, and failed, to contact the departmental Permanent Secretary, leaked parts of the Mayhew letter to Chris Moncrieff of the Press Association on the instructions of Leon Brittan after obtaining 'cover' from Bernard Ingham, the Prime Minister's Chief Press Secretary, and Charles Powell, the Downing Street private secretary specializing in foreign and defence matters. She was, however, clearly anxious about the correctness of her action, and had wished to consult her Permanent Secretary, but knew that he was out of London for the day and could not be contacted. 'The conflict of evidence,' as the Defence Select Committee put it, 'arises from the fact that the Committee was told that the method of disclosure was agreed between Mr Ingham and Miss Bowe, and was also told that Mr Ingham did not give instructions.'[11]

The Defence Committee concluded that 'the unattributable communication of tendentious extracts from the letter was disreputable', and expressed its astonishment that the advice given to the Government by one of the Law Officers should have been disclosed without his consent. The Committee concluded that 'at the heart of this problem lies the question of accountability to Parliament'.[12]

The Committee argued that 'a Minister does not discharge his accountability to Parliament merely by acknowledging a general responsibility, and, if the circumstances warrant it, by resigning. Accountability involves accounting in detail for actions as a minister ... The fact that ministers have not made themselves fully accountable to Parliament in this matter has called into question the conduct of the civil servants involved.'[13] Ministers are supposed to be accountable for the actions of their civil servants, and the latter are supposed to be anonymous 'servants of the Crown'. But the Prime Minister herself named the five civil servants involved in the leaking of the Solicitor-General's letter in her Commons statement.

Yet the inquiry was conducted without Parliament or the Select Committee being allowed to question the individual civil servants involved, or knowing who they were or even what they said to Sir Robert Armstrong. These were not the only obstacles placed in the way of the Select Committee, as the list it drew up shows. The Government refused for a long time to make relevant documents available; rejected the Committee's proper request to cross-examine named officials, and ministers were not interviewed in the course of the leak inquiry.

All of this serves to underline the fundamental weakness in the doctrine of ministerial accountability – as long as ministers control information and access to it, the doctrine has little real content. Parliament has few real sanctions it can exercise. The Defence and Treasury and Civil Service Select Committee produced valuable evidence and trenchant criticisms of the blatant way in which constitutional considerations had been set aside in the Prime Minister's determination to curb a minister whose insistence on getting his own way led him to flout the conventions of collective responsibility.

The Government, however, blandly replied to the Treasury and Civil Service Select Committee's Report on the duties and responsibilities of civil servants as though nothing had happened:

> The Government endorses the Committee's two basic propositions on accountability: that ministers and not officials are responsible and accountable for policy; and that officials' advice to ministers is and should remain confidential. Constitutionally, ministers are responsible and accountable for all actions carried out by civil servants of their departments in pursuit of Government policies or in the discharge of responsibilities laid upon them by Parliament.[14]

Peter Hennessy, writing on the Westland affair in 1986, summed up its impact:

> It was the Prime Minister's attempt to gag Heseltine by insisting at the Cabinet meeting of 9 January that in future he clear all his statements on Westland with the Cabinet Office which finally triggered his resignation. Pressure from Conservative backbenchers forced Leon Brittan to follow Heseltine out of the Government, not the requirements of ministerial

responsibility. The need to preserve the position of the Prime Minister and not constitutional doctrine led the Conservative majority on the Defence Select Committee to 'clear' Mrs Thatcher. Naming and blaming the civil servants involved, albeit on a sliding scale of culpability, was done without a moment's pause to consider the conventions of ministerial and official responsibility ... In the Westland affair [procedure] provided not one jot of protection or guidance for the system or the people who worked in it. The constitution really was reduced to what happened.[15]

Ministerial Accountability – a Myth?

Plainly Parliament cannot hold ministers accountable if it lacks access to the relevant information. Ministers control that access to information. They may even conceal or distort information, release information not with the intent to inform, but to protect their own interests, or they may even deny that they themselves have access to information. Parliament may request information but has no independent means of checking the correctness of the information they receive.

That has led some, such as Peter Kellner of the *Independent*, to propose a Code of Ethics for ministers which includes an obligation on ministers to act in accordance with the United Nations Charter, the European Convention on Human Rights and the laws of the United Kingdom. They should act in ways consistent with the decisions of Parliament and of the Cabinet. Above all, 'Ministers should not lie; nor should they wilfully conceal information that it is reasonable for Parliament and the people to possess.' They cannot appeal to the national interest in defending concealment without proof. The public recognition of ministerial obligations of this kind would play a part in proper public access to information. Where civil servants believe that ministers are engaged in some kind of cover-up, the ensuing dispute should be referred to some kind of independent machinery, 'the existence of [which] ... and the right of officials to use it, is likely to encourage ministers and officials to observe the rules and to seek to resolve disputes with the minimum of fuss or disturbance to the progress of the Government's legitimate business'.[16] A code for ministers seems to be an essential balance to a code of ethics for civil servants, and an independent appeal tribunal of some kind would help, simply by its existence.

Ministerial control of access to information is not the only reason for the claim that ministerial accountability is a myth. Sir John Hoskyns, more recently Director of the Institute of Directors, but former head of the Downing Street policy unit, and former member of the central policy unit, the private free-market think-tank established by Mrs Thatcher and Sir Keith Joseph in 1974, argued that 'it is completely unrealistic for a Secretary of State to act as *de facto* chief executive of his department. Once again the minister is necessarily, though not entirely, concerned with policy development and change, not with the day-to-day running of what is already there'.[17] In the same memorandum, he stresses the extent to which ministers are involved in so many activities and 'conflicting responsibilities' – departmental and Cabinet committees, Cabinet, constituencies and Parliament – making it impossible for them to know every administrative detail of their own departments or 'to think deeply about the formulation of policy'.[18]

The view that ministerial accountability has any content was dismissed by Lord Rayner saying it was an 'absurd convention' that a 'single individual can be responsible for all the actions of a department'.[19] This interpretation was shared by D.J. Derx, then Director of the Policy Studies Institute and formerly a civil servant, who pointed out that 'the mistakes of the department are no longer necessarily all their personal mistakes, but that has been the reality for years'.[20]

The changes in the structure of the civil service the Government introduced almost inevitably have an impact on ministerial responsibility, at least if devolving responsibility is taken seriously. It was perhaps a certain cynicism about the Financial Management Initiative that led some of the witnesses to the Treasury and Civil Service Select Committee, which considered duties and responsibilities of civil servants and ministers, to claim that devolved budgeting would have little effect in practice. 'In principle there should be no practical effect on ministerial accountability to Parliament',[21] because, 'presumably the minister would still be questioned about the extent of delegation to managers and the continued delegation to managers with an inadequate track record'.[22]

But two witnesses to the Select Committee recognized that the Financial Management Initiative raised important questions about the meaning of ministerial answerability and responsibility. D.J. Derx considered that: 'The Government's efficiency strategy has ... implications which merit more consideration. First the extent to which it treats ministers as managers of departments ... Ministers ... should concentrate on policy initiative and development ... it will mean less ministerial advance control over decisions that may prove controversial. There may be more "mistaken" administrative decisions for which ministers have to answer in the House.'[23]

143

Sir Patrick Nairne, former Permanent Secretary at the Department of Health and Social Security, argued the need for new guidelines to replace those in the Armstrong Memorandum:

> I believe that there is a need for careful evaluation of the current degree of delegation 'down the line to civil service managers at all levels' with a view at least to exploring whether new guidelines replacing in some degree 'traditional' doctrines could usefully be produced. The greater degree of accountability which, in recent years, has been emphasized down the line needs to be reviewed against the background of some important precedent cases affecting ministerial responsibilities.[24]

Sir Patrick clearly took the view that devolved budgeting had created a new situation and accompanying problems:

> I think there is a problem ... it is crucially important that civil servants down the line should feel they are really responsible themselves and that they can be brought to account within their department for what has gone wrong, for what can be laid at their door. I think it does still remain the doctrine that it is the ministers who must account for this and accept responsibility to Parliament. In practice there have been a number of cases over the years in which I think ministers have accepted that there was no need for them to resign ... the result of this doctrine of managerial responsibility down the line has been a certain fuzziness ... I believe it would be a worthwhile exercise to see whether one could analyse and examine rather carefully the way in which, since Crichel Down, doctrine has evolved about the precise responsibility of ministers in taking a personal responsibility on matters where the actions were taken very low down in the machine.[25]

The 'fuzziness' about ministerial accountability became even more obvious when the Select Committee questioned witnesses about the 'Next Steps' initiative. Curiously enough, the Government's responses to the Treasury and Civil Service Select Committee shows its unwillingness to face up to the implications of the introduction of agencies. In the Fifth Report from the Treasury and Civil Service Committee, published in July 1989, the Minister for the Civil Service, Richard Luce, stressed that as civil servants, chief executives will continue to be answerable to their ministers: 'It will be the minister in charge who carries the ultimate accountability and that is a factor that we will always have to keep in mind.'[26] The Government did, however, accept the Committee's recommendation that the chief executives should be formally appointed as 'Agency Accounting Officers', a change which the Project Manager for the 'Next Steps' programme described to the Committee as 'quite remarkable ... a breakthrough'.[27] It was announced on 10 November 1988.[28] It is significant because the chief executives can be called directly to account by Parliament.

The chief executives themselves, in evidence to the Select Committee, said that the creation of the agencies meant that they now dealt more directly with Members of Parliament, rather than corresponding with them through ministers, and that MPs were likely to deal directly with lower grades of staff such as district managers. The procedure is spelt out in several Agency Framework documents, and is thought to increase the ability of MPs to pursue questions about the operations of a particular department.[29]

This should not be regarded as quite as innovative as the chief executives seem to think. Most MPs seek to establish good working relations with the local managers of various administrative bodies, from the health authority to the Department of Social Security, and would normally correspond with them over constituents' problems. Writing to the Secretary of State is usually reserved for some matter of policy that cannot be resolved at local level, or if, for some reason, the local management are unwilling to settle the issue, or, perhaps, to make a political point.

But the way in which questions from Members of Parliament to ministers concerning the work of agencies are handled remains a problem. The Framework Agreements all emphasize that although ministers remain fully accountable for the activities of the agency, Members of Parliament are advised that it would be better to deal with the chief executives on operational matters. But the Treasury and Civil Service Select Committee pointed out in its Eighth Report[30] that there are differences between the agencies on the question of accountability. The Patent Office's Framework Agreement states that 'DTI ministers will answer to Parliament on the work of the Agency', while that of the Companies House explains that there may be cases in which the minister will 'decide to reply', in addition to cases involving wider policy issues. The Framework Agreements of the Central Office of Information and the Occupational Health Service state that ministers will answer from Members of Parliament, who particularly ask for a ministerial response, which is in line with the Government's commitment to a ministerial reply 'in any cases where a Member of Parliament specifically seeks a reply from a minister'.[31]

Neither MPs nor the Treasury and Civil Service Select Committee were content to leave the matter there. In an adjournment debate in May 1990, the minister replying to the debate made it clear that the minister decides whether the question concerns a 'strategic, resource or operational matter'. If the former, it will be answered by the minister, and if the latter, that is, simply an operational matter, it will be sent to the chief executive, who replies to the member. If the MP concerned wishes, a copy of the reply will be placed in the Library of the House of Commons. The Minister of State for the Civil Service explained that this method was designed to ensure that Hon. Members 'deal direct with the person ... who is best placed to answer on the matter in hand'.[32] The Committee was quick to point out the disadvantages of this method. First of all, the distinction between strategic and resource-allocation questions, and purely oper- ational ones, is not as clear-cut as all that. Furthermore, it is left to the minister to make the distinction, without any indication as to what his criteria may be. Indeed, the whole point of raising an individual case with a minister is often a way of illustrating strategic and resource issues, and regarding such a case as a purely operational matter could be an easy way out for a minister.

Secondly, placing a copy of the chief executive's reply in the Library is no substitute for a written parliamentary answer. It can be read in the Library by other MPs, if they happen to know of its existence, but a written parliamentary answer attracts the attention of MPs and the media: particularly assiduous members of the lobby spend a great deal of time studying written answers, and MPs use them in press releases for lobby correspondents, their local press, constituents and relevant pressure groups. That is why the Select Committee on Procedure recommended in its report of July 1991 that the chief executives' replies should be published in Hansard. However, in its response to the Select Committee report, 1991, the Government stated that the chief executive's replies to MPs' questions would be published, but not as part of Hansard. This is still unsatisfactory because it is not clear that these replies enjoy the same parliamentary privileges as Hansard.

Ministers should only be regarded as being responsible to Parliament for policy decisions and the administration of their departments. That, of course, is to state the obvious. Yet neither the sense in which ministers are responsible to Parliament, nor the range of activities for which they can reasonably be held accountable, have been properly considered. The Government contented itself with restating the traditional position in response to the Treasury and Civil Service Select Committee's reports on the 'Next Steps' developments and grudgingly allowed the chief executives to reply to queries from Members of Parliament, and for the replies to be placed in the House of Commons Library. Understandably, Members of

Parliament consider that their inability to question ministers on the floor of the House or through written parliamentary questions in Hansard limits ministerial accountability.

Ministerial Accountability – Its Limits

It is time to come to a frank recognition of the limits of ministerial accountability for the activities of their departments and the executive agencies. It is refreshing to read the Final Report of the Canadian Royal Commission on Financial Management and Accountability (1979): 'Today, ministers are not necessarily held responsible for all the mistakes or failings of public service subordinates unless they clearly knew about and ignored them, or ought to have known about them.'[33]

This statement of principle at least has the merits of honesty, and should be applied in the British context as well. It may not, however, be as easy to apply as it appears at first sight. Even when all the evidence points to the fact that the minister knew that the issue is an important one, the minister may not resign, leaving the notion of ministerial responsibility as defined above as coherent as ever, but honoured in the breach, not the observance. An example of this occurred in July 1991, when two IRA suspects, Nessan Quinlivian and Pearse McAuley, broke out of Brixton gaol. The break-out took place on 7 July after the two had attended Mass in prison. It later transpired that the Home Office had been warned from two different sources that the break-out would take place and that the two prisoners planned to get hold of a gun to facilitate their escape. A Brixton prison officer warned the prison governor, who passed on the warning to the Home Office, and at the same time police sources warned the Home Office quite independently. Furthermore, the Home Office had received a report from Her Majesty's Inspector of Prisons, warning that the prison was in no fit state to receive, or contain, high-risk prisoners. The Home Secretary, Kenneth Baker, said publicly: 'I considered my position ... But I do not believe a ministerial resignation is necessary in this case.' That leaves the impression, as one commentator pointed out, that 'the Government itself does not believe that the escape of two suspected terrorists is important enough to merit ministerial resignation'.[34]

Some still claim that ministers should be accountable in some sense for administrative decisions they have not personally authorized, but that the sense in which they are accountable has to be carefully defined. The minister is still under an obligation to explain what has happened to Parliament and to alter administrative decisions where they are considered to be unjust or lead to inappropriate or inefficient use of the department's resources, to name but a few examples. The problem is, of course, that this assumes that, on the one hand, ministers know every detail of what is happening in their own departments and can take full managerial responsibility, and that, on the other, Members of Parliament have access to such information. Ministers control the information Parliament is given. Members of Parliament can only seek such information through the select committees, parliamentary questions, adjournment debates, etc. Their suspicions that the full truth has not been revealed may be aroused from the nature of ministerial replies, information from other sources, or even from issues their constituents raise with them. Persistent questioning may bring rewards, but that does not alter the fact that in the last resort the flow of information is controlled by ministers. The secrecy which surrounds public administration in Britain does undermine the grandiose claims made for the traditional concept of ministerial accountability to Parliament.

Ministers are traditionally held to be responsible for the efficient management of their departments. Most ministers accept that they are responsible for both the policy and management of their departments, although it is not feasible for ministers to act as the 'chief executives' for their departments.

The constitutional position was set out by Sir Ian Bancroft, a former Head of the Home Civil Service, in the 1982 Treasury and Civil Service Committee report to which the Efficiency Unit referred. 'The minister in charge of a department is ... responsible, and accountable to Parliament, for the effectiveness of his department's policies and the efficient and economical use of the resources allocated to it. It is part of that responsibility to ensure that his department has the systems, procedures, organization and staffing necessary to promote efficient management.'[35]

But that statement of the constitutional position was set out in 1982, before the introduction of the Financial Management Initiative and the 'Next Steps' programme. The aim is to devolve responsibility for just such managerial considerations to cost centres in the first instance and now to the executive agencies. From the debate which has taken place in the reports of the Treasury and Civil Service Select Committee and the Government's replies, and, to a limited extent on the floor of the Chamber, it is clear that the issues has not been satisfactorily resolved. The chief executives of the agencies can, with some justification, argue that their responsibility for running the agencies is undermined if ministers interfere in their work in order to respond to parliamentary questions; hence the arrangements the Government has made, outlined above, which do not satisfy Members of Parliament.

The Westland affair was a stark revelation of the emptiness of the traditional theory of ministerial responsibility. But the matter cannot and should not be left there. It is not enough to say, as Professor George Jones has done, in his contribution to a symposium on ministerial responsibility, that 'ministers are accountable, that is, answerable, to Parliament for everything done by their departments, whether committed by themselves, or by high, middle-ranking, or the lowest grade civil servants in their departments, and whether located in headquarters, regional or local offices . . . So there is no problem about who is accountable to Parliament: the minister is . . . The minister is also legally responsible, since powers are laid down by statute and under the prerogative by common law and convention on the minister.'[36] This is all part of the 'democratic control of bureaucracy'.[37]

The fact that a minister has 'to account in Parliament, strengthens his political control over the department, since the issues that arise in Parliament focus his attention on specific topics inside his department . . . It keeps not only him but also his civil servants on their toes'.[38] There is no question of wishing to undermine ministerial accountability, but of making it effective. This is particularly important in the new context of the establishment of agencies in which the thrust of the development is towards devolving responsibility and making the chief executives as accounting officers responsible to Parliament.

The most important way in which the democratic accountability of the bureaucracy can be strengthened is through giving the public the right of access to information about the operations of the agencies. Just what form that access should take has to be spelt out. But its value as a means of making the bureaucracy more careful, more efficient, at least in the sense of being more accurate and more accountable as well should not be underestimated. Professor Jones's description of the 'random manner' of the 'spotlight of parliamentary concern can alert the ministers to where he should be directing his gaze within the department'[39] is accurate. The trouble is just that – that parliamentary scrutiny is inevitably intermittent, and dependent on what issues happen to come to light from other sources, whether through the media or through letters, telephone calls to Members of Parliament or arising out of their advice surgeries. In such circumstances, MPs can pursue the matter through all the parliamentary means open to them and, where relevant, through the adept use of publicity. When the system works, it can be pursued effectively, depending on the energy and effort of the MP concerned or on media attention.

But, as one former civil servant, who had worked in the fraud section of the Department of Trade and Industry, pointed out, parliamentary scrutiny does serve to bring one particular case to the fore. 'It's a case of all hands to the deck. Meanwhile, the files relating to other possible cases of fraud on the part of financial services companies continue to pile up.'[40] The Department of Trade and Industry's dilatory investigation of allegations of fraud was notorious, and resulted in innocent and sometimes foolish citizens losing their life savings or redundancy payments, which they had invested with companies regulated by the DTI.

Random, indeed, parliamentary scrutiny may be, but its randomness does not have quite the desired effect. The bureaucracy is simply too large for the occasional spotlight to have much effect and too large for ministers, however assiduous they are, to supervise and therefore be answerable to Parliament in any meaningful sense. And, of course, ministers can and do control the information available to Parliament. Other forms of account-ability must be developed to reinforce ministerial accountability, taking accountability to mean the duty, whether legally imposed or not, to explain and justify actions and decisions and to admit errors or misjudgements if well-founded criticisms are made; and then either to put things right if this is possible, or suffer from some penalty, again legal or of some other kind such as embarrassment, or loss of office. Accountability is supposed to achieve the eliciting of information, putting wrongs right, settling the citizen's grievances, and safeguarding the quality of government and public administration.[41] Given this wide, but entirely acceptable, statement of what accountability is expected to achieve, ministerial accountability obvi-ously falls short, and should be strengthened by other forms of account-ability. Of these, public access to information is the key, a theme which will be developed in the next chapter.

Accountability Through Public Access to Information

The framework documents of the agencies could provide a much more useful vehicle than they do at present for setting out the target agencies should achieve, the policies they are designed to implement, the resources available to them and the methods used to achieve the anticipated results. The Treasury and Civil Service Select Committee has commented on the 'blandness' of the framework documents. If the framework documents were more detailed, the select committees, including the Public Accounts Committee, would be able to examine more easily the work of the agencies in terms of clearly defined targets and policies. But there will be problems in 'enforcing' the results of their investigations, because the whole point of establishing the agencies is to relieve the minister of responsibility for operational matters. The framework documents could themselves recognize the need for a wider public accountability by imposing on chief executives a duty to disclose certain kinds of information, particularly the files of the agency's 'clients' and other information about its performance, such as the annual review of its activities, or correspondence over operational matters with the department. An incoming government could implement this straight away without waiting for the introduction of Freedom of Information legislation.

The public, however, do not merely need to know about the activities of agencies, or simply be able to read their own files: they need to be able to seek redress of grievances against the bureaucracy. Constituents often appeal to their Members of Parliament to combat bureaucratic errors or inefficiencies on their behalf. But this is not the only way to secure a review of administrative decisions. A tribunal system provides for the review of decisions by benefit officers and inspectors of taxes for example, and covers a wide range of issues, such as conditions of employment in the industrial tribunals. It also includes a range of specialist tribunals, such as the Performing Rights tribunal, which together handle well over a quarter of a million cases annually. The chief problem with the tribunals is that of access and adequate support for the individual citizens involved in tribunal proceedings. With such a large and varied mass of tribunals, it is difficult for the average person to find out which, if any, is the appropriate body to which to bring his complaint, and to obtain the right sort of support.

Better provision for dealing with individual grievances should be made. It is true that in addition to the tribunal system, individuals may appeal to the ombudsman or the Parliamentary Commissioner for Administration, but only through the Member of Parliament. The scope of the ombudsman's powers is limited to a citizen's 'sustained injustice in consequence of maladministration in connection with' the administrative actions of a Government department or authority subject to the ombudsman's jurisdiction, provided the complaint is one which, in the ombudsman's judgment, he can investigate. JUSTICE, the British section of the International Commission of Jurists, has argued that the terms of reference are too narrow and should extend to 'unreasonable, unjust or oppressive action' by Government departments, but Parliament has not yet been persuaded of the desirability of this extension. The authorities are under an obligation to respond to the Parliamentary Commissioner's criticism and to improve their procedures accordingly, but, unlike a judge, he cannot make an enforceable order, only a recommendation for redress, although Parliament can enforce a remedy. The Parliamentary Commissioner publishes quarterly reports of his work, which are considered by the Select Committee on the Parliamentary Commissioner for Administration, whose role it is to ensure that the Commissioner considers cases thoroughly and does not engage in any attempt to whitewash the authorities.

Plainly the individual citizen does not have clear and simple enough means for obtaining redress for grievances. One possibility would be to establish an ombudsman for each of the agencies dealing with the public, such as the Social Security Benefits Agency, the Employment Service or the Passport Office, with powers to handle complaints without referral from an MP. The chief executive could be required to establish an agency ombudsman in the framework document with given terms of reference, and to set out the procedures in the agency for responding to the ombudsman's recommendations. If a chief executive was reluctant to accept the ombudsman's judgment, then the matter could be considered by the Parliamentary Commissioner for Administration or the appropriate select committee.[42]

The only problem with this approach is the proliferation of ombudsmen. It may well be better to extend the scope and powers of the Parliamentary Ombudsman to cover the work of all the agencies providing services to the public and to allow the public to have direct access to the ombudsman. This should be accompanied by a publicity campaign to provide the ombudsman with a high media profile. MPs could refer appropriate cases to the Parliamentary Ombudsman.

Ombudsmen and the Swedish System

When the Labour Government introduced the 1967 Act establishing the Parliamentary Ombudsman in the British system, they had looked to Sweden as a model, but significantly altered the powers granted to the office. The main difference is that the Swedish public have direct access to the ombudsman, a move which would increase the number of complaints and strengthen the ombudsman's influence. At present, the number of complaints the Parliamentary Commissioner dealt with, 704 in 1990, is fewer than the Swedish Parliamentary Ombudsman's 3000 complaints in the same year. The Swedish Parliamentary Ombudsman has a wide range of responsibilities in overseeing the courts of law and all the administrative authorities, including all state and municipal agencies and bodies as well as their personnel, but not Cabinet ministers, Members of Parliament or the Chancellor of Justice.

The ombudsman may be present at the deliberations of a court or an administrative authority, but cannot take part in the proceedings. They have access to all official files and documents; indeed, all officials are obliged by law to give the ombudsmen all the information they require and every assistance with investigations. They cannot, however, alter a decision made by the court or the administrative authority, nor can they instruct a court or any executive agency to make certain decisions or act in a certain way.

The ombudsman can, however, and does criticize the officials concerned, describe how the matter should have been handled and recommend ways of putting the matter right. The executive agencies can be asked to improve their procedures on the recommendation of the ombudsman. All of the ombudsman's reports and recommendations are published, and often covered by the media. The Ombudsman's Office carries immense authority, so that, although its decisions cannot be enforced, the executive agencies act upon them. As far as redress and compensation on the part of the individual citizen is concerned, this is not a matter for the ombudsman but for the administrative courts. A report from the ombudsman, supporting the individual citizen's case, will generally ensure that the administrative court will find in his favour.

Anyone can complain to the ombudsman, even citizens of other countries or those living outside Sweden, nor need the complaint be personally involved in the issue. The complaint should normally refer to an event which took place less than two years before the complaint was made, but an older case may still be investigated in exceptional circumstances. The complaints may concern the tax authorities or the police; prisoners may complain about prison conditions, and both journalists and members of the public may complain about the authorities failing in their statutory duties to allow public access to documents. The remit is very wide.

In addition, Members of the Riksdag refer their constituents' complaints to the ombudsman, and this is not in any way regarded as passing the buck. Sometimes the ombudsman receives anonymous complaints, and although no action is taken on these, they sometimes inspire the ombudsman to initiate an investigation. The ombudsman does not only respond to individual complaints, but may also decide to start an investigation, perhaps as the result of media reports of the activities of the courts or administrative agencies. The Office also carries out routine inspections of the courts, prisons, and administrative agencies, studying files and documents, interviewing staff, prisoners and hospital patients. The ombudsman's decisions are frequently reported in the mass media, and, of course, the reports of decisions are public documents. A lengthy annual report covers the ombudsman's findings and decisions on all cases of general interest and the report is studied by the Riksdag's standing committee on the Constitution and is debated in Parliament. The recommendations cover the practices of the agency concerned and may lead to recommendations to amend existing legislation.

Extending the powers and the role of the Parliamentary Ombudsman in Britain would be an additional source of accountability. Giving the citizen the right to approach the ombudsman directly is the first step, and would bring his work into line with international standards: only two ombudsmen, the French *médiateur* and the British ombudsman, cannot receive complaints directly from the public. Few people know about the ombudsman's existence, so publicizing his work and the results more widely than the annual report would create further pressures to which the civil service and the agencies would have to respond. That pressure arises only from the Select Committee or the Parliamentary Commissioner for Administration, which considers the quarterly reports on selected cases which the ombudsman provides. If a Government department does not provide a remedy when the ombudsman has upheld a complaint, the Select Committee can make recommendations. Their reports have helped to encourage Government departments to accept the ombudsman's criticisms, which they would otherwise have continued to dispute.

Like the Swedish ombudsman, the Parliamentary Ombudsman should be able to investigate the administration, including the executive agencies, on his own initiative. The impetus to carry out such work would arise from an analysis of his own case work, out of complaints from members of the public about one particular Government department or agency, or from reports in the media of alleged incompetence. The mere fact that the Parliamentary Commissioner had embarked on an investigation, and the publicity that would follow, would no doubt encourage the agency to start sorting out its administrative procedures. These reports, together with the reports on individual cases, which are at present included in the Select Committee reports, could also be used, as the Justice-All Souls Review of Administrative Law suggested, as the basis of 'good practice' for the civil service.

Since the ombudsman makes recommendations but cannot enforce them, other methods are necessary to bring that about. Reference has already been made to the system of tribunals, but extensive as they are, they do not cover all the areas in which citizens might want to have decisions reviewed or to obtain redress. One possibility would be to establish a proper system of administrative courts, covering every aspect of the administration and incorporating existing tribunals. Special administrative judges would adjudicate over the cases which the citizen, without incurring any costs, would be able to present in writing. That is the kind of back-up provided for the Swedish ombudsman and would appear to be the simplest system. There are problems, however, in providing adequate resources in terms of staff and finance, and in making sure that the public does not have to face long delays before their grievances are heard.

The Justice-All Souls Review made two other proposals, one of which should apply, whatever system of adjudication and enforcement is in place. It is the duty to 'give reasons' which would apply to administrative authorities as an enforceable legal duty. This duty is recognized in other legal systems, such as the United States, and in the reforms in administrative law carried out in Australia in the 1970s. The review argues that requiring the administration to give reasons on demand when a decision has been challenged in the courts or tribunals makes for better decision-making, and provides a check on arbitrary behaviour. Tribunals have had to provide reasons for their decisions since 1958, and the review points out, 'it is generally believed that the quality of decision-making has improved' since then.[43] The fact that the court or tribunal has to provide reasons for its decisions means that, in turn, the administration has to be able to defend its actions at any time. Care must be taken to ensure that the right kind of reasons are adopted, perhaps along the lines of the Australian formulation, which require the decision-maker to state the 'findings on material questions of fact, referring to evidence or other material on which these findings were based and giving the reasons for the decisions'.[44]

The other proposal is to improve the procedures for judicial review, introduced in England and Wales in 1977, and in Scotland in 1985. The grounds on which judicial review may be sought should also be clarified. JUSTICE believes that this could be done along the lines of the Australian Administrative Decisions (Judicial Review) Act, 1977, which is a brave attempt to set out as precisely as possible the general principles on which a judicial review may be sought. Given the system is already in place and that it has been used with increasing frequency, the procedures should be improved, and the basis of judicial review should be made clearer. But it would be far better to rely on other ways of making departments and executive agencies efficient and effective and dealing with the public's complaints.

Apart from individual complaints or even the wider issues raised in judicial review, there are other means of bringing about administrative accountability. The present Government has provided itself with a tool in the framework documents but has failed to exploit these to the full. The documents at the moment are generally too bland, but they could follow the Employment Agency model more closely, with its annual 'performance targets' for the agency to attain.[45] Here, there are some financial penalties for failing to reach the targets – a reduction in the chief executive's pay, as occurred with Michael Fogden at the end of the Employment Agency's first year, for failing to reach the job-placement targets during one of the most serious post-war recessions (a penalty which some might think should apply to the Chancellor and the Secretary of State for Employment as well!). An operational plan has to be agreed with the Secretary of State, which provides a yardstick against which the agency's performance can be judged. The National Audit Office looks for value for money, and, of course, at financial propriety. Its attention has turned to estimating the effectiveness of the spending programmes which the departments and agencies manage. A wide range of performance indicators and institutions should be used to check public administration and ensure its effectiveness.

All of these elements taken together will make the accountability of the departments and the executive agencies to the public a reality, provided that the essential element of the right to information has been established. Without that, accountability, even the much-vaunted parliamentary accountability, exists only in the shadow, not the substance.

Notes

1 G. Fry, Memorandum to the Treasury and Civil Service Select Committee, 'Civil Servants and Ministers: Duties and Responsibilities', 1985–6, Vol. 2, p. 316.
2 D. Wass, *Government and the Governed*, 1984, p. 45.
3 as quoted by P. Hennessy in *Whitehall*.
4 H. Morrison, *Government and Parliament*, 3rd ed., 1964, p. 265.
5 ibid., para. 28.
6 HC Deb., 13 January 1986, col. 515.
7 HC Deb, 15 January 1986, cols. 1093–1103.
8 Fourth Report from the Defence Committee, 1985–6, p. xxxix, HC 519.
9 ibid., p. xl.

[10] HC Deb., 27 January 1986, col. 652.
[11] Fourth Report from the Defence Committee, Session 1985–6, *Westland plc: The Government's Decision Making*, HC 519, para. 158, p. xivii.
[12] ibid., paras. 234–8, pp. lxvi–lxvii.
[13] ibid.
[14] 'Civil Servants and Ministers: duties and responsibilities': Government response to the 7th report from the Treasury and Civil Service Committee, 1985–6, HC 92, 1986, Cmnd 9841, p. 6.
[15] P. Hennessy, 'Constitutional issues of the Westland affair, Helicopter crashes into Cabinet: Prime Minister and constitution hurt, *Journal of Law and Society*, 1986, Vol. 13, p. 432.
[16] P. Kellner, Memorandum in Treasury and Civil Service Select Committee, 'Civil Servants and Ministers: Duties and Responsibilities', 1985–6, Vol. 2, p. 327.
[17] ibid., J. Hoskyns, p. 275.
[18] ibid., p. 274.
[19] ibid., D. Rayner, p. 272.
[20] ibid., D.J. Derx, p. 324.
[21] ibid., p. 268.
[22] ibid., p. 256.
[23] ibid., D.J. Derx, p. 324.
[24] ibid., P. Nairne, p. 48.
[25] ibid., P. Nairne, Q. 184, p. 51; Q. 191, p. 53.
[26] R. Luce, Treasury and Civil Service Select Committee, Fifth Report, July 1989, Q. 323.
[27] Q. 344.
[28] HC Deb., cols. 249–50W.
[29] QQ. 81, 117, Treasury and Civil Service Select Committee, Fifth Report, Developments in the Next Steps Programme, HC 348 and the Vehicle Inspectorate Policy and Resources Framework.
[30] Treasury and Civil Service Select Committee, Eighth Report, 1989–90, HC 481.
[31] Cmnd 524, November 1988, p. 9.
[32] HC Deb., 21 May 1990, cols. 150–51, see also 9 July 1991, col. 102W.
[33] Final Report of the Canadian Royal Commission on Financial Management and Accountability, 1979, p. 190.
[34] A. Bevins, 'Making the Best of a Bad Job', *Independent*, 8 August 1991.
[35] I. Bancroft, Memorandum in Treasury and Civil Service Select Committee, Third Report, Vol. 2, Evidence HC 236–II, p. 174, para. 1.
[36] G. Jones, 'Symposium on Ministerial Responsibility', *Public Administration*, 1987, Vol. 65, No. 1, Spring, p. 87.
[37] ibid., p. 89.
[38] ibid.
[39] ibid.
[40] private information.
[41] D. Oliver, 'Machinery of Government' seminars, 'Labour and Whitehall: A Fabian Inquiry into the Machinery of Government', paper to Fabian Society, 6 June 1991.

42 ibid.
43 Report of the Justice-All Souls Review of the Administrative Law in the United Kingdom, 'Administrative Justice – Some Necessary Reforms', 1988, p. 71.
44 ibid., p. 72.
45 *Independent*, 1 July 1991.

SEVEN

Open Government

The traditional doctrine of ministerial responsibility is now interpreted in a more limited fashion as the doctrine that ministers should be held personally responsible for those policies, acts and omissions of their departments which they authorized or of which they were or ought to have been aware. That concept of responsibility has been attenuated over the years since the Crichel Down affair, in that ministers do not resign even if gross errors are committed by their departments. As regards the actions or mistakes which the minister has not personally authorized, or of which he or she could not reasonably have been aware, the minister fulfils his or her responsibilities to Parliament and the public by explaining what has happened. In these circumstances, the minister would normally inform the House of Commons of any steps taken or plans to discipline the civil servants concerned and of the practical steps which should be taken to prevent any recurrence.

Ministerial responsibility for the executive agencies has become more remote, since the minister is only responsible for matters concerning resource allocation or strategy, not for operational matters. With the increasing devolution of administration to the agencies, the area for which ministers are accountable in the first sense will continue to decline. This is a modern version of the traditional doctrine, but one which would command widespread support as a reasonable interpretation of it. The problem is that the reality bears little resemblance even to the modern version of much-vaunted traditions. Ministerial accountability, it was argued in the previous chapter, is undermined by the fact that the minister can choose what information will be disclosed to Parliament. The House of Commons no longer has the power it once had to move the motion to 'send for papers' or to set up select committees to investigate and extract information about a particular issue, and to punish those who refuse to produce the papers. This right disappeared towards the end of the nineteenth century as part of what one historian of Parliament, J. Redlich, has described as 'the continuous extension of the rights of the government over the direction of parliamentary action in the House and ... the complete suppression of the private member, both as to his legislative initiative and as to the scope of action allowed to him by the rules'. This arose from the 'completion in the nineteenth century of the system of parliamentary government'.[1] Redlich is right, of course, in that the parliamentary system we have now, and the dominant concept of the relationship between Government and Parliament, is essentially a nineteenth-century one and increasingly inappropriate for the twentieth century.

The Official Secrets Act, 1889

The first Official Secrets Act was passed in 1889, finally removing any right Parliament had to demand information from the government of the day, though that was not its primary intention. The Act arose out of the long-standing concerns of government and senior civil servants about the unauthorized disclosure of official information of all kinds. The Government eventually decided to act and introduced the bill which dealt with both spying and breaches of official trust, two distinct but related problems. These two elements are found in all the subsequent official secrets legislation, which is designed both to protect national security, and also to put control of information in the hands of the executive.

The first attempt was faulty. The 'catch-all' Section 2 of the 1889 Act defined an offence under this section as one committed by a Crown servant or a Government contractor whose contract contained an obligation of secrecy, if he communicated official information 'corruptly or contrary to his official duty' to a person to whom it 'ought not, in the interest of the State or otherwise in the public interest to be communicated at that time'.[2] The breaches in this Act, however, had to be shown to be contrary to the public interest. It is curious that exactly one hundred years later the government of the day introduced yet another bill in Parliament to protect official information and to define a satisfactory alternative to this end as a replacement of Section 2 of the 1911 Act – that is, the 1989 Official Secrets Act.

The Official Secrets Act, 1911

By 1903, the War Office had concluded that the 1889 Act was defective. The provisions on spying were unsatisfactory. It had proved impossible to punish newspapers which published leaked information and convictions could only be secured where the Government testified to the truth of the information published. The Government's concerns all seem very familiar. They were supported by an official report of 1909 which recommended greater powers of arrest, search, and seizure, with persuasive and useful evidence about the existence of German spies. This gave the Asquith Government the excuse it needed to introduce the 1911 Official Secrets Act, passed by Parliament in a single day in the midst of hysteria over German spies. The Act did much more than strengthen counter-espionage measures. Section 2 of the Act imposed the most extensive restrictions yet on unauthorized dissemination of official information and allowed for criminal prosecutions of anyone found guilty of revealing it. Section 2 was not mentioned once in the parliamentary debates, nor did the Government give a proper explanation of the bill during the debate.

The Franks Committee, set up in 1971 to 'review the operation of Section 2 of the Official Secrets Act 1911 and to make recommendations' described the way in which the Act was passed in their report:

It was in these circumstances that the 1911 legislation was passed through Parliament with little debate. The country was in crisis and it was late summer. The debates on the Act in the House of Lords were brief and the House of Commons passed it in one afternoon with no detailed scrutiny and virtually without debate. The debates give a clear impression of crisis legislation, aimed mainly at espionage. Closer study, and references to official sources, reveal a different story. This legislation had been long desired by governments. It had been carefully prepared over a period of years. One of its objects was to give greater protection against leakages of any kind of official information whether or not connected with defence and national security. This was clear enough from the text of the bill alone. Although Section 2 of the 1911 Act was much wider in a number of respects than Section 2 of the 1889 Act, the files suggest that the Government in 1911 honestly believed that it introduced no new principle, but merely put into practice more effectually the principle of using criminal sanctions to protect official information. At all events, the Government elected not to volunteer complete explanations of their bill in Parliament. And Parliament, in the special circumstances of that summer, did not look behind the explanation offered.[3]

Reporting in 1972, the Franks Committee found the case for reform 'overwhelming', and added that 'section 2 is a mess. Its scope is enormously wide. Any law which impinges on the freedom of information in a democracy should be much more tightly drawn. A catch-all provision is saved from absurdity in operation only by the sparing exercise of the Attorney General's discretion to prosecute. Yet the very width of this discretion, and the inevitably selective way in which it is exercised give rise to considerable unease. The drafting and interpretation of the section are obscure. People are not sure what it means, or how it operates in practice, or what kinds of action involve real risk of prosecution under it.'[4]

But the then Conservative Government took no further action apart from publishing the report and allowing Parliament to debate the issue under a 'Take Note' motion. The Labour Party's manifesto of October 1974 promised to 'replace the Official Secrets Act by a measure to put the burden on the public authorities to justify withholding information'. But no action was taken until the belated production of a White Paper in July 1978, timed no doubt for an anticipated October election, which in the event did not take place until 1979. Attempts at reform were left to backbench MPs. Despite repeated attempts in the 1970s and 1980s to reform the Official Secrets Act or to replace it with freedom of information legislation, the Government decided to reform the original Act with its own legislation, significantly entitled the Official Secrets Act, 1989.

The Official Secrets Act, 1989

The 1989 Act can at first sight be presented as a more liberal measure than the 1911 Act. The Government argued that the Act should be seen in this light, when they replaced the infamous catch-all Section 2 with a new measure, making it an offence to disclose information under certain conditions. It is true that much official information will no longer be protected by the criminal law, but as freedom of information campaigners were quick to point out, 'It is about the efficient protection of information, not its disclosure . . . The public will have no new rights to information, and ministers will continue to be able to withhold information embarrassing to their case, or damning of their performance.'[5]

What is subject to the criminal law is information about security or intelligence (defined only as 'the work of, or in support of the security and intelligence services or any part of them'); the 'damaging disclosure' by a Crown servant or Government contractor of any information relating to 'defence'; information relating to international relations or any confidential information obtained from another state or international organization; information 'which results in the commission of an offence, facilitates an escape from legal custody, or impedes the prevention or detection of offences or the arrest or prosecution of suspected offenders'.[6]

The final category of disclosure that may constitute an offence under the Act covers information given in confidence by the British Government to other states or international organizations. This is an odd provision, to say the least. It means that if a civil servant or an official of another state leaks information given by a British Government to that state, it could be unlawful to disclose that information here. The information could be published in newspapers all over the world, perhaps even in those on sale in this country or certainly available to anyone who goes abroad. But the media in Britain would be unable to publish the information in question even if it did pose a threat to national security such as position papers issued by the Government, say, to the European Community or the International Labour Organisation, explaining why the British Government wishes to continue with the breaches of international law. Edward Heath delightfully took the Government to task over this clause in the *Spectator*:

> The term 'international organization' is laughably wide. The Foreign Office says that it is impractical to produce a full list of organizations. This is an extraordinary statement, given that we are voting whether or not to apply the criminal law. There is no reason to suppose that the Senegal Groundnut Company is not covered by the law. It would also be instructive for the Lords to consider in greater detail whether information flowing between the UK and the EC should be covered by such a blanket term, given that we are asked to reap the benefits of a Single European Market by 1992. This cannot be achieved without greater coordination; we must ask ourselves whether a process that affects us all should be so secretive.[7]

Under the 1989 Act, not only the person who leaks the information, but also the person who publishes it, is liable to prosecution, provided the editors of newspapers or programmes have reasonable cause to believe that the information is protected against disclosure. In the White Paper preceding the bill, the Government argued that 'what justifies making the unauthorized disclosure of certain information a criminal offence is the degree of harm to the public interest in which it is likely to result. Since the unauthorized disclosure of certain information by, say, a newspaper may be as harmful as disclosure of the same information by a Crown servant, the Government believes that it would not be sufficient for the new legislation to apply only to disclosure by Crown servants.'[8]

This, of course, entirely sets aside any constitutional role for the media in a democracy; indeed, at no stage in the discussions which preceded the passage of the bill through Parliament, or during the parliamentary debates, did the Government show any sign of understanding the vital necessity of such freedom.

What makes the Act even more alarming is that the legislation covers a wide range of information and is imprecisely defined. It restrains the media from publishing any information unlawfully revealed, if its publication would be damaging. It could even apply to any information, which has not been classified, provided it could be said to cause 'harm', however unimportant. Of course, the prosecution will have to convince a jury that harm has been caused, but the fact that it is possible for such a case to be brought against the media will create a certain hesitation to run risks and public information which might land them in court.

In the discussions which took place before the legislation was introduced into Parliament, the Government rejected any kind of defence on which the media might rely in court. There are two possible justifications: 'prior publication' and the claim that publication is justified 'in the public interest'. As far as the first type of defence is concerned, the Government argued in its White Paper that 'a newspaper story about a certain matter may carry little weight in the absence of firm evidence of its validity. But confirmation of that study by, say, a senior official of the relevant Government department would be very much more damaging. In such circumstances, the Government considers that the official should still be subject to criminal sanctions.'[9]

But refusing to allow the possibility of a prior publication defence has more far-reaching implications than the Government is prepared to admit. Section 5 of the Act makes it an offence for anyone, not just a civil servant, to disclose the information, whatever its source. Take, for example, the Spycatcher case. Under this legislation, both the *Guardian* and the *Observer* could have been successfully prosecuted, even though the information had already been published by Chapman Pincher and Nigel West and was well known throughout the world.

The Government also refused to allow any public interest defence to become part of the bill, an omission which Edward Heath insisted in the course of the parliamentary debate as being 'integral to the bill's failure to weigh the rights of the individual against possible abuses of state powers'.[10] The Government, however, argued that it is essential to 'concentrate the protection of the criminal law on information which demonstrably requires its protection in the public interest'.[11] In the Government's view it is always in the public interest to protect information from disclosure, whatever the nature of that information or the circumstances – a 'nanny state' *par excellence*. The result is that the media will be liable for publishing documents or information showing that a Government minister has withheld information from Parliament, deceived or misled Parliament, or disclosed allegations published by a former security officer overseas which suggests or indicates that members of the service have been engaged in subversive activities. This led Edward Heath to ask, 'Under this measure, in this country, if it occurred, would we know about Irangate? That is still my test, though my question has not been answered. We would not have known anything about it. We would not have known about the evil policies, the hypocrisy, the corruption and lies of President Reagan's regime. Is that justifiable in a modern democracy? Not for one moment.'[12]

Even debate on the bill was guillotined, which meant that a number of clauses of the bill were not scrutinized by Parliament at all, and once again the Executive was able to use its power and its majority to ensure that its legislation was passed unscathed and without proper consideration. But again, as Heath pointed out in the same *Spectator* article, 'these reforms go to the heart of the relationship between the individual and the Executive'. The balance of power has swung strongly in favour of the Government as a result of this Act, and the 'countervailing balance of the public' has been ignored. In these circumstances, the 'risk' is that the Government will 'equate the interests of the State with that of the Government',[13] precisely the view the judge expressed in his summing-up in the Ponting trial.

Both the Government's White Paper and the 1989 Act exclude any possibility of a 'public interest' defence for disclosure of information falling under the categories outlined above which attract criminal sanctions. The White Paper firmly rejected the proposal that

> the law should provide a general defence that disclosure was in the public interest ... the Government recognises that some people who make unauthorized disclosures do so for what they themselves see as altruistic reasons and without the desire for personal gain ... The general principle which the law follows is that the criminality of what people do ought not to depend on their ultimate motives – though these may be

a factor to be taken into account in sentencing – but on the nature and degree of harm which their acts may cause.

In the Government's view, there are good grounds for not departing from the general model in this context; and two features of the present proposals particularly reinforce this conclusion. First, a central objective of reform is to achieve the maximum clarity in the law and in its application. A general public interest defence would make it impossible to achieve such clarity. Secondly, the proposals in this White Paper are designed to concentrate the protection of the criminal law on information which demonstrably requires its protection in the public interest. It cannot be acceptable that a person can lawfully disclose information which he knows may, for example, lead to loss of life simply because he conceives that he has a general reason of a public character for doing so.

So far as the criminal law relating to the protection of official information is concerned, therefore, the Government is of the mind that there should be no general public interest defence and that any argument as to the effect of disclosure on the public interest should take place within the context of the proposed damage test where applicable.[14]

But this argument simply does not get to grips with the issues at stake. Someone who discloses official information in order to expose crime, fraud, corruption, negligence or danger to life, will not be able to cite these reasons as his or her defence. Such a person will be as guilty as if the information had been released just to make money or for some other kind of personal gain. Suppose such a person released information, say, about the causes of environmental pollution, which was concealed on the grounds of national security, that person could not argue that the benefit to the public from the release of information outweighed the minimal harm disclosure brought about, even if the information clearly did benefit the public. The Government has the power to refuse to reveal information about the causes of environmental pollution on the grounds of national security under the 1990 Environmental Protection Act, 1990. A public interest defence does not mean that a civil servant can reveal anything he likes, whenever he likes. A proper justification has to be provided and argued.

That has never been the case with the law of confidence to which reference was made during the Spycatcher case. The All-England Law Report on the House of Lords' case included the following point: 'The Court would not grant an injunction restraining the publication of confidential information acquired by a Crown servant in the course of his employment by the Crown if it could be shown that publication of the information would not be contrary to the public interest. Thus it was incumbent on the Crown to show not only that the information was confidential but also that it was in the public interest that it should not be published if it wished to restrain the disclosure of Government secrets. Accordingly, an injunction would not be granted if all possible damage to the Crown's interest had already been done by publication of the information abroad.'[15]

Some of the bills introduced by backbench MPs and supported by the Campaign for Freedom of Information in fact deal with the arguments presented in the White Paper. Take, for example, Richard Shepherd's 1988 bill, which was dismissed on a three-line Government whip, an unprecedented invasion of the limited time available for private members' bills, which are not normally subject to a three-line whip on party lines. The bill allowed for a public interest defence provided the person who leaked the information had 'reasonable cause to believe that it indicated the existence of crime, fraud, abuse of authority, neglect in the performance of duty or other misconduct'. If a civil servant was involved the defence would only apply 'if he has taken reasonable steps to comply with any established procedures for drawing such misconduct to the attention of the appropriate authorities without effect'. Even then the civil servant must show that other ways of dealing with the problem have been exhausted; the information has to 'relate to specific types of misconduct', and the 'misconduct would have to be sufficient to justify, in the public interest, disclosing information which should normally not be revealed'. Nor can the defence rely on 'unsubstantiated suspicion', but must be able to persuade other 'reasonable people that an abuse was occurring'.[16] Conditions of this kind provide a reasonable form of public interest defence, yet the Government refused to consider any such possibilities. When the bill was introduced in Parliament, it did not allow a public interest defence. The Home Secretary, however, did make the following statement when the bill was published: 'At present there is no defence of public interest. Under these proposals, where there is a harm test and the defendant could argue that the disclosure caused good not harm to the public interest, it would be for the jury to decide. What a defendant could not argue is that his disclosure did cause this degree of harm but, because it did some good then the harm didn't matter',[17] but this hardly seems a sufficient concession to the notion of a public interest defence, since a jury would only be asked to consider whether or not a disclosure of information would cause a particular kind of harm and if it did, the jury would have to convict the accused.

The opportunity to extend public access to information was lost in 1989. Again, as Edward Heath concluded, 'In our society now the balance is all too often coming down on the side of secrecy, against the press and information in general.'[18] Other countries have no difficulty in recognizing a public interest defence; and indeed some, such as the United States, have made arrangements, however inadequate, to protect the 'whistle-blowers'. Furthermore, not only is the 1989 Act decidedly illiberal, but it does not establish any kind of rights to information. All the legislation introduced over the past twenty years in the United States, Canada, Australia, New Zealand, France and Germany runs entirely in the opposite direction. They have all started from the presumption that the public has a right to know, and have restricted that right in limited and more or less carefully defined areas. But the 1989 Act has left the British Government even more firmly in control of information, with effective sanctions to prevent and restrict, even where the criminal law no longer applies. The Act and the White Paper preceding it only set out to reduce the excessively wide scope of the criminal law of official secrecy. The Government explicitly rejected the aim of extending public access to official information.

Freedom of Information Legislation in Britain

Britain sticks out like a sore thumb amongst advanced democracies in passing legislation with such a title and purpose. It appears to be one of the few democracies which cannot bring itself to trust its own citizens with information. Britain may, however, find that its membership of the European Community may oblige Parliament to extend the public right of access to information in some areas at least. A new European directive on access to environmental information has been adopted which requires member states to introduce new rights of access by January 1993. These and perhaps other EC directives may bring Britain more closely into line with other Western democracies, willy nilly.

France and Germany both extended public access to government documents in the 1970s. Australia, Canada and New Zealand, all with 'Westminster-style' parliaments, passed freedom of information legislation in 1982. This puts paid to the argument that freedom of information is incompatible with a Westminster-style government. Parliament would itself define the exemptions of freedom of information and would be free to revise them in the light of experience, as indeed Australia has done on two occasions.

Each of these governments commissioned extensive reports on secrecy and freedom of information before introducing legislation, and each has found that freedom of information has worked satisfactorily, at least from the point of view of government. In the course of their pre-legislative considerations, Australia, Canada and New Zealand examined the question of the compatibility of freedom of information with ministerial accountability. As Robert Hazell points out, 'before the introduction of the legislation all three countries devoted much thought to the compatibility of [freedom of information] with a Westminster constitution based on the convention of ministerial accountability to Parliament. Whole chapters are devoted to the subject; but in the subsequent reviews ministerial responsibility does not rate a mention. In the comprehensive evidence of the Australian Attorney General's Department to the Senate Committee it is not even mentioned under the heading of "past concerns".'[19]

Those seeking access to information in these three countries and the United States may still find that there are obstacles in the way, and that recourse to the courts or to an independent tribunal or an information commissioner is necessary in order to obtain the desired information. An examination of such systems and obstacles would be necessary before freedom of information legislation is introduced in the UK to make sure that there are no unnecessary bureaucratic hurdles to overcome, or that citizens are not barred by undue expense in obtaining information.

One of the significant arguments in favour of the introduction of freedom of information in this country, and one which highlights the absurdity of the 1989 Official Secrets Act, is that the desired information can easily and rightfully be obtained elsewhere. A telling example of that occurred at a meeting of the Defence Select Committee, when the following exchange took place between Michael Mates MP, Chairman of the Defence Select Committee, and David Gould, a civil servant from the Ministry of Defence:

Q78. How many Phantoms are there at Wildenrath?
(Gould) I am afraid that is not something we can give in public session – two squadrons.

79. The published CFE declaration says twenty-eight.
(Gould) That sounds all right.

80. You told the Russians but you cannot tell us in public session?

(Gould) I hesitate to make new policies even in such an august session as this. I agree perhaps there is scope for doing so.

81. We are getting into an absurd position. I just accepted what you told me about closures because there might be one or two sensitivities in

consultations with the German allies. If the Russians know how many Phantoms there are, why cannot the British public?[20]

This is but one example of the way in which information may be published in other parts of the world but is not made publicly available here. Very often that information is directly relevant to people's everyday lives; for example, car safety figures relating to specific car models was published by the Department of Transport for the first time in April 1991, as a result of pressure from the Consumers' Association. The latter organization had publicized the car safety record of the Suzuki four-wheel drive model, popularly known as the Suzuki 'Jeep' 410 in 1989 on the basis of its own tests, but also drew on information available in the United States from its safety checks.

Quite apart from the absurdities arising from the fact that such information is available, and often made available by the British Government, to other organizations in other parts of the world, the public still has no right of access to information about the decisions their elected Government is making on their behalf. The 'price of freedom is eternal vigilance' but the public are in no position to exercise that vigilance without proper access to information. Nor can they play any part in the process of making the policies which influence their lives, and the result of that exclusion is to make those policies poorer and ill-considered. Britain has become a secretive state to the extent that not only is democratic debate crippled, but the public is uncertain where real power and influence lies, and those who exercise it can evade full accountability for their actions. Where the public does become aware of, or suspect, serious errors, they see that the cloak of secrecy enables those whom they suspect are at fault to get away with it. Justice, in other words, is seen not to be done. In such circumstances error and inefficiency is likely to increase and remain undetected.

The failure to acknowledge such fundamental democratic principles has important practical consequences for people's daily lives; indeed, in some instances such failure can prove fatal. Take a few examples in the area of transport safety: enforcement notices served on ships which breach safety regulations are secret, so although officials may know that lifeboats, jackets, fire equipment or other safety measures are below standard, the public does not.

In his report on the King's Cross underground fire, which led to the loss of thirty-one lives in November 1987, Desmond Fennell QC revealed that London Underground internal inquiries into earlier fires had previously identified fire hazards. Similarly, reports by the fire brigade, police,

Railway Fire Prevention and the Fire Safety Standards Committee had also pointed out the fire risks. The report concluded that London Underground's failure to implement earlier recommendations had contributed to the fire. London Underground now publishes such information, but British Rail does not.

Investigations into air disasters carried out by the Air Accidents Investigation Branch of the Department of Transport are carried out in secret. All inquiries are held in private, and any written submissions are confidential. Furthermore, before the reports are published, those who are directly involved, and anyone whose reputation may be adversely affected, must be consulted and can have their case examined by a review board. Only when that process has been carried out can the report be published.

Over recent years, the relatives of those who died in the Lockerbie aircrash, the Zeebrugge ferry disaster and the sinking of the *Marchioness*, have all found that the secrecy and delays have added almost too much to their grief.[21]

In Britain, especially in the context of the current reforms of the civil service, public access to Government information has a particular importance. Establishing agencies does weaken ministerial accountability still further. The Government insists that Members of Parliament should correspond with chief executives about operational matters, leaving ministers free to decide which matters are operational and which are strategic and concerned with resource allocation; it also insists that the replies should simply be placed in the Library of the House of Commons, a matter which is now in dispute, as it were, between Parliament and the Executive. The National Audit Office and the select committees, from their own vantage points, review the workings of the agencies. But with the best will in the world their examination of any particular agency will be occasional. The result could be even less access to information about the operations of the executive agencies than Members of Parliament and the public have about the workings of the departments. The accountability of the administration has undoubtedly been weakened by the introduction of the agency system.

This is not to say that the 'Next Steps' initiative should be abandoned. It does, however, mean that some other more effective means of ensuring ministers' accountability should be found. This is where public access to information held by the agency comes in. Access of this kind has two functions, the first of which has already been suggested by looking at the secrecy surrounding the work of so many regulatory authorities and investigations into transport safety. The point is that open government does help to protect the citizen against maladministration, and will undoubtedly help to encourage greater efficiency on the part of civil servants working in the agency. As one ex-civil servant put it: 'The fact that your professional colleagues could read what you have written to a member of the public would certainly make you take far more care over what you were doing.'[22]

Other practical effects follow from the introduction of freedom of information. Civil servants document their work more carefully and apply policy more consistently. Grievances are settled more easily when the reasons for administrative decisions are explained and when citizens' personal files are kept more accurately.

The 'culture of secrecy' endemic in British government will be hard to break. It is reinforced in so many ways within the civil service; for example, one of the professional criteria for judging civil servants is their ability to keep a secret. Indeed, those in particularly sensitive positions within the civil service, working closely with ministers, may well take care not to be seen on close or intimate terms with members of Opposition parties. Secrecy itself is seen as an inevitable consequence of the doctrines of individual and collective ministerial responsibility. All too obviously, it is greatly to the advantage of the government of the day. Mistakes can be concealed from public gaze. Ill-considered policies, such as the now-notorious poll tax, can be rushed through Parliament. The Opposition's hands are tied through limited access to information. It may well be for this reason that the major political parties have not in the past endorsed the many attempts over the last twenty years to counter this tradition. Indeed, one former Cabinet minister declared that the public already had more information that it can handle, both that which the Government already makes available and the extensive leaks in the press. He frequently read full and accurate accounts of Cabinet meetings which he had attended in the national newspapers the following day, and asked what more the public could possibly wish to know.

Yet there are rifts in the tradition of secrecy. Both the Labour Party and the Liberal-Democrats, preparing for the 1992 general election, have made a clear commitment to legislating freedom of information. Despite the fact that senior civil servants have been brought up in the culture of secrecy, many would prefer more open government. The First Division Association has for some years been firmly committed to the introduction of freedom of information. Its resolution to the 1991 Trades Union Congress states:

Congress calls for the introduction in the United Kingdom of freedom of information through legislation establishing for citizens a statutory right of access to all official information, with provision for such information to be withheld only against specifically defined criteria. Where information is withheld a citizen should have the right of appeal to an independent review process with powers to order disclosure.

Congress recognizes that the introduction of freedom of information would no longer be a radical step but a rather well-proven reform which would bring the United Kingdom back in step with other countries such as the USA, Canada, Australia, New Zealand and France, where freedom of information is an established right underpinning democratic and accountable government.

Congress also urges a review of the Official Secrets Act and the reintroduction of a public interest defence.[23]

Quite apart from the commitment as a matter of principle on the part of the First Division Association, its members would benefit from it. For 'many of the dilemmas faced by individual civil servants would disappear if it was clear that in most cases official information was legitimately accessible to the press and public. There would be far less conflict between a civil servant's perception of his "public" or civic duty and his official obligations'.[24]

Freedom of Information in Britain − The Way Forward

The way forward is to establish in legislation the right of public access to government-held information and to allow only carefully defined exceptions to this fundamental principle, with an appropriate appeals system for those faced with the government's refusal to disclose information. In Sweden, whose principles of open government were first established in 1766, official information is disclosed not in response to individual requests but automatically and generally. The right of free access has not only become an integral part of the Swedish way of life, but is also part of the Swedish constitution. This ensures continued public access to government-held information, since even if the government of the day sought to limit access and got the legislation through Parliament, it would be ineffective if it clashed with constitutional law. The latter has to be passed twice by Parliament by a simple majority with a general election in between, and is thus distinguished from other laws.

Of course, the right of access to public documents is limited. The Freedom of the Press Act lists seven types of documents which may be classified as secret in order to protect certain kinds of interests. These include the security of the realm, relations with a foreign state or an international organization; central financial monetary or foreign exchange policy; the activities of a public authority for the purposes of inspection, control or other supervision; preventing or prosecuting crime; the economic interest of the State or local authorities; protecting individuals' personal integrity or economic conditions (though individuals can obtain information about themselves in public documents or on computer files), and preserving plant or animal species. It may well seem that such broad categories would give a government considerable freedom to insist that a wide range of documents should remain secret. But the justification for such a claim has to be found in the extremely detailed provisions of the Secrecy Act 1980, and can only be made by the authority, whether a local, or regional or central government board. The public have a general understanding of the documents which are likely to be kept secret – foreign policy and military affairs, State commercial transactions, the inspection and control of individuals and their medical and social treatment, as well as taxation.

The authority which holds the document has the sole right to decide whether or not to allow access to a document it holds. Access can only be refused on the basis of the authority's interpretation of the provisions of the Secrecy Act. However small and local the authority, it cannot turn to any higher authority for advice, since each authority is independent. If a member of the public is refused access to a particular document, he then has the right of appeal to one of the four regional administrative courts of appeal, and may take the issue further to the Supreme Administrative Court. The court has to study the document, interpret the relevant section of the Secrecy Act and assess the degree of risk to the interests which have to be protected under the Act. Judges in the administrative courts assess the strength of the alleged risk themselves; they do not bring in or consult any outside experts. The Supreme Court publishes an annual report on the most significant decisions they have made in the course of the year, which provides the authorities with further guidelines on the question of access.

No statistics are kept about the number of applications for access to documents to every Swedish authority in any given year; only the number of applications to the administrative courts. Requests for information of all kinds, ranging from personal files to matters relating to government policy, are referred to the administrative courts, to which any citizen may bring their application knowing that they will not incur any costs in so doing.

There are two kinds of government-held information; that relating to the Government, and that held by Parliament. All parliamentary documents are open to public view. A government document only comes into existence when it leaves the Chancery, of which the twenty or so ministries are divisions. Any application to see these documents must be made to the minister, who can refuse; and appeal can only be made to the Government as a whole but not to individual ministers. That could well be construed as an effective block on access to government documents, and in other cultures it could well operate in this way. It does so less in Sweden because there are other ways of gaining access to ministerial documents. Copies of most of these documents are held by other government agencies, which may well decide to grant access to them, and if the agency does not, then the applicant can appeal to the administrative courts, and finally to the Supreme Administrative Court. Journalists have been known to use the first method and to rely on the second only if they do not succeed in gaining access to ministerial documents through another agency.

The Swedish system probably leads to the most open form of government. Civil servants take it for granted that anything they put in writing is open to inspection by the public, more often by the press. Most government agencies have a press room where incoming and outgoing documents are displayed each day, and the media have, of course, learnt to identify and publicize the most important ones. Public discussions of the latter enhances the much more open process of policy-making there.

Plainly, access to files is very important from the point of view of the individual. It means that an ordinary citizen can so much more easily deal with any matter bringing them into conflict with the authorities. Compared with the rough ride too many people get from various public authorities in Britain, as any Member of Parliament knows from their constituency post-bags, the Swedish approach has obvious advantages. Access is, of course, backed up by the administrative courts, not only to ensure access but also to give the citizen redress for grievances.

Access to information on request is the usual system in those countries which have freedom of information legislation – Canada, Australia and New Zealand. The scope of the authorities covered by the legislation is limited in its application to only those authorities for which the federal government is responsible, and, in all cases excludes courts and tribunals, royal commissions and commissions of inquiry and state trading corporations. Canada restricts access to citizens and permanent residents; New Zealand excludes companies overseas and foreigners, but Australia extended access to government documents to all residents, companies and foreigners. Access may be granted to all kinds of records, including documents, plans, maps, tapes, computer records and videos, and in New Zealand it is possible to ask what happened at a meeting of which there is no record of any kind.

In all three countries, the public are denied access to certain kinds of information, typically, national security and defence; international relations; law enforcement; Cabinet discussions; civil service advice; legal advice; damage to the economy; commercial information; personal information and information protected by other statutes. In Australia and Canada, it is still an offence to reveal official information without authority, but the leaks continue unabated.

Three kinds of appeal have been established in Australia, New Zealand and Canada: to the courts which function as a second tier to a tribunal or to an ombudsman. The first step in appealing against the decision to refuse access to information is to appeal to the specialist commissioner in Canada, to the ombudsman in New Zealand and to a tribunal or the ombudsman in Australia. An ombudsman or commissioner can only recommend disclosure of documents, but a tribunal can order their release, and is therefore much more effective. A tribunal is better able to handle legal arguments over disclosure and the meaning of the freedom of information legislation and therefore builds up good case law. They are cheaper and quicker than the courts and produce much more case law than the latter. For that reason, applicants in Australia prefer the tribunal route and applications to the tribunal outnumber applications to the ombudsman by three to one. The barrier to access to information in Australia is the cost, about $30 per hour for the search for the information the applicant has requested. The costs are not prohibitive if the applicant knows exactly what to ask for, but a general or open request for information is too expensive for most applicants. For freedom of information legislation to work effectively it must be accompanied by good information systems within all government departments and agencies and low charges – not surprisingly the courts in the shape of an ombudsman in the former and a commissioner in the latter. Their powers are limited, though, since they can only recommend disclosure. They cannot order the release of government records. Australia set up a tribunal system as an alternative to an appeal to an ombudsman, and experience since then has shown that most people prefer the former for the reasons set out above.

The Australian experience suggests the system might work much more effectively if the ombudsman deals with minor delays and difficulties in gaining access to government records, and the tribunals handle the more complex cases, and also cases referred to them by the ombudsman, as the Senate Committee in Australia recommended.

This brief review of the freedom of information legislation introduced recently in Canada, Australia and New Zealand gives some idea of the pitfalls to be avoided in any future freedom of information bill in the UK. It must ensure that there is real, as opposed to nominal, access by providing an effective right of appeal against any refusal by the authorities to disclose information; and that the costs of any search should not be prohibitive. The signs are that the hourly charges in Australia are a real barrier to access to information which is theoretically available to the public.

An information commissioner and the commissioner's office can play a valuable role in advising the authorities on better and more precise documentation and good information retrieval systems. The latter is important in the British context, when, as Maurice Frankel points out, ministers with growing frequency claim that it is not possible to provide information in answer to written parliamentary questions. The cost limit is £250 per question, although ministers may decide to spend more, but, apart from the question about the administrative costs of the civil service referred to in Chapter 1, the Government has also refused to answer questions about details of defence procurement projects on which money has been spent in the last five years, but which have not directly resulted in equipment being adopted by the armed services[25] and a question about how much TV advertising time the department had purchased from each ITV network on grounds of costs.[26] Plainly, if this is truly the case, Whitehall needs much better information systems than it apparently has at its disposal. It does not bear comparison with the costs of freedom of information legislation in Australia and Canada of around £7 million a year.

Wherever freedom of information legislation has been introduced, it has given the citizen a vital weapon in the fight against 'sloppy standards, lame excuses and attitudes that patronize the public', to use Prime Minister Major's words. It has provided the citizen with a weapon to protect himself against safety hazards or discrimination in the allocation of contracts or the enforcement of standards; to ensure that he is not being denied benefits through error or arbitrary action, and to ensure that his money as a taxpayer is not being wasted on expensive, prestigious but unnecessary projects. The Citizens Charter, produced by the Conservative Government in July 1991, promised to 'give more power to the citizen ... [it] is not a recipe for more State action; it is a testament of our belief in people's right to be informed and choose for themselves. The White Paper sets out the mechanics for improving choice, quality, value and accountability. Not all apply to every service. But all have a common objective: to raise the standard of public services, up to and beyond the best at present available.'[27]

The Prime Minister recognized the vital importance of information in the Charter when he addressed the Conservative Women's Conference a month before the Charter was presented to the public. He promised that the Charter would meet the public demand for full and clear information about services and how they performed. But when the Charter was published it did not contain any such commitment. Whitehall will once more decide what information the public will be given.

There can be no real charter for citizens without the right of public access. To make sure that the right to know is fully utilized the Act should be accompanied by programmes of education to explain that the Act exists, how it works, what it does and how citizens can best use it. Freedom of information must be accompanied by changes in attitude if society is to be better informed and more open. Establishing the right to know is part of that process. And it is certain that, without the right to know, democracy cannot flourish.

Notes

[1] J. Redlich, 'The Procedure of the House of Commons', Vol. I, pp. 57, 207, in R. Chapman and M. Hunt (eds), *Open Government*, 1987.
[2] Official Secrets Act 1889, Section 2.
[3] Departmental Committee in Section 2 of the Official Secrets Act, 1911, Cmnd 5104, Vol. 1, 1972, para. 50.
[4] ibid., para. 88.
[5] D. Wilson, 'Not in the Public Interest', *The Times*, 1 December 1988.
[6] Official Secrets Act 1989, clauses 2–6.
[7] E. Heath, *Spectator*, 10 March 1989.
[8] White Paper, 1988, CM408, p. 12.
[9] ibid., p. 13.
[10] HC Deb., 21 December 1988, col. 479.
[11] White Paper, 1988, CM408, p. 7.
[12] HC Deb., 2 February 1989, col. 491.
[13] E. Heath, *Spectator* op. cit.
[14] White Paper 1988, paras 58–61.
[15] Attorney General *v. Guardian* Newspapers, 1988, No. 2, 3 Aller, 545–6.
[16] quotes from Richard Shepherd's Protection of Official Information Bill, 1988.
[17] Home Secretary's Statement on publication of the Shepherd Bill.
[18] Edward Heath, *Spectator*, op. cit.
[19] R. Hazell, 'Freedom of Information in Australia, Canada and New Zealand', *Public Administration*, 1989, Vol. 67, No. 2, pp. 189–210.

[20] Defence Select Committee, Fifth Report, minutes of the Evidence, session 1990–91, HC 393, p. 9.
[21] E. Russell, Report for the Campaign for Freedom of Information, published in 'Secrets', No. 22, July 1991.
[22] private information.
[23] Resolution submitted to the 1991 TUC Congress by the FDA.
[24] R. Holme, Memorandum to the Treasury and Civil Service Select Committee, 'Civil Servants and Ministers: Duties and Responsibilities', Vol. 2, HC 92, p. 330.
[25] HC Deb. 160, col. 187, 14 November 1989.
[26] quoted by M. Frankel; N. Lewis (ed), *Parliamentary Accountability, Happy and Glorious: The Constitution in Transition*, 1990, pp. 37–8.
[27] The Citizen's Charter, Raising the Standard, July 1991, CM 1599.

EIGHT

Looking to the Future

Whitehall and the European Community

The whole environment in which Whitehall operates could well change dramatically during the 1990s, not only as a result of the establishment of the Single Market, but also with the development of economic and monetary union. This will inevitably bring about further changes in the management and culture of Whitehall. It is, however, not often recognized that the decision-making process in the European Community already has a considerable impact on policy formation in Whitehall, requiring effective cooperation between departments as well as responsiveness to developments within the Community.

The European Secretariat of the Cabinet Office selects or accepts the issues requiring interdepartmental discussion, organizes all the necessary meetings and back-up, and ensures that ministers are aware of, and deal with, all the key problems. Altogether, the Cabinet Office chairs about 200 meetings a year on Community issues and circulates over 300 papers, since so many more Whitehall departments are involved in negotiating and implementing the 300 or so Community directives, which will bring about the Single Market by 1 January 1993.

Whitehall's role is primarily a reactive one, developing a British response to the Commission's initiatives, which must inevitably be in line with the Government's overall objectives. Not all of the discussions relate to specific directives, but to the ongoing policies of the Community, such as the Common Agricultural Policy. The Foreign and Commonwealth Office keeps a watching brief on the overall development of the European Community policy, but could not take on the role of the European Secretariat in the Cabinet Office, because the former has 'a particular departmental point of view on EC issues. They could not do this and at the same time hold the ring in Whitehall discussions."

Once decisions have been taken, the Foreign Office plays its particular role in the process of coordinating policy, since UKRep. Brussels, its branch there, rather than an ambassador (or permanent representative), is responsible for carrying out instructions as well as helping to formulate them. Its members of staff usually attend weekly meetings at the Cabinet Office to discuss tactics for dealing with any current issues of concern. Civil servants, far more than ministers, are deeply involved in negotiating the details of draft directives and regulations. Parliament plays no part in this process at all; Community negotiations by-pass it completely.

Most Whitehall departments now find themselves taking a lead in negotiations on the many directives on one or other aspect of the Single Market, but frequently involve several departments. For example, the Treasury took the lead on the directive to liberalize public purchasing by utilities (which was adopted by the Council in September 1990), but the Department of Trade and Industry, the Departments of Energy, Environment and Transport and, of course, the Foreign and Commonwealth Office, had a major part to play in the whole process of discussion in interdepartmental meetings arranged by the Cabinet Office. These discussions led to an agreement on the line to be taken in Brussels.

The demands of the Single Market have increased the workload in Whitehall, and the speed with which draft directives are considered and then adopted by the Council of Ministers. These now take two to three years instead of well over ten; the Non-Life Insurance Services Directive was adopted in 1988 about seventeen years after the proposal had first been tabled, the Second Banking Directive was adopted in 1989 within three years of its first being drafted.

Of course, long before a draft directive is considered by the Council, the government of the day has sought to influence the proposals for legislation through its civil servants in Brussels and from Whitehall. The draft directives themselves are the result of a long process of consultation with leading representatives of Euro-level interest groups, national experts, senior civil servants and politicians (where appropriate). There is a continuing exchange of views between Commission officials and civil servants from national bureaucracies in an informal way or through COREPER, the Committee of Permanent Representatives of ambassadorial rank. Once the directive has been considered and possibly amended by the European Parliament and then adopted by the Council of Ministers, it has to be implemented by the national parliaments of the member states and incorporated into their legislation. Margaret Thatcher took pride in the fact that, by 1989, Britain led the way in the implementation in national legislation of the directives constituting the Single Market.

These descriptions of Whitehall's arrangements for handling EC directives suggest that the process of policy formation is essentially reactive. The Government and the Whitehall machine appear to respond to the Commission's initiatives, instead of developing policy within a Community perspective. That can sometimes lead to serious errors, as with the 1988 Merchant Shipping Act, which introduced restrictions to prevent foreign owners of ships from 'quota-hopping' by registering their ships under British flags and then fishing British quotas. The European Court of Justice ruled that member states must comply with the rules of Community law, since which it follows that Part II of the Act has to be set aside, since Community law must prevail according to the Community Treaties. The ruling itself should have been anticipated, and the Government should not have introduced the restrictions it did, whatever the political advantages. Nor should the European Court's decision have caused the fluttering in the political dovecotes that it did.

The reactive approach adopted in Whitehall does mean that the Government does not have the influence in the early stages of drafting directives that it should have. It is alleged that this is because 'the British government has taken a deliberate decision not to send its top administrative talent to the decision-making machinery in Brussels ... The British ... seem to ignore the claims of long-serving British Eurocrats who operate more effectively than any newcomer within the Brussels corridors of power ... The result is that a number of line jobs – where, say, the first submission is made on a price of interest to British farmers – quietly go to non-Brits ... Overall, it means that British influence on decision-making in the Commission is significantly less than some of the other member states.'[2]

No single national government can set the agenda, since that is determined by the Commission's own programme, pressures from the European Parliament, Council decisions, external events and the priorities of the Presidency in office, to name but a few. Recently some Presidencies, such as Luxembourg in the first part of 1991, have attempted to set their stamp on Community developments. Bender claims that 'in the second decade of UK membership of the EC we [have] learned how to influence this process and found ourselves about to argue much more with the grain of EC policies and priorities than we had in the first decade ...', and that 'of the eight major issues facing the Community', such as 'completing the Single Market, successful conclusion of the GATT/Uruguay round, relations with EFTA, relations with Eastern Europe, German unification, the Social Action programme and Preparation of the Inter-Governmental Conference on Institutional Reform/Political Union, the UK is in the forefront of EC opinion or the mainstream on five, while three of the issues, EMU, Political Union and the Social Action Programme would not be on the agendas of the UK's devising.'[3] The claim is an extraordinary one, since, for example, Mrs Thatcher, the then Prime Minister, thought that German reunification was years away and the last three items are all fundamental to future developments in the Community in the eyes of all the other member states. The responsibility for the failure to judge the readiness for progress in the Community lies partly with the Government's advisers, comforting themselves with doses of Euro-scepticism, especially about the speed of these developments, but primarily with the politicians.

The scepticism arises from the failure to appreciate the forces for change set in motion by the Single European Act, which is designed to complete the Single Market in 1992 by removing the physical, technical and fiscal barriers to trade within the Community, and to reach agreement on the necessary steps by extending qualified majority voting. This Single Market is required if the European Monetary System (now the Exchange Rate Mechanism) is to be maintained, bearing in mind that its original purpose was 'to maintain exchange rates between the currencies as stable as possible in order to foster monetary and price stability as well as intra-European trade and thereby also economic integration within the boundaries of the European Community'.[4] In view of the Commission, the EMS provided the 'necessary framework' for 'progress towards economic policy convergence'.[5] That convergence made both the Single Market possible and the barriers to trade an obstacle to economic growth. At the same time, the system of fixed exchange rates, with its advantage of price stability, eventually deprives an open economy of its long-term monetary independence. This is the dynamic which has led to the proposals to establish economic and monetary union, Stage 1 of which will include the full implementation of the Single European Act, closer coordination of economic and monetary policies, the abolition of exchange controls and the entry by all member states into the ERM. Stages 2 and 3 raise the most controversial issues. Stage 2 as envisaged by the Delors Report includes the establishment of a European Central Bank, and precise, but not binding, Community rules on national budget deficits; and Stage 3, the introduction of a single currency, this last stage to be reached by 1997.

The precise nature of these proposals has to be decided in the forthcoming Inter-Governmental Conference in December 1991 at Maastricht.

Once a common currency area has been established, then there has to be a common monetary and debt management policy, which could easily be disrupted by one of the member states running up large budget deficits. The Commission has proposed in its draft treaty that multinational guidelines be issued to member states concerning their budget balances as well as other aspects of its economic and budgetary policy. The Community will not bale out any member state which fails to comply by allowing it to finance budget deficits 'by direct assistance from Eurofed or through privileged access by the public authorities to the capital market', or 'by granting [it] ... an unconditional guarantee', though member states in difficulties may be given assistance through a Community support programme of some kind.[6] The Commission does not, however, spell out what action the Community should take against a member state which refuses to comply, or what counts as an excessive budgetary deficit. The French and the Germans have prepared draft treaties which deal with these substantial issues, but the British have not tackled these problems at all to date, preferring to stand by the 'hard ecu' plan and the belief that the introduction of a single currency will be long delayed, which is not the consensus amongst experts.

The Commission also deals with the transition to Stage 3, that is, the move to a single currency. The decision has to be taken by the Council of Ministers on the basis of reports produced by the Commission and the Central Bank to the effect that the 'conditions for moving from the transitional period to the final stage of economic and monetary union have been met.'[7] The ECU would then become the single currency of the Community, and exchange rates would be fixed irrevocably. This decision has to be taken by the Council acting unanimously. The Commission has not defined what counts as the appropriate kind of convergence before the move to Stage 3 could take place, although the French Government, and the German Government in particular, sought to set out the criteria for convergence, such as a high level of price stability, close alignment of interest rates and the reduction of budget deficits to a level which can be sustained in the long term and is consistent with stability.

Linked with these developments, the Draft Statute of the Committee of Governors of the Central Banks proposes the establishment of an independent Central Bank of the European Community. The Bank is modelled on the Bundesbank, and would exercise its powers entirely independently of 'Community institutions, governments of Member States or any other body'.[8] It is unclear, however, whether this applies to the exchange rate. The European Central Bank is due to be established at the beginning of Stage 2 in January 1994, but the British Government baulks at the idea of a Central Bank which is entirely independent of political control and which has such wide responsibilities for the management of monetary and economic policy. The British Government put up alternative proposals for the 'hard ecu' in an attempt to avoid any set timetable for moves towards economic and monetary union, but it is unlikely to make headway with these plans.

Economic and Monetary Union

The establishment of economic and monetary union plainly has fundamental implications for the structure of the European Community and for its democratic processes. The existence of the 'democratic deficit' was acknowledged by Jacques Delors, the President of the Commission, in a speech to the European Parliament on 6 July 1988 in which he expressed his surprise that national parliaments, apart from Germany and Britain, had not yet realized the displacement of decision-making to the centre and that in ten years' time, 80 per cent of economic and perhaps even fiscal and social legislation will be of Community origin. In the early 1980s, it was the widely accepted view that the democratic legitimacy of the Community has been settled by direct elections to the European Parliament, first held in 1979.

The elected European Parliament then began to challenge the democratic legitimacy of the other institutions of the Community, and demanded a greater part in the legislation process. The Council of Ministers is not accountable to the European Parliament, nor can Council members effectively be held accountable at the national level to their national parliaments for legislative decisions. It is the supreme legislative body of the Community; its members negotiate and decide on vital policy issues for the Community as a whole, but which directly affect both member states and their citizens, yet its proceedings are held in secret. 'In short, the Euro-elections have not justified the manner in which political power is exercised in the EC: they have challenged it. It took a long time for national political élites to recognize the persistence of the democratic deficit.'[9] The 'democratic deficit' arises from the limited role the European Parliament plays in the legislative process and the fact that national parliaments, such as the British Parliament, have little opportunity to scrutinize EC legislation, and has virtually no powers to change any of the decisions of the Community.

The European Parliament itself, following the Single European Act (which took effect in British law under the 1972 European Communities Act by means of the European Communities (Amendment) Act, 1986), acquired a more influential role in the legislative process in the 'cooperation procedure', which involves dividing the legislative process into first and second readings. At the first stage, the Parliament can only give an 'opinion', which the Council of Ministers has before it when it adopts a 'common position'. When the Council of Ministers arrives at a common position, the second stage of the procedure is set in motion. At this stage the European Parliament may reject or amend the common position on a majority vote. The Commission then has to re-examine its position and puts forward another proposal taking account of the Parliament's views. The Council of Ministers may then decide to adopt the resubmitted proposal by a qualified majority. But if the Council wishes to change the new proposal or reinstate the one rejected or amended by the Parliament, it can only do so by unanimity. These powers are in addition to its original but limited powers over the Budget to alter or increase it within legally defined limits or to reject it completely, which it has done from time to time. When that happens the Community continues with its expenditure under the 'twelfths system'. A two-thirds majority of the Parliament can dismiss the whole Commission, but these powers are so draconian that they have never been used. The 'democratic deficit' clearly arises from the limited powers the European Parliament has over the executive of the Community, the Council of Ministers, and the fact that the national parliaments play virtually no part in the Community's legislation or in its executive decisions.

National leaders have finally recognized that economic and monetary union and extending the competence of the Commission to other spheres such as social policy requires clear democratic legitimacy. The European Council meetings of April and June 1990 decided to convene a second and parallel Inter-Governmental Conference (IGC) to deal with the issue of political union. This was in response to the Kohl–Mitterand letter of April 1990, which set out the major issues which the second IGC should discuss. These are to examine ways of making the Community institutions more effective, to ensure the unity and coherence of the Community's activity in the economic, monetary and political areas, and to define and implement a common foreign and security policy. The Conference will also consider ways of reinforcing the democratic legitimacy of the Community.

The Inter-Governmental Conference on Political Union has been under way since the European Council meetings in April and June 1990. Community foreign ministers, the Commission and the national parliaments all contributed preliminary studies during 1990, with the original aim of establishing Economic and Monetary Union and Political Union on 1 January 1991. The original aim was overtaken by events, with the decision of the Rome Summit in October 1990 to 'progressively transform the Community into a European Union'. The Commission set out its proposals for European Political Union, which include extending majority voting to cover almost all of the Community's competence. The Commission document stressed the importance of the 'principle of subsidiarity' which would '[leave] Member States full powers in matters which have not been deemed necessary for the Union, subject to recourse to inter-governmental cooperation for questions of general interest'.[10] Out of these and other submissions from member states, the European Parliament and the conference of the Parliaments of the Community, held in Rome in November 1990, came the Presidency conclusions at the end of the December Rome Summit, which were that five major subjects should be considered at the Inter-Governmental Conference. These consist of democratic legitimacy, common foreign and security policy, European citizenship, extension and strengthening of Community action, the effectiveness and efficiency of the Union.

The Inter-Governmental Conference in Luxembourg in June 1991 merely reiterated the principles guiding the development of the Community which had already been laid down six months before. Decisions about the 'defence identity' of the Community were postponed until the Maastricht conference in December 1991. The European Council agreed that the European Parliament's political, legislative and monitoring role should be strengthened as part of the development of the Union, and that agreement must be reached on the co-decision procedure, which in the view of some member states is an essential part of establishing a more democratic Community. The final decision about the Treaty on Political Union and on Economic and Monetary Union was taken by the Maastricht European Council in December 1991 so that the results of the two Inter-Governmental Conferences can be submitted for ratification during 1992 and the new Treaty will come into force on 1 January 1993 with a further European Council in 1996, which will examine the institutions of the Community to deal with the 'democratic deficit' and to look at the changes which may be necessary as a result of the enlargement of the Community.

Apart from that, the Maastricht conference agreed that full economic and monetary union would be established by 1999, provided that a minimum of seven member states agreed. The conference also decided that the Community should have a common foreign and security policy with elements of majority voting; a common immigration policy and to extend the competence of the Community to deal with certain elements of economic, health, education and cultural policies. The conference decided to extend the powers of the European Parliament, giving it the right of veto over certain decisions taken by the Council of Ministers, provided the latter were subject to majority voting and not unanimity. To the amazement of the other eleven members of the Community, Britain refused to sign the Social Charter (concerned with employment rights). To rescue the whole Maastricht conference, the Social Charter was removed from the Treaty and instead became a protocol of the Treaty signed by eleven out of the twelve member states. Maastricht therefore marks a significant step towards economic and monetary union and even towards political union as well.

The Loss of Sovereignty

The two Treaties on Economic and Monetary Union and on Political Union imply fundamental changes in the nature of the European Community and will have a significant impact on the status of the member states. But just how these two Treaties and subsequent developments will alter the status of the member states has to be determined. In Britain, attention has focused on the issue of sovereignty and the potential loss of it if all the proposals currently under consideration within the Community are accepted. Indeed, the debate in this country has been described as amounting to an 'obsession', a 'dangerous distraction from facing up to real problems'.[11]

Couching the entire debate in these terms prevents Britain from making any constructive contribution to the debate on the future shape of the Community. The initiative has been taken by France and Germany, with an entirely negative and sceptical response from Britain. The forces for change were set in motion by the Single European Act, the logic of which demands structural changes in the process of decision-making in the Community. The need for such a debate is merely obscured by the 'obsession' with sovereignty.

This obsession is due in part to the fact that, as the Foreign Affairs Select Committee concluded, 'The British notion of sovereignty differs from that of our European partners. Since it is derived from a different historical experience, ours is founded not necessarily upon a concept of national identity but upon a very particular definition of sovereignty arising from our parliamentary history and procedure. This "parliamentary"

definition of sovereignty is not shared by most of our European parliamentary colleagues.'[12] It is quite simply the traditional definition of
parliamentary sovereignty as Parliament's 'right to make and unmake any
law whatsoever' and the claim that no one else has the 'right to override
or set aside the legislation of Parliament' to use Dicey's words to describe
one of the fundamental doctrines of constitutional law in the United
Kingdom.[13] Any discussion of political integration of the Community in
terms of a loss of sovereignty in this sense is plainly sterile. The European Court of Justice stresses the fact that Community law must be
uniformly applicable throughout the Community. 'The law stemming
from the treaty, an independent source of law, could not, because of
its special and original nature, be overridden by domestic legal provisions,
however framed, without being deprived of its character as Community
law and without the legal basis of the Community being called into
question.'[14]

Parliament has already ceded the right to the Community to make
decisions and issue regulations which override legislation by Parliament.
That decision was taken in 1972, when Parliament passed the European
Communities Act, and repeated when that Act was amended in 1986,
extending the Community's powers over the British Parliament. In theory,
Parliament could reverse these decisions and repeal these two Acts of
Parliament. In practice it is extremely unlikely that this will happen, just
because Britain's economy, after almost twenty years of membership of
the Community, is closely integrated with that of the other member states.
But the debate continues as though sovereignty is an absolutist conception,
deriving from the notion of Parliament as the sole law-making body.
Sovereignty, as Mrs Thatcher's speeches suggested, is something you either
have or you do not have. Sovereignty can be lost to a European Political
Union, but not shared within such a Union on this view.

Parliamentary sovereignty, in the terms in which Dicey described it, is
plainly a myth, since Parliament has already, albeit voluntarily, limited its
powers by virtue of the international agreements into which the Government has entered and which Parliament has endorsed. In the case of
membership of the European Community, 'acceptance of the Treaty of
Rome carries with it a permanent limitation of [the member states']
sovereign rights'.[15] As the *acquis communitaire* (that is, the Community rules
in the relevant areas laid down by the Treaties, by Council and Commission
legislation and case law − the achievements of the Community, in other
words) has continued to accumulate, member states have accepted further
limitations on their powers because they consider it to be in their national

interest. Once that has been recognized, then the discussion about sovereignty can take the only appropriate form at this stage – that is, the political rather than the legal sense of the term, the only sense in which sovereignty can be 'shared' or 'pooled'. The pooling of sovereignty therefore refers to the joint use of political power. That can be seen as a matter of choice for member states, a choice which they will exercise if they consider it to be to their advantage to do so, though they may not always be realistic about the extent to which they have effective powers.

It is in this field of monetary policy that governments are most likely to delude themselves. As Lord Jenkins, former President of the European Council and former Chancellor, put it in his evidence to the House of Lords Select Committee: 'As far as governments are concerned as opposed to parliaments, monetary policy, interest rate policy, and an exchange rate policy are the supreme field in which you can cling to the shadow of sovereignty but the substance has flown out of your grasp some time ago.'[16] Parliament is certainly 'deluding itself if it thinks it has control over monetary policy'[17] and, specifically, it has little control over budgetary deficits and government borrowing. The conclusion is plain: parliamentary sovereignty is not at risk and there is nothing to prevent the Government from entering into economic and monetary union from the point of view of state sovereignty. Lacking control over monetary policy as a sovereign state, a member state has little to lose and may have much to gain by sharing power in such a union.

A decision of this kind can only be made by a sovereign state in the sense of the terms used in international law, where it is used to refer to the characteristics of a state. It must have a settled population, a defined territory, independence in conducting international relations and it must have power and authority to uphold internal legal order. A sovereign state can transfer or pool sovereignty, but the question of whether or not a state has transferred or pooled sovereignty has been obscured by the 'Luxembourg compromise', an agreement reached in 1966 at the instigation of de Gaulle. It was not a formal agreement in the sense of being part of the Treaties of the Community, nor did it meet with the approval of all the member states. The Luxembourg compromise allowed a member state to veto any issue which it regarded as clashing with its fundamental national importance. The Luxembourg compromise undoubtedly influenced, and some would say, stunted the development of the Community between 1966 and 1984. Both Britain and Denmark found the Luxembourg compromise made their membership of the Community more congenial: it meant that they could veto proposals they did not like, and all decisions required unanimity and therefore a long drawn-out process of reaching consensus.

In 1985, the European Council came to its momentous decision to complete the internal market by 1992, though its far-reaching implications were understood by few at the time. The Council also decided to establish the Single Market by qualified majority voting, since allowing the veto to continue and to reach consensus on the 300 or so directives would mean that the internal market would never be established. The Council and the Commission were also responding to external pressures such as the globalization of the market and fierce competition from other trading blocs, together with the recession 1979–84. The Commission and the Council realized that decision-making in the Community would have to be speeded up, and the ponderous bureaucracy of harmonizing regulations abandoned. All of these pressures and considerations combined to produce the Draft Treaty of European Union in 1984, the Single European Act of 1985 and the decisive move towards majority voting. Under the new arrangements sovereign states would no longer strike deals with each other, often at head of governmental level. They would, instead, pool sovereignty, an entirely different process. It is this shift which has caused consternation and misunderstanding in the British debate about the future of Europe.

The commitment to establish the Single Market by 1992 led to 'dynamic adjustment processes in the economic sphere whose political repercussions have all the force of a self-fulfilling prophecy'.[18] The economic consequences are plain enough, but the political consequences are also momentous. As a result, the way in which decisions are made in the Community has become vitally important in a way in which it was not and could not be prior to the Single European Act. Abandoning the right of veto on Community proposals, and therefore the right of national governments to protect national interests, means that it is even more important to ensure that the Community's decision-making processes are democratic.

The Democratic Deficit

The British Government currently rejects the view that there is a democratic deficit in the Community, generally defined as the gap between the powers transferred to the Community and the effectiveness of the European Parliament's oversight and control. Underlying this view is the belief that the European Parliament should not have such a role, which usurps the function of the national parliament. The Community should, of course, be democratic, but that democracy should be exercised through accountability. National governments represented in the Council should be accountable to their national parliaments and through them to the people they represent. The advantage of this approach, according to the Thatcher and Major governments, is that it preserves national sovereignty in the sense of parliamentary sovereignty in a way which is simply not possible through the European Parliament. The Government acknowledges that the latter is democratic, since it is, after all, directly elected, but is suspicious of this institution because it is supra-national. The only way to deal with the democratic deficit in the Community is to strengthen the Council's accountability to national parliaments. The Government therefore welcomed the proposals of the Select Committee on Procedure to reform the scrutiny procedures for proposed European Community legislation and other Community activities.

No doubt any such improvements are welcome, but they do not address the fundamental issues at all. The House of Commons spends a considerable time on Community matters with its debates on proposed legislation: debates on the Government's six-monthly reports on developments in the European Community, which now allow for a discussion of developments up to the time of debate, so the debates have a more contemporaneous air than they had in the past; ministerial and Prime Ministerial statements on Council of Ministers and European Council meetings; general Foreign Affairs debates and *ad hoc* debates on major Community issues as and when they arise. It is rare indeed for such debates to lead to votes of any kind, and even if they did, the Government would not be bound by them. The fact remains that the House of Commons has no part to play in shaping the content of the Community legislation, which will play an increasing part in the lives of British citizens. They do not initiate such legislation since that is the role of the Commission, and the Commission's proposals become law if the Council of Ministers so decides, although the European Parliament does have a part to play through the cooperation procedure. Nor is Parliament in a position to comment on draft legislation in time; sometimes the drafts are out of date, or insufficient texts are available, or the texts arrive so late that hardly anyone taking part in the debates has time to read them properly. It is increasingly difficult for national parliaments to keep up with the speed and volume of EC legislation, particularly since consideration of amendments to the proposed legislation has become so much more important. 'Time, different legislative timetables, and the different nature and work of national parliaments all militate against them making an effective input into the daily EC legislative process. In 1988, the Commons' Scrutiny Committees received over 800 reports, and managed to consider only 109 of them in 39 debates. Commons scrutiny of EC legislation is largely symbolic and will remain so.'[19]

As far as the Council of Ministers or the European Council are concerned, Parliament can only hold the Government to account for decisions which have already been taken, but cannot impose its will on the government of the day. The Government reports to Parliament after the event. Within the Council of Ministers, national governments may find themselves out-voted or may need to make certain stances through political expediency or because certain bargains have to be struck. Parliament can have no say over such actions and has to accept the Government's account of the proceedings, since the Council meetings are held in secret and are not subject to public examination. Whatever changes are made in Parliament, they cannot provide any effective scrutiny or control, a fact of which the Government must be aware.

If strengthening parliamentary procedures in the British Parliament, and indeed in other national parliaments, does not provide the way forward in overcoming the democratic deficit, then attention naturally turns to the European Parliament. The elected members of the European Parliament, 518 in all, do not constitute national delegations, but are members of Community-wide political parties and much of their time is taken up with party meetings and party committees, providing them with entirely different networks across the Community from those of members of the national parliaments.

The European Parliament has some powers over the Community Budget, as we have seen, but, unlike the parliaments of member states, it has no power to raise taxes. The European Parliament has been able to use its powers over the Community Budget to good effect, and the areas of the Budget over which the Parliament can exercise detailed control has been increased. The cooperation procedure has improved parliamentary scrutiny of the Commission's proposed legislation and provides an opportunity for amending it. But Parliament cannot initiate legislation, and even its power to influence proposals for legislation is marginal. The Commissioner and his or her 'cabinet' consult widely before tabling draft legislation, but they consult the committees of experts, composed largely of national civil servants in a non-official capacity of which there may be over 500 at any one time, and receive delegations from interested parties of all kinds. They may consult Members of the European Parliament, especially influential ones, but Commissioners may well not consider it essential to do so. After wide consultation, the Commission puts its draft proposals to the Committee of Permanent Representatives, which meet for two to three days per week. Their working groups consider every aspect of the Commission's proposals, and may even decide the outcome without the proposals ever being presented to the Council of Ministers, and the latter may merely decide to accept COREPER's recommendations without discussing them. Once the Council has adopted the Commission's proposals, regulation, management and consultation committees examine the process of implementation before the legislation reaches the national administrations.

It is clear from this account that the European Parliament has only a bit-part in the whole process and indeed that is true of democracy as well. The process of policy-making does involve wide consultation, hence the exponential growth in lobbying in Brussels, but it is bureaucrats and not politicians whom the lobbyists target.

This is the democratic gap which must be closed. Most national politicians have no part to play in the whole process, nor do members of the European Parliament. 'The "losers" are the parliamentarians and parties; their patterns of interaction have not developed resources and forms comparable to those of national bureaucrats and [governmental] politicians.'[20] The European Parliament is intensely critical of the inefficiency of the Community's decision-making processes and of the 'dilatoriness of the Council in its legislative role'. It has proposed in three reports from the European Parliament Institutional Affairs Committee, whose rapporteur was David Martin, the Labour MEP for East Lothian, that the European Parliament should be an equal partner with the Commission in a Political Union, proposals which were later supported by the 'Assizes'.

The Commission in its 'opinion' has taken account of some of these proposals and has suggested further changes to the procedure of adopting draft proposals for legislation. These include incorporating the Parliament's amendments in the Commission's proposals which, once resubmitted, could be rejected by a simple majority. The Commission also recommended that the cooperation procedure should apply to all the new areas of policy to which qualified majority voting is to apply. It even envisages a role for the European Parliament in Commission appointments, such as appointing a Commission President on the basis of a recommendation from the European Council; appointing Commission members by agreement between the states after consulting the President; and then allowing the Parliament to confirm the whole Commission, having considered its programme. The Commission, in other words, has primarily considered details of the legislative procedure. The Kohl–

Mitterand Declaration did not conduct a detailed examination of parliamentary procedure or rules for the appointment of Commissioners, but suggested that the European Parliament's role should be extended into one of co-decision on legislation.

The Conference of the Parliaments of the European Community, the 'Assizes', met at Rome in November 1990. It consisted of meetings between 85 MEPs and 173 MPs, including 26 from the UK (interestingly enough, the national delegations of MPs soon broke up into transnational party groupings). The Assizes concluded that 'in order to carry out the new tasks facing it at the monetary level and in external relations, the Community must transform itself into a European Union in order to meet the requirements of democracy, which entails adapting its Institutions and other bodies'.[21] To this end, the European Parliament must play an equal part with the Council in the legislative and budgetary functions of the Union and its assent must be sought for all significant international agreements. The Assizes also recommends cooperation between the national parliaments and the European Parliament through regular meetings of specialized committees and conferences of parliaments. Not surprisingly the Conference of Parliaments supported the European Parliaments in the role it demands in the appointment of commissioners. Above all, the parliamentarians of the Community call for meetings of the Council in its legislative role to be open to the public and for it to act by majority voting except in connection with amendments to the Treaties, the accession of new member states and extension of powers. This is only to be expected from parliamentarians whose own proceedings are broadcast, televised, reported in the media, observed by the public, and all of whom would regard it as entirely undemocratic to hold their debates in private.

All of these proposals were considered in the run-up to the June Summit during the Inter-Governmental Conference on European Political Union. Monthly meetings at ministerial level took place, but the negotiations were designed to take place in secret. Some of the papers submitted by individual states were published by Agence Europe. The German-Italian Declaration supported the co-decision procedure; giving the European Parliament a right of initiative and participation in the nomination of the Commission; a larger part to play in the Community's international agreements and more control over the powers of the Commission, especially in the management of Community finances. It also supports the principle of the European Parliament's participation in revising Treaties, the power to instigate investigations into breaches of EC law and the right of Community citizens to submit petitions to the European Parliament. These and other submissions led to the Luxembourg Presidency of the IGC on European Parliamentary Union presentation of a 'non-paper' or draft treaty of articles 'with a view to achieving political union'.

The Luxembourg Draft Treaty

The Luxembourg draft Treaty covers a wide range of issues, including cooperation on home affairs and judicial cooperation, social policy, economic and social cohesion, European citizenship, research and development, subsidiarity, energy, public health and education, the environment, transport, consumer and cultural protection and development cooperation. But the most controversial chapters of the Treaty deal with the joint decision-making procedure and foreign and security policy. The former builds on the present Treaty cooperation procedure, with the significant difference being that in the event of any disagreement the final decision rests with the Council and the European Parliament on an equal footing. A failure on the part of the Conciliators and persistent disagreement would result in the whole process starting all over again. The co-decision procedure would remove the Commission's right to initiate legislation, thus alerting the institutional balance as laid down in the original Treaties. These proposals do not find favour with the Commission itself. Jacques Delors no doubt expressed the views of the Commissioner when he claims that these proposals would reduce the Commission to little more than a 'general secretariat', and that the co-decision formula would be a 'serious infringement' of the fundamental principles of the Treaties.

The Luxembourg Summit did not take any final decisions about the Luxembourg 'non-paper' or indeed about any of the proposals concerning European Political Union. These decisions are expected to be taken at the Maastricht Summit in December 1991. Whatever form the final proposals take, it is vital that measures are taken to overcome the democratic deficit by increasing the powers of the European Parliament to carry out valid legislative control and scrutiny functions. Indeed, the 'democratic deficit in the EC can only be remedied if the three key actors in the legislative process cooperate in an open and constructive manner. The issue is not, therefore, democracy as an end in itself but how the EC can be managed in a responsible, responsive, open and democratic manner to ensure that it serves the interests of its component parts and citizens under complex and difficult conditions'.[22]

There is, however, a serious problem with one of the proposed ways of overcoming the democratic deficit, the co-decision procedure. The proposal itself has not won the unequivocal support of all the member states. Belgium, Ireland and the Netherlands, in particular, consider that the draft Treaty weakens the role of the Commission in unacceptable ways. Apart from criticisms of this kind, the proposed co-decision procedure is complicated and cumbersome and could impede the decision-making process in the Community. The whole point of the Single European Act was to streamline decision-making in the Community, to enable it to overcome the creeping 'Euro-sclerosis' of the early 1980s so that the Community could respond more quickly to structural changes in the world economy.

The Single European Act took the Community forward, but in turn the logic of the single market requires a single currency and inevitably economic and monetary union. Decisions about what would then have to be a single monetary policy will then have to be taken centrally; hence the Community's decision to establish a Central Bank of Europe, although, at the time of writing, its political independence has yet to be agreed by member states. The implications of a single monetary policy for the whole Community are far-reaching since a single currency imposes fiscal and budgetary disciplines on the member stages. The former President of the Bundesbank, Karl Otto Pohl, emphasized the necessity of a very 'high degree of economic cohesion and convergence' for monetary union, which 'might take rather a long time, if one takes into account the difference in the economic, social and cultural environment of member states'[23] but despite that, 'one cannot wait and should not wait for the last ship in the convoy, so to speak'.[24]

There is, however, considerable disagreement about the nature of economic convergence, whether it should refer only to what many see as the key measure of convergence-inflation rates, or whether it should refer to other aspects of economic development, such as growth and unemployment, as well. Witnesses to the House of Lords Select Committee such as Karl Otto Pohl pointed out, however, that 'membership [of the Exchange Rate Mechanism] has helped the members to achieve the same degree of price stability as in Germany, as the country which has served as a kind of standard for the monetary system'.[25] Using the experience of the ERM it could be argued, as indeed others giving evidence to the Select Committee did, that economic convergence should be seen as a consequence or monetary union and not as a prerequisite. Lord Cockfield pointed out that the 'effect of the EMS has been to encourage greater convergence in the economies of those members who are fully participating members of the EMS, and the same will happen with a common currency –

it will lead to much greater economic convergence'.[26] Lord Jenkins argued that the ERM had been successful with less convergence than some economists had predicted, and had brought about greater convergence. He added that 'you will never get anywhere' if 'economic union [is] forced to wait for monetary union and economic convergence'.[27]

Even if we take the view that economic convergence will follow from monetary union rather than being a necessary condition of it, the transition may not be without pain for some member states. The European Parliament therefore called for the 'legal, budgetary and institutional means [to ensure] greater coordination and convergence between Member States' respective economic policies'.[28] This would involve the 'close coordination' of budgetary policies and an increase in the funds for regional policy. The European Trade Union Confederation has argued that the 'Community will have to have its own budget, capable of macroeconomic management', which would inevitably mean a direct transfer of resources. Commissioner Bruce Millan reflected the views of the member states with relatively weak economies, which were 'fearful that they would fall further behind after economic and monetary union ... there was no confidence that economic and monetary union would help to promote cohesion ... These fears need to be met, and in any case the unacceptably high regional disparities in the Community would need to be addressed in the 1991 review of the Structural Funds and the subsequent decisions on the Community Budget for the period after 1992'.[29]

All the trends in the developments currently taking place within the Community point towards centralized decision-making. The Delors Report of 1989 argued that collective monetary policy would have to respond to the dynamics of economic integration and the cross-border effects of likely structural adjustments. The report suggested some central powers for the Community, but also for coordination between national authorities and for a degree of member state autonomy to be retained in member state decision-making to strike a balance between national and Community competences. Economic and monetary union entails a single monetary policy throughout the community, requiring coordination of the fiscal and budgetary policies of the member states. This will in turn bring about greater economic convergence, which will be assisted, if only in response to the anxieties of the economically weaker member states. The Community will have to devote more resources to the Structural Funds, and that will require changes in the methods of calculating the Community's 'own resources' and obtaining the necessary funds from the member states. In addition to these considerations, the Community is actively planning to extend the Community's competence to new areas, yet to be agreed.

Attention has rightly focused on the 'democratic deficit' in the Community, but the question of its executive powers has been neglected. Some of the proposals before the Council of Ministers, such as the cooperation procedure, would plainly hamper the Community's ability to maintain the momentum of the legislative programme designed to establish the Single Market. The assumption appears to be that the Council of Ministers, with ECOFIN (the Council of Economic and Finance Ministers (of the European Community)) in particular taking the responsibility for coordinating the macroeconomic policies of member states of the Community, if not planning the Community' macroeconomic policies, and the biannual European Council are adequate. The only argument has been about making the Council's proceedings open and public, at least as far as its legislative work is concerned. That view has been taken not only in the interests of democracy, but also in the belief that it would improve the quality of legislation. The Council's remit is, however, wider than legislating for the Community; it includes taking decisions of principle on future developments of the Community and on external relations, and in this sense its work is similar to that of the British Cabinet when it takes major policy decisions. The Council also engages in 'diplomatic' work, such as the preparation of Community positions for negotiation. In these areas and in the deals and discussions which must still take place despite the move to weighted majority voting, it is difficult to envisage the Council accepting the proposal to make its proceedings public. Indeed, the Foreign Secretary, Douglas Hurd, expressed the view that, if the Council met in public 'arthritis would seize the institutions of the Community in a very big way'. Sir Leon Brittan, one of the Commissioners, predicted that in an open Council 'there would be no question of ever reaching agreement'.

Whatever the merits of the case from the point of view of increasing democracy in the Community, it looks as though forcing the Council out into the open is fraught with difficulty. Even if this problem could be resolved, the Council may still be an inappropriate body to act as the final decision-making institution in the Community. It is a 'hybrid organization, because its Members are national members with their lines of responsibility through their own national systems. But collectively it operates for the Community purposes and, of course, it is the case that the Council should have to justify its collective decisions and it can only justify its collective decisions to a body which is collectively representative and that can only be the European Parliament.'[30]

It is the hybrid element in the Council which is the core of the problem. The ambivalence of Members of the Council is bound to emerge when the Council and the Community face the issues arising from ensuring a single monetary policy and the disciplines that entails and acting to encourage economic convergence. The inappropriateness of the Council for playing its part in this task is but part of the problem in which the Community seeks to extend its decision-making powers, but lacks the appropriate instruments. The Community suffers not only from a democratic deficit, but also from what might be called an 'executive deficit'. It seeks to function as a federal government, but lacks the institutions to enable it to fulfil the demands which will be made upon the Community as a result of economic and monetary union. This is the issue which now has to be addressed, and from which some member states, notably Britain and Denmark, shy away. The nature of the deficit has not been properly examined, but when it is it is unlikely that it can be resolved by looking to the Council of Ministers in view of the problems arising out of its hybridity. An elected federal government of some kind is the only solution.

An Elected Federal Government

Britain and Denmark's denial of such a possibility is an unrealistic approach, since the Community, to all intents and purposes, acts as a federation at present. Judge David Edward of the European Court of the First Instance argued that one acceptable definition of federalism is a 'form of government of which the essential principle is that there is a union of two or more states under one central body for certain permanent common objects. In the most perfect form of federation the states agree to delegate to a supreme federal government certain powers or functions inherent in themselves in their sovereign or separate capacity, and the federal government, in turn, in the exercise of those specific powers act directly, not only on the communities but on each individual citizen ... If that is the definition ... we are already a substantial way down the road to what in a very loose and broad sense, could be called a federal government'.[31] The Community has four institutions, although only three of them have been considered here. As the Community seeks to establish full economic and monetary union by 1997, arguments about federalism are beside the point; the only issue to be addressed is the adequacy of the institutions, and the powers they should have.

If however, the Council cannot take on the tasks which would be required in the context of economic and monetary union, then a federal government should be created. Plainly such a commitment involves a radical reappraisal of the existing institutions of the Community and their relations to each other. Finding a suitable model of a federal government for the European Community, composed as it is of the twelve member states with so many different languages and traditions, with its sometimes restless ethnic minorities and disparate regions, is an almost impossible task. The means by which a federal government should be elected, whether it should be elected separately from the European Parliament, or whether it should be headed up by a separately elected president, are but a few of the issues which would face the whole Community with its varied democratic traditions; but they are issues which the Community will ultimately have to face. Widening the Community would simply add to the problems. Despite the immensity of the task, the dynamic created by the establishment of economic and monetary union will help to bring this about.

It is in partial recognition of the pressures for centralization of government that the Community has created by seeking economic and monetary union, that attention has focused on the principle of subsidiarity. The term 'subsidiarity' has become 'shorthand for a cluster of issues about the sharing of powers between different levels of government in Western Europe', although the term has many different meanings, which Helen Wallace and Marck Wilke carefully defined.[32] There are of course different views about the interpretation of the principle, which depend on one's view about the degree of centralization the Community requires. Two examples will serve to illustrate this point.

The Martin Report expounded the relationship between competence and subsidiarity by singling out four main areas in which the present level of Community responsibilities was thought to be insufficient. These include economic and monetary union, action in the social sphere and on the environment, foreign and security policy and on the people's Europe in the context of European citizenship, especially the protection of fundamental rights.

The term does not appear in the Treaties but the principle is contained in Article 130R of the Single European Act on environment policy. The note by Counsel to the Speaker recorded in the Foreign Affairs Committee Report is interesting because it shows the way in which the principle can be used to avoid the issues outlined above. The Article itself reads: 'The Community shall take action relating to the environment to the extent that the objectives referred to in paragraph 1 can be attained better at Community level than at the level of individual Member States.' Counsel's note explains: 'Article 130R(4) is helpful because it illustrates how subsidiarity might be invoked on a practical level to draw a line between Community action and Member State action. In this context, because the basic rule laid down by Article 130s is unanimity, Member States have a simple way to prevent action at Community level which they might prefer to discharge themselves.'[33]

The fact that the principle can be interpreted in this way suggests that a deal definition of subsidiarity should be part of the Treaty or at least part of the preamble to it. That would mean the Member States have come to recognize that subsidiarity is intrinsic to any federal system. It is about the way in which powers and competences are shared between the different levels of government. The Community has embarked on that process by its determination, or at least the determination of almost all the Member States, to establish economic and monetary union. For the rest, the Community has proceeded on a case-by-case basis, but must now move on to clarify the criteria for deciding which powers are to be centralized and which to be relegated to national or regional levels of government.

For some Member States of the European Community, contemplating a federal European Community in which the powers ascribed to each level of government are as carefully set out as they can be in a written constitution does not present the same causes of anxiety as it does in the British context. It is seen as a decentralization of power instead of its centralization in Germany, for example, as Helen Wallace's reference to the Bonn meeting in spring 1988 between Jacques Delors and representatives of the Lander show. 'Delors listened carefully to the concerns they expressed and went away convinced that the Community did indeed have to take account of fears that the vigour of local or regional government might be undermined by over-weaning legislators in Brussels. The language used at the meeting in Bonn included the term subsidiarity; it was intended as a shorthand way of stressing the point that powers exercised at the EC level must depend on their conferral and acceptance by those who exercise the most direct and most localized political responsibility, i.e. power and accountability from the bottom up, not the top down.'[34]

This debate, despite the difficulty of defining subsidiarity as a legal concept, is plainly a crucial one for the future shape of government in Britain, depending on the level of government here to which the relevant powers are ascribed.

Developments in the Community imply the concentration of significant powers, particularly over macroeconomic policy in Brussels, which will affect not only the shape of government in Britain but also the shape of

Whitehall. The 'Next Steps' initiative, with its range of executive agencies responsible for the administration of policy, may well turn out to be a more timely move than at first intended. Their function would be unaffected by any move to a federal European Community. But if the concentration of certain powers are concentrated in Brussels and this is accompanied, as well it might be given a change of government in Britain, by the establishment of regional government, then powers which it is decided should not be exercised by a central government, might well be referred to regional government. Once again the executive agencies, perhaps with certain modifications – more regional control or regional outlets – could be adapted to fit with such a scheme of government.

It is the core departments which face the real problems, even without or until a federal government of the Community. So much attention has been paid to the executive agencies as the exciting new development in the British civil service that the role and function of the core departments has been neglected. Their role as policy advisers remains, but is itself affected by the changes which are taking place. Key policy-makers should have had practical experience of policy implementation, but the existing arrangements could militate against that, unless they can gain such practical experience without affecting their career prospects in the department. Open competition of the kind, suggested in Chapter 4, could assist with that. Their remaining functions are linked with the management and supply of the programmes on which central government decides; they will increasingly act as quasi-'purchasers' of these services and that will shift their concerns for being administrators of services. The notion of 'purchaser' in this context will also require careful definition, since they will not only be concerned with the quality of the services delivered but also with their fair distribution. If this is accompanied by the changes proposed in this book – public access to information, a powerful ombudsman and a proper system of administrative courts – then they themselves and the agencies will be 'supervised' by the public.

The civil service is already described as 'unified' as opposed to the 'uniform' civil service bequeathed by the Northcote Trevelyan Report and brought into being in 1920 under Warren Fisher. It has to be remembered that the civil service consisted of a mere 193,000 in 1919, an increase of 120,000 as a result of the First World War and before the establishment of the welfare state. The concept of a unified civil service, a single career civil service, was therefore developed in quite different circumstances, and may not be appropriate in a period of rapid change.

The present Head of the Home Civil Service no longer describes the service as 'uniform' because of the impact of the executive agencies and the limited freedoms given to the chief executives to negotiate pay and conditions for their own staff in their own particular circumstances. But so far another aspect of its unity has remained: it is still a closed entry system in which the senior civil service positions are exclusively or mainly open to those who have come through the ranks. They enjoy a type of tenure which they are expected to serve until their retirement in the same grade, although they may not necessarily remain in the same department or in the same office. The argument for tenure is that it enables the individual to take an independent stance, a stance which it has apparently proved difficult (though not impossible) for civil servants to maintain from the evidence of the last decade. Professor Christopher Hood has pointed out that this independence could be achieved through some of the proposals outlined earlier – a system of administrative law, freedom of information and protection for whistle-blowers.

The closed entry system is alleged to improve the calibre of recruits at every level; an argument put forward by Northcote Trevelyan but against such a different background in which corruption and nepotism was rife. Open entry in the way in which the Swedish civil service handles it could bring in candidates of merit at any level (to a greater extent than the current arrangements for late entry). Furthermore, 'a closed-entry system may depend on a definition of merit which is too narrow, preventing late developers, or black or women candidates, from getting into the system'.[35]

The arguments may not be as compelling as they once were for a uniform civil service. However, even if they were, it is clear that the reforms already in train and the external pressures arising from developments in the European Community have radically changed the character of the central departments. The latter may even find themselves attached to regional governments in the United Kingdom instead of occupying Whitehall, and much will be lost in that process.

Notes

[1] B.G. Bender, 'Governmental Processes, Whitehall, Central Government and 1992', *Public Policy and Aministration*, Spring 1991, Vol. 6, No. 1, p. 18.
[2] R. Denman, 'There are Not Enough Sir Humphreys in Europe', *Independent*, 6 March 1990.
[3] op. cit., B.G. Bender, p. 19.
[4] H. Schmidt, 'The European Money System: Proposals For Further Progress', *The World Today*, 1985, Vol. 41, p. 89.

⁵ Commission of the European Communities, 'Five Years of Monetary Co-operation in Europe', COM, 125, final 1984, p. 18.
⁶ Draft Treaty amending Treaty establishing European Community with a view to achieving Economic and Monetary Union, Articles 102c, 102d, 103, 104, 104a.
⁷ ibid., Articles 109f, g.
⁸ ibid., Article 7.
⁹ J. Lodge, 'Democratic Legitimacy and European Union', *Public Policy and Administration*, Spring 1991, Vol. 6, No. 1, p. 23.
¹⁰ Commission's proposals, Agence Europe No. 1697/8.
¹¹ D. Edwards, Select Committee on the European Communities, 'Economic and Monetary Union', Vol. 1, HL 88–1, QQ 561, 818, 1155, pp. 117, 252.
¹² The Operation of the Single European Act, 14 March 1990, HC 82–1, Foreign Affairs Committee, Second Report.
¹³ A. V. Dicey, *The Law of the Constitution*, 1885, p. 40.
¹⁴ in A. V. Bradley, *The Sovereignty of Parliament in the Changing Constitution*, J. Jowell and D. Oliver (eds), 1989, p. 36.
¹⁵ Costs *v.* Enel, 1964.
¹⁶ op. cit., Select Committee on European Communities, HC 88, Vol. 2, p. 46.
¹⁷ ibid.
¹⁸ F. Sharp, 'The Decision-making Trap Five Years Later', Max Planck Institut für Gesellschaftforschung, 1990.
¹⁹ J. Lodge, 'The Democratic Deficit and the European Parliament', Fabian Society Discussion Paper, January 1991, No. 4, p. 11.
²⁰ Wessels, p. 10.
²¹ 'Final Declaration of the Conference of European Parliaments' issued in Rome, 30 November 1990 by the President of the European Parliament.
²² op. cit., J. Lodge.
²³ evidence to the House of Lords Select Committee, Session 1989–90, Twenty-seventh Report, Vol. 2, p. 73.
²⁴ ibid.
²⁵ ibid., p. 74.
²⁶ ibid., p. 135.
²⁷ ibid., p. 46.
²⁸ Resolution of 16 May 1990.
²⁹ op. cit., p. 65.
³⁰ op. cit., H. Wallace.
³¹ op. cit., p. 13.
³² H. Wallace and M. Wilke, 'Subsidiarity: Approaches to Power Sharing in the European Community', Royal Institute of International Affairs, 1990, London, p. 6.
³³ Foreign Affairs Committee, 14 March 1990, HC 82–II (see above, n. 12).
³⁴ op. cit., p. 3.
³⁵ C. Hood, 'Do We Still Need a Career Civil Service?', Labour and Whitehall, A Fabian Inquiry into the Machinery of Government, 1991, p. 15.

Index